THE DETOX COOKBOOK

THE DETOX COOKBOOK

AN EASY-TO-USE, SAFE, REVITALIZING AND BODY-CLEANSING DIET WITH
EXPERT ADVICE, 150 RECIPES, AND 750 STEP-BY-STEP PHOTOGRAPHS

Contributing Editor: Maggie Pannell

Published by World Publications Group, Inc.
140 Laurel Street, East Bridgewater, MA 02333
www.wrldpub.net

Produced by Anness Publishing Ltd
Hermes House, 88–89 Blackfriars Road
London SE1 8HA
tel. 020 7401 2077; fax 020 7633 9499
www.annesspublishing.com

If you like the images in this book and would like to investigate using them for publishing, promotions
or advertising, please visit our website www.practicalpictures.com for more information.

Publisher: Joanna Lorenz
Project Editor: Lucy Doncaster
Editorial Reader: Lindsay Zamponi
Production Controller: Don Campaniello
Designer: Nigel Partridge

ETHICAL TRADING POLICY
At Anness Publishing we believe that business should be conducted in an ethical and ecologically
sustainable way, with respect for the environment and a proper regard to the replacement of the
natural resources we employ.
As a publisher, we use a lot of wood pulp to make high-quality paper for printing, and that wood
commonly comes from spruce trees. We are therefore currently growing more than 500,000 trees
in two Scottish forest plantations near Aberdeen – Berrymoss (130 hectares/320 acres) and West
Touxhill (125 hectares/305 acres). The forests we manage contain twice the number of trees
employed each year in paper-making for our books.
Because of this ongoing ecological investment programme, you, as our customer, can have the
pleasure and reassurance of knowing that a tree is being cultivated on your behalf to naturally
replace the materials used to make the book you are holding.
Our forestry programme is run in accordance with the UK Woodland Assurance Scheme (UKWAS)
and will be certified by the internationally recognized Forest Stewardship Council (FSC). The FSC is
a non-government organization dedicated to promoting responsible management of the world's
forests. Certification ensures forests are managed in an environmentally sustainable and socially
responsible way. For further information about this scheme, go to www.annesspublishing.com/trees

A CIP catalogue record for this book is available from the British Library.

ISBN-10: 1-57215-516-7
ISBN-13: 978-1-57215-516-9

Printed and bound in China

Main front cover image shows Seared Mixed Onion Salad with Parsley and
Balsamic Dressing – for recipe, see page 214.

NOTES
Standard spoon and cup measures are level.

Large eggs are used unless otherwise stated.

Electric oven temperatures in this book are for
conventional ovens. When using a fan oven, the
temperature will probably need to be reduced
by about 20–40°F. Since ovens vary, you should
check with your manufacturer's instruction book
for guidance.

The nutritional analysis given for each recipe
is calculated per portion (i.e. serving or item),
unless otherwise stated. If the recipe gives
a range, such as Serves 4–6, then the
nutritional analysis will be for the smaller
portion size, i.e. 6 servings. Measurements for
sodium do not include salt added to taste.

The diets and information in this book are not
intended to replace advice from a qualified
practitioner, doctor or dietician. Always consult
your health practitioner before adopting any of
the suggestions in this book. Neither the
author nor the publisher can accept any liability
for failure to follow this advice. A detox diet is
not recommended for children, the elderly or
pregnant women.

CONTENTS

Introduction 6

The Detox Diet 8

What are toxins and where do they come from? 10

How diet affects your health 12

Food allergy and intolerance 16

Benefits of a detox 18

The body's natural detoxifiers 20

How to boost your vital organs 21

Foods to avoid 22

Foods to include 26

Vital nutrients 34

Essential minerals and vitamins 36

Herbs and spices for health 38

Detox supplements 40

Healthy shopping 42

Healthy cooking 44

Exercise for body and mind 46

Complementary therapies and relaxation techniques 48

Preparing to detox 52

Following the detox programme 56

A weekend detox 60

One- and two-week detox meal planners 64

Long-term healthy eating 68

Safe drinking 74

Health problems and how to help to prevent them with diet 76

Juices, Smoothies and Breakfast Ideas 78

Appetizers and Snacks 102

Simply Sensational Soups 114

Main Dish Salads 140

Vegetable Main Dishes 162

Tofu, Egg, Fish, Shellfish and Chicken Dishes 188

Simple Salads and Side Dishes 208

Delicious Healthy Desserts 234

Index 252

Acknowledgements 256

Introduction

Detox diets have become increasingly popular and no wonder, as they offer fantastic health benefits, claiming to leave you feeling relaxed, refreshed and rejuvenated. In an increasingly toxic world, a detox programme can help your body's in-built detoxifiers to counter the effects of pollution and the many potentially harmful, chemical substances with a spring–clean that leaves you looking and feeling brighter and healthier.

What is detoxing?

Detoxing is an ancient therapy that has been practised in various forms for hundreds of years. It is believed to cleanse the digestive system and help the body eliminate waste products and various toxins absorbed from the air, soil, water and food, as well as toxic substances produced by the body itself. Although this has not been medically or scientifically proven, a detox diet offers many health benefits and is useful for giving the body's own detoxification system a helping hand occasionally, especially since the body has to deal with an ever-increasing toxic load in the modern world.

Detox diets, although based on the same idea, vary in the length of time they're recommended for and the foods that are allowed or avoided. Strict detox diets allow just fruit and vegetables, ideally raw and often taken as juices,

Below: Raw vegetables are key detox foods, so eat them in abundance.

Above: Drinking plenty of water is essential for health at all times.

with plenty of water for just one or two days. This is a light fasting regime, designed to give the body's digestive system a rest, and it should not be continued for a longer period. A less restrictive regime is based on eating healthy meals, consisting of plenty of fruit and vegetables, home-made soups, whole grains, beans, peas, lentils, fish, skinless poultry, seeds and nuts. Wheat and dairy products, caffeine drinks and alcohol, are not allowed.

The detox diet regime should also be combined with regular exercise and complementary therapies, including pampering beauty treatments and relaxing techniques, in order to gain the full holistic benefit.

Benefits

A detox programme can improve your digestion, boost your immune system and give you a renewed zest for life. Benefits may include better sleep, improved hair, nails and skin, more energy, stress relief, weight loss and possibly even the reduction of cellulite. This is achieved by restricting the intake of toxins and chemical substances, eating a healthy diet and including regular exercise, all of which have the combined effect of making you feel and look better and adopt a positive attitude towards your health.

Beyond detox

For the long-term, a detox should
be followed by choosing a healthy
balanced diet, including a wide variety of
foods, as discussed under 'Long-term
healthy eating' (see page 68). This can
aid in the prevention of chronic illnesses,
such as cancer and heart disease.

Is it for you?

The checklist in the following column will
tell you if you could be suffering from
toxic overload. Basically if you have
ticked at least five of the questions, you
are likely to be feeling below par and
could benefit from a detox.

As long as you are fit and healthy,
it is safe for you to follow a detox
programme. However, you must first
check with your doctor, especially if
you suffer from any health conditions
or are taking any medication. Do
not attempt to self-diagnose any
troublesome symptoms that may have
an underlying physical cause and
require medical investigation.

Remember that a detox diet is not
designed to be a weight-reducing diet,
nor is it an elimination diet for identifying
the cause of food allergies, although
it may be successful in helping with
weight loss or spotlighting a food
sensitivity. For successful weight loss
and long-term maintenance, a healthy
balanced diet combined with regular
exercise is essential.

How to use this book

You can choose to follow either a strict
weekend detox programme based on
fruit and vegetable dishes, or a one-
or two-week detox diet designed to
give your body a full internal cleanse,
and allowing a wider variety of foods.
It is entirely up to you which you
choose. Certainly you will feel the
benefit after one week or just after a
weekend detox, but if you are able to
continue for two weeks, the benefits
will be more noticeable

Another approach could be to follow
the detox for just one week, then to
reintroduce some wholegrain wheat
products and reduced-fat dairy
products to add greater variety to your
diet for a more flexible eating plan.

It is not recommended that you
follow a detox diet for longer than two
weeks, since certain food groups are
restricted and a healthy diet should
include a wide variety of foods and not
remove any foods long-term, without
sound medical or health reasons.
However, once you've completed your
detox, gradually reintroduce food and
drinks that were restricted, but avoid
junk foods, which are high in fat and
sugar and with poor nutritional value.
Maintain and build on the benefits
gained by following the basic principles
of leading a healthy lifestyle.

*Below: Frequent headaches can be a
symptom of toxic overload.*

the
detox
diet

Discover how to detox your body and mind safely
and efficiently through healthy eating combined
with exercise and relaxing complementary
therapies. All aspects are discussed, including
advice on shopping and cooking, food sensitivities,
nutritional information and healthy eating
guidelines for beyond your detox.

What are toxins and where do they come from?

Overload of toxins can be responsible for causing a range of health problems. So what are the different toxins that we are now exposed to in the modern industrial world and what can we do to restrict our exposure?

What are toxins?

Toxins are potentially harmful substances that pollute and irritate our bodies, putting a strain on the efficiency of our vital organs. There are many different kinds of toxins and they are nothing new, but we are now living in an increasingly toxic world, due to modern technology, intensive farming and food production methods, and a greater use of chemicals, all of which may affect our health and well-being.

Although the human body is designed to deal with these unwanted substances, a build-up of toxins puts an extra strain on our natural detoxifying system, especially with increasing age. This can lead to troublesome symptoms and health conditions,

Below: Traffic exhaust fumes are a major air pollutant.

particularly affecting the digestive and respiratory systems. Asthma, for example, is becoming increasingly common, and although environmental pollution is not necessarily the cause, it is certainly a contributing factor and can be responsible for making the symptoms worse. Increasing evidence and scientific research now suggest that many health conditions and chronic diseases may be linked to toxins in our world and lifestyle.

Where do toxins come from?

Toxins bombard us every day. Not only are they produced naturally in the body, but they can enter the body in the air we breathe, from pollutants in the atmosphere and our environment, and in the food, drinks, drugs and medicines that we consume. Toxic chemical substances are also absorbed through the skin from cosmetics, toiletries and household products, including everyday materials such as paint, glue and electrical products. In fact, unless you live in a sterile bubble, it is impossible to avoid everyday exposure to toxins.

Environment

Pollutants in the air include car exhaust fumes, cigarette smoke, fumes from industrial waste, air-conditioning and heating systems, cleaning fluids, air fresheners, paints, detergents, deodorants and hairsprays.

Tap water

Water quality regulations are imposed to ensure that tap water is safe to drink. It also contains valuable minerals, depending on the source and region. However, there is increasing concern about levels of pollutants, including nitrates from fertilizers, weedkillers, industrial chemicals, poisonous metals (such as lead and mercury) and oestrogen-like chemicals, that may be present (albeit in minute quantities) and their possible effect on our health. You can easily find out about the quality of water in your area. If you are concerned, buy a water filter or choose bottled water.

Chemical residues

Agricultural land is treated with fertilizers, crops are sprayed with pesticides and growth regulators, and animals and farmed fish may be fed antibiotics. All of these practices can leave artificial chemical residues either on or in our food, as well as contaminating the environment and water supplies. Increasing concern about these pollutants and a desire to move towards a greener future has led to more and more farms converting to an organic system and more people choosing organic foods.

Free radicals

The body constantly makes and breaks down free radicals, and in small amounts they are helpful as a natural defence against invading bacteria and viruses. However, certain factors such as cigarette smoke, environmental pollution and over-exposure to sunlight,

can accelerate their production. In large amounts, they are thought to cause damage to cell walls and DNA (the genetic material found in cells), speeding up the ageing process and contributing to the development of heart disease and some cancers. Antioxidant enzymes and nutrients in the blood (produced naturally and ingested in food) help to neutralize and deactivate free radicals and render them harmless.

Food additives

Due to a diet that tends to be largely made up of processed foods, manufactured to suit a fast modern lifestyle, where speed and convenience are often key to the choices we make, much of our food now contains a wide array of additives. Preservatives are added to prevent the food spoiling, to protect against contamination and to increase the shelf life; emulsifiers improve the texture and consistency of foods; colours, flavourings, flavour enhancers and sweeteners are used to alter the appearance or taste of a food or drink, and various other additives may be used for miscellaneous purposes such as for glazing or as anti-foaming agents. All these additives would not be necessary if we chose to eat more fresh food that was seasonal and produced locally. Although only some people may be sensitive to certain additives, the combined effect adds up to a considerable intake, of which we don't really know the effect over a long period of time.

Alcohol

Drinking alcohol in moderation is relaxing and sociable and can be positively good for your health, but alcohol is basically a poison to the body and puts strain on the liver. Alcoholic drinks, such as wine, beer, cider and alcopops, may also contain chemical additives such as sulphite preservatives that some people can be allergic too. Sulphites can trigger an asthma attack in susceptible individuals.

Cigarettes

Tobacco smoke, which is inhaled into the lungs, contains nicotine and tar as well as many other chemical substances. Not only is the nicotine extremely addictive, but the smoke exposes the body to powerful and harmful chemical compounds that are known to cause cancer and other tobacco-related diseases, such as heart disease and bronchitis.

Left: Highly processed convenience foods are loaded with additives.

Above: Organic farming avoids the use of chemical fertilizers and pesticides.

HOW TO RESTRICT EXPOSURE TO TOXINS

- Avoid smoky environments and if you're a smoker, seek help and advice on how to kick the habit.
- Avoid walking in built-up areas, close to traffic or in industrial areas.
- If you live in a town or city, try to escape to the seaside or country as often as you can for fresh air.
- Wear a mask if you cycle in heavy traffic conditions.
- Cut down on or cease using unnecessary household chemical products, such as aerosol air fresheners.
- Buy eco-friendly household cleaners, washing powder and washing-up liquid.
- Choose organic produce whenever possible.
- Adopt a 'greener' lifestyle.

How diet affects health

Diet is a complex affair. Just think about all the foods you have eaten over the past few days and imagine how their substance and value may affect your body. Then consider all the other factors in your life that may influence your health and you can begin to see why it is generally so difficult to identify the causes of troublesome symptoms and conditions.

Diet in general, or a particular food or group of foods may well be at the root of the problem, but it's important to consider and examine a broad view of possibilities before eliminating foods indiscriminately from your diet.

Symptoms may be attributable to other medical conditions so it's vital to always check with your doctor in the first instance to safely rule out any possible underlying physical causes.

Below: Wheat products can cause gastrointestinal complaints.

Above: Always discuss troublesome symptoms with your doctor.

Digestive problems

Wheat and dairy products are frequently suspected and sometimes identified as causing bloating, abdominal pain and wind in susceptible individuals. Symptoms of a digestive disorder may also include diarrhoea and constipation. This may be due to a true allergy or an intolerance. The degree of sensitivity may be slight, moderate or severe and there may also be other symptoms present, such as asthma, eczema, rashes and wheezing. Food intolerance or a food allergy, however mild it may seem, should always be taken seriously, so seeking professional diagnosis is very important.

Could also be due to:

• Irritable bowel syndrome (IBS). This is the most common bowel disorder in the Western world although sufferers are often too embarrassed to discuss the condition with their doctor. It is twice as common in women as in men and is most likely to affect people between the ages of 20 and 40 years. Typical symptoms include stomach-ache, bloating and wind, as well as constipation and/or diarrhoea. The condition may be triggered by stress,

a hormone imbalance or different types of food. Wheat (especially bran), beans, peas, lentils and dairy products are common food culprits. There is no single effective treatment, but generally a dietician will recommend a special diet that may exclude suspected offending foods. If you think that you may be suffering from this condition, keep a food diary together with a record of your symptoms and consult your doctor for referral to a dietician.

• Coeliac disease. This life-long inflammatory condition is caused by a permanent adverse reaction to gluten, a protein in wheat, as well as other similar proteins in rye, barley and oats. Diarrhoea, abdominal pain and wind are common symptoms and adults may find that they lose weight and become anaemic. Coeliac disease used to be rare, but more and more doctors are beginning to recognize the disorder. The average incidence in the West is 1 in 100 people and about one in 1000–1500 people are affected worldwide. Once diagnosed, the condition can be controlled by following a strict gluten-free diet for life, under the guidance of a dietician. There is now a wide variety of gluten-free foods readily available, allowing you to have a less limited diet.

Above: Dairy products could be responsible for sinus problems.

Respiratory problems

Dairy products can lead to excess mucus in the sinuses and nasal passages, so if you suffer from a persistent stuffy or runny nose (perennial rhinitis) or congested sinuses (sinusitis), dairy foods could be the culprit. A short detox, eliminating all dairy products from your diet, will help to highlight if this could be the cause of your symptoms.

Could also be due to: An allergic reaction to any substance that may trigger an individual reaction. This could be a food or an additive in the food, or it could be a household or cosmetic product or something in the environment that the body regards as alien and potentially harmful. House-dust mites, pollen, feathers, animal fur, air fresheners and washing powders may all be offending triggers. Allergic reactions can be responsible for triggering asthma attacks, so it is important to always seek medical advice. Some asthmatics are sensitive to sulphite preservatives, commonly used in beer, wine and cider. Labelling laws now require alcoholic drinks to be labelled if they contain sulphites.

Food cravings and addictions

The body can get hooked on certain foods that are eaten frequently and suffer withdrawal symptoms when they are not eaten. This can be caused by foods believed to boost serotonin and endorphin levels in the brain, which provide a feel-good effect, or by sugary foods that give an instant, but temporary blood-sugar fix. Addiction to caffeine is also common. Symptoms include fatigue and mood swings and binging on the culprit food, which can then cause weight gain and bad skin. In effect you can find yourself trapped in an addictive cycle of craving and withdrawal. Refined and sugary foods tend to be responsible, including cereals, cakes, biscuits, chocolate and sugar as well as tea and coffee. Sometimes a food craving can indicate a sensitivity to it, and this should be investigated by a dietician or a professional allergy specialist.

Skin problems

Common complaints include rashes, eczema and spots, and although acne is generally a teenage problem, it can strike as late as middle-age. Eczema, characterized by red, itchy, dry and flaky skin that may bleed or blister, is often brought on by allergens. This may be an external irritant, such as wool, metal or a detergent, to which the skin is sensitive, or a reaction to something eaten. Milk, eggs, fish, shellfish, tomatoes, nuts and wheat are

Above: Eggs may be a problem food and exacerbate eczema.

common culprits. A medically supervised exclusion diet can identify the offending trigger, if symptoms improve or disappear when a suspect food is avoided. Drinking plenty of water daily will help improve the general condition of the skin by flushing out the body's waste products.

Could also be due to:
• Emotional stress.
• Hormonal fluctuations, especially in the week before a menstrual period.
   • Nutrient deficiencies.

Right: Chocolate is a common food addiction.

Left: Drinking a cup of hot water with a generous squeeze of lemon juice in the morning will stimulate the liver and the gall bladder to kickstart the process of detoxing the body.

Headaches

These may be triggered by a food sensitivity, additives used in certain processed foods, or by consuming excessive amounts of caffeine, which alters the blood supply to the brain. Chocolate, cheese, citrus fruits and alcohol, especially red wine and port, are also commonly cited dietary culprits associated with migraine attacks. Headaches may also be due to an irregular eating pattern. Skipping meals causes blood sugar to plummet, which in turn can precipitate a headache. Try eating regular light meals, do not skip breakfast and if you often wake up with a headache, have a light snack before bedtime to prevent blood sugar levels from dropping too low overnight.

Dehydration can also trigger headaches so be sure to drink plenty of water, especially during hot weather spells, or following strenuous exercise or excessive alcohol consumption.

Could also be due to:

• Poor posture.
• Eye strain.
• Hormonal fluctuations.
• Stress and tension.
• Nasal congestion.
• High blood pressure.
• Poor liver or kidney function.

HEADACHES

Frequent or severe headaches should always be investigated by a medical professional to establish their cause, especially if ordinary painkillers do not help and certainly if you experience other symptoms such as blurred vision, muscle weakness, weight loss or vomiting.

Below: Frequent or severe headaches could be due to a toxic overload, and may be alleviated by making simple changes to the diet.

Tiredness and lack of energy

Sweet snacks, caffeine, alcohol and chocolate can all play havoc with your energy levels, giving you a quick energy boost followed by a rapid fall in sugar levels and an energy dive. Drowsiness may also sometimes be due to a food intolerance. While it is normal to feel sleepy after a big meal, constant lethargy is not normal, and may be due to a sensitivity to grains – particularly wheat, as the process of digestion may induce excessive sleepiness in susceptible individuals.

Could also be due to:

• Coeliac disease.
• Anaemia resulting from poor iron and folic acid absorption.
• An underactive thyroid or a viral infection.
• Stress in your professional and/or personal life.
• Mild dehydration resulting from insufficient fluid intake.
• Diabetes.

Mood swings and depression

There are many reasons for changing moods, and ups and downs are part of everyday life. It may be because you are unhappy, under pressure or worried. Stress makes you feel depressed and may be accompanied by various aches and pains. Over a long time, stress can lead to serious illness, including high blood pressure and heart disease. Identify the root cause and think of ways to cope and reduce the strain. Everyday foods can affect your mood and nutritional deficiencies, food intolerances and the level of blood sugar in the bloodstream can all influence your mental state. Regular meals, eating foods rich in B vitamins (which are good for the nervous system) and cutting down on caffeine and alcohol will all help to maintain a steady blood sugar level.

Could also be due to:
• Premenstrual syndrome (PMS).
• Clinical depression.

Below: Close contact with a loved one provides comfort when you are down.

Above: Snack on fresh fruit rather than processed foods when you are hungry.

Premenstrual syndrome (PMS)

This is a common female complaint brought on by fluctuating hormone levels, which can be responsible for causing bloating, headaches, breast pain and depression. Research shows that nutrition can influence hormone production, so a change of diet may help to relieve symptoms. Cutting down on saturated fats may relieve breast tenderness and lowering the intake of salt can reduce bloating and water retention. Also avoid coffee and alcohol for 1–2 weeks before a period is due. Small frequent meals, including nutritious snacks, such as fruit, nuts and seeds, will maintain blood sugar levels. Obesity can affect hormone balance so try to keep your weight within acceptable limits. Regular exercise helps to relieve symptoms.

Joint pains

An allergy or intolerance to particular foods could be a contributing factor to joint pain. Pinpointing the culprit foods can be difficult, but common suspects include dairy products, eggs and cereals. An exclusion diet, followed under medical supervision, will help to identify problem foods. Scientific evidence suggests that a diet deficient in antioxidants, particularly vitamins A, C and E and the mineral selenium, may also predispose some people to joint problems. To increase your intake of these nutrients, you should eat a healthy balanced diet, rich in oily fish and shellfish, fresh fruit and vegetables, wholegrain cereals, eggs, nuts and seeds.

Could also be due to:
• Excessive body weight. Not only can this be a cause of joint problems, particularly affecting the hips and knees, but carrying excess weight can add to the pain caused by other factors.
• Lack of exercise. Regular exercise helps to strengthen the muscles responsible for protecting the joints and helps to prevent stiffness.
• Injury or over-exertion. Cut back your exercise routine or change to a less physically demanding activity.

Food allergy and intolerance

Allergies and intolerances are becoming increasingly common and it has been estimated that around 25 per cent of the population may suffer from a sensitivity at some point in their lives. This appears to be a consequence of a number of factors, including increased air pollution, greater use of chemicals, modern living conditions, over-use of antibiotics and other drugs and more stressful lives, all of which weaken the immune system and make us more vulnerable. The potential causes of allergy or intolerance are numerous and can be difficult to identify. Pollen, house-dust mites, pet hair, insect stings and chemicals, as well as food and drink, can trigger an adverse reaction in susceptible individuals.

What's the difference between allergy and intolerance?

These two terms are frequently confused. The main difference between them is that an allergy involves a reaction by the body's immune system, whereas an intolerance does not. Only a small percentage of individuals with sensitivities are truly allergic. Allergies have a genetic link and are more likely to occur in families where there is a history of allergic conditions, including asthma, hay fever and eczema. Allergies and intolerances can occur at any age and stress can be a trigger.

Above: Shellfish can trigger an allergic reaction in people with sensitivities.

Food allergy

This is an extreme immune (defence) system response to a food that the body mistakenly believes to be harmful, causing the production of antibodies. This triggers the release of powerful irritating chemicals, such as histamine, into the bloodstream which cause inflammation and symptoms such as vomiting, diarrhoea, skin rashes, oral and facial swelling, breathing difficulties and plummeting blood pressure. Reactions in some cases can be so severe that they may be life threatening. This is known as anaphylactic shock and requires immediate medical attention.

Food intolerance

This may result from a number of different conditions, such as a lack of a digestive enzyme or a damaged intestine (known as leaky gut). Symptoms may be delayed, so it can be difficult to identify the culprit, and are generally not as severe as those experienced with an allergic reaction. They can include bloating, indigestion, migraines, rashes, joint pains and fatigue. It is important to remember that these symptoms may be associated with other conditions so always seek medical advice.

MEDICAL DIAGNOSIS

Following a detox diet may help to relieve symptoms and to identify a problem food, but it should not be used to self-diagnose. Allergic reactions, however mild, need to be taken seriously and professional medical diagnosis is essential. If you think you have a food allergy or intolerance, consult your family doctor. Blood and skin prick tests can be reliable for identifying 'classic' allergies, or an exclusion diet may be recommended in which suspect foods are systematically eliminated from your diet, then reintroduced to see if the symptoms return.

Above: Wheat, nuts and dairy products are some of the foods that can cause sensitivity in susceptible people.

Which foods can cause problems?

No food is harmful in itself, but those that are known to cause the greatest percentage of reactions in susceptible people are milk and dairy products, gluten (sometimes just wheat), eggs, fish and shellfish, nuts and soya. Food additives, such as sulphites and benzoates (both used as preservatives) and colourings, may also be culprits.

Gluten

This protein is found in wheat and rye and is related to similar proteins found in rye, barley and oats. People who experience a permanent adverse reaction to gluten are diagnosed as having coeliac disease. This occurs in genetically susceptible individuals and is a lifelong condition. In a coeliac, gluten damages the lining of the small intestine which greatly reduces the ability of the gut to absorb adequate nutrients from food. Coeliac patients may be severely ill with weight loss, vomiting and diarrhoea or they may have chronic, almost trivial symptoms, such as tiredness, lethargy and breathlessness. Adults may have a history of abdominal pain and intestinal upsets, or they may suddenly develop the condition at any time. Anaemia and mouth ulcers, resulting from nutrient deficiencies are also common features. If these symptoms are evident always seek medical advice and do not attempt to self-diagnose. Another possible side effect of intestinal damage is an increased sensitivity to other foods such as soya or lactose in milk.

If coeliac disease is diagnosed, it means cutting out all wheat-based foods including bread, flour, wheat pasta, semolina, couscous, bulghur wheat and certain breakfast cereals as well as cakes, biscuits, pastries and puddings and any processed foods that may include wheat, such as soups, sauces, sausages and stuffing mixes. You will also need to avoid rye and barley (beer, stout and malted drinks) and possibly oats, although a moderate amount can usually be tolerated as they contain less gluten. A gluten-free diet should include plenty of potatoes, rice, beans, peas, lentils, corn and nuts to replace the prohibited foods.

Below: Dairy products can cause an adverse reaction in some people.

Wheat

Many people are intolerant to the whole wheat grain, including wheat starch. Symptoms include bloating, indigestion, lethargy, asthma and skin disorders. Sufferers need to follow a completely wheat-free diet, including many gluten-free products, such as gluten-free bread, which may contain wheat starch. However, other types of cereal such as oats, rye, barley, rice and corn may be included in the diet.

Milk

Lactose intolerance A lack of the enzyme lactase results in an inability to digest lactose, the sugar in milk. Symptoms may include bloating, abdominal pain, wind and diarrhoea. Hard cheese (which is very low in lactose) and yogurt, especially probiotic yogurt (as the bacteria help to digest the lactose), are usually well tolerated. Nut, rice or soya 'milks' or special lactose-reduced milk provide good alternatives, although research suggests that the best way of dealing with the problem is not to avoid lactose-containing foods and potentially risk low calcium intake, but to stabilize symptoms by including small amounts of dairy foods.

Lactose intolerance is usually genetically inherited and is more common among non-white races. It is a relatively common complaint.

Milk allergy Some people have trouble with milk-based products because they cannot tolerate certain milk proteins and the human immune system reacts adversely to them. Symptoms can include eczema, rashes, digestive problems, wheezing, stuffy nose and runny eyes and in rare cases, anaphylactic shock. Generally, all dairy products need to be avoided, including butter, cheese, yogurt and cream and also products with a milk content. Soya, rice and oat 'milks' can be used as alternatives to cow's milk. (These are not suitable for babies under 12 months.) Ideally they should be fortified with calcium and vitamins to ensure an adequate intake of these essential nutrients.

Nuts

Allergies to nuts can develop at any age and are usually life-long. Peanuts are the most likely offender, but other varieties may also cause a reaction. It is essential to avoid all contact with the nuts concerned as a reaction can be very serious. In severe allergy, even slight contact from nut dust in the air may trigger anaphylactic shock, which can be fatal. Nut-allergy sufferers should carry an epi-pen containing adrenaline to counteract a nut reaction if triggered. People with nut allergy may be more prone to anaphylactic reactions if they have asthma or at times of stress.

Eggs

Symptoms of an allergy to eggs may include skin rashes, swelling and stomach upsets as well as asthma and eczema. It is usually the egg white (protein) that causes a problem, but if you are allergic then all eggs and egg products should be avoided, including mayonnaise, cakes, desserts, mousses, meringues and quiches. A powdered, dry egg substitute can be bought from many health food stores.

Benefits of a detox

The benefits you will enjoy from following a detox programme will vary depending on the length and strictness of the regime, the degree of change to your usual lifestyle and eating habits, and your current state of health and well-being. Benefits vary from person to person, but these are the main physical and mental improvements frequently experienced.

Better health
As well as helping to relieve bothersome ailments like headaches and bloating that may be due to food intolerances, a detox diet including plenty of vitamin C from fruit and vegetables can also help to boost your immune system and fight off minor infections – or at least reduce their severity. Including a wide and plentiful variety of fruit and vegetables, packed with antioxidant vitamins and minerals,

Below: Regular exercise, especially when taken in the fresh air, helps to promote mental and physical health.

and other valuable compounds called phytochemicals, also helps to protect against chronic diseases such as heart disease and cancer. Regular consumption of low-fat probiotic yogurt also tops up the good bacteria in the gut, which improves the digestion and helps to relieve disorders such as IBS and constipation, and strengthen the immune system.

Improved appearance
A diet that is rich in vitamins and minerals, with plenty of fruit and vegetables, and that avoids alcohol and cigarettes, will improve the condition of your skin, hair and nails and can help to slow down the ageing process. Fruit and vegetables provide a rich source of vitamin C, needed for the production of collagen (a protein needed for healthy skin, teeth and gums) and also betacarotene, which helps to generate new cells. Overall skin health also depends on proper hydration, so drinking plenty of water helps to promote clearer skin. Regular exercise,

especially if taken in the fresh air, boosts the circulation, delivering oxygen to all body cells, and giving the complexion a healthy glow. Teeth will look brighter if not discoloured by tannins present in red wine and black tea.

Improved mood and inner calm
By choosing nutrient-rich foods, your body is better equipped for coping with stress. You will feel calmer and more relaxed and better able to concentrate and think clearly. Regulating blood sugar levels will help you to avoid mood swings, and a break from alcohol will prevent the depressive effect that dulls the brain and affects the memory. Complementary therapies, such as visualization and meditation, are excellent for helping to declutter the mind and induce a relaxed sense of well-being. Feeling happy, optimistic and having a positive outlook on life all help to boost your confidence and self-esteem and promote good health, and a long life span.

Above: A detox diet will help you to sleep better.

Restful sleep

Alcohol, cigarettes and caffeine drinks all interfere with sleep patterns and can cause insomnia. As these should all be ideally eliminated during your detox, you will begin to have a better night's sleep. Also, you will not be eating highly processed junk foods that tend to be high in fat and difficult to digest, especially if they are eaten late at night. Regular exercise and many of the complementary and relaxation therapies, chamomile or valerian tea, all of which are recommended while detoxing, will also help you to sleep.

Increased energy

Fatigue can be made worse by not eating the right foods and therefore not getting enough nutrients to promote sustained energy and vitality. Maintaining good nutrition by eating a wide variety of foods, combined with more sleep and a better ability to cope with stress through complementary relaxation techniques, will all help to banish tiredness and replenish your energy levels.

Weight loss

A detox is not designed to be a weight-reducing diet. However, because you are choosing healthy foods (whole grains, low-fat protein foods and plenty of fruit and vegetables), and cutting out foods that are high in fat and sugar, as well as alcohol, you will naturally consume fewer calories and are therefore likely to lose some weight. Also, gentle but regular exercise will encourage weight loss as well as improving muscle tone.

Reduction of cellulite

Some women also notice a reduction in the appearance of cellulite, although there's no sound scientific evidence to support the claim that cellulite is actually caused by a build up of toxins, and therefore by following a detox diet the appearance of cellulite can be reduced or removed. Cellulite has a dimpled, orange-peel-like appearance on the skin and can affect women's thighs, buttocks and upper arms – even if you are slim. The female hormone oestrogen is responsible for women acquiring fat in these areas, and because it is stored just under the skin, it can affect its appearance. Many

naturopaths and beauticians claim that a diet high in processed and refined foods and low in fruit and vegetables can be to blame for causing cellulite. Certainly a low-fat diet that includes plenty of fruit and vegetables may help to reduce it, and regular exercise will definitely help too. Dry skin brushing and massage treatments can also help to improve the appearance of cellulite.

Improved long-term diet

Although certain foods and drinks are restricted temporarily while following a detox programme, the basic principles of the diet should help you to kick bad habits and adopt a pattern of healthy eating that you will be able to maintain afterwards. It is important to remember that a restrictive diet is not recommended as a continued or long-term eating plan.

Below: A slimmer, more toned figure results from cutting out foods that are high in fat and sugar.

The body's natural detoxifiers

The body is a remarkable system of organic engineering, working to eliminate undesirable substances via the liver, kidneys, lungs, skin, and digestive and lymphatic systems. Generally toxins are dealt with and cleared out routinely and efficiently, but a detox 'spring clean' provides the body with extra help in coping with an increased toxic load.

The digestive system

Your health is often governed by your digestive system. Everything you eat travels from the stomach to the intestines where nutrients are absorbed and waste is eliminated via the bowel. Food is broken down by digestive enzymes and 'friendly' bacteria in the gut. If these are out of sync, due to poor diet, stress, over-use of antibiotics, food intolerances or toxin overload, food remains semi-digested and problems such as constipation, leaky gut, irritable bowel syndrome (IBS), nausea and bloating arise. Food itself can also become toxic if not digested properly.

The liver

This is the most complex human organ and it is responsible for handling almost everything that enters the body. It has hundreds of functions including the removal of toxins from the bloodstream. It is the body's main detoxifier, removing and neutralizing poisons, drugs, alcohol and nicotine. Once made 'safe', these substances can then be eliminated from the body via the kidneys, lungs and bowel. The liver also converts the energy from food into the metabolic nutrients that are needed for cells to function efficiently.

Optimum health depends on the efficient functioning of the liver. If it becomes overloaded with toxins, these are not eliminated and are instead stored in the liver and in fat cells throughout the body. Signs that may indicate an unhappy liver range from: headaches, IBS, poor digestion,

Above: Exercise aids the effective functioning of the internal organs.

bloating, depression and mood changes to the more serious problems of hepatitis and cirrhosis.

The kidneys

These organs basically act as filters to clean the blood. They are responsible for the removal of urea (a toxic waste product from the liver), removal of excess ions (such as sodium) and adjustment of water content in the blood. These waste products are then eliminated in urine, via the bladder. During this filtration process, the kidneys reabsorb useful nutrients and recycle them for further use. It is very important to drink plenty of water at all times to help the kidneys carry out their function efficiently.

The lymphatic system

This system carries toxins, unwanted waste, dead cells and excess fluid to the lymph nodes, where the waste is filtered before being passed into the bloodstream. Poor circulation and a weakened immune system may be signs that the lymphatic system is not functioning efficiently. Higher levels of toxins are believed to slow down your lymphatic system.

The lungs

When we breathe, the lungs deal with air-borne pollutants, such as carbon monoxide from traffic pollution. They allow oxygen to enter the bloodstream and waste products to be removed as carbon dioxide.

Correct breathing is essential if the body's metabolism and organs are to work properly. However many of us do not inhale enough oxygen and so do not expel all the unwanted waste gases. Catarrh, blocked sinuses and a constant runny nose are signs of a poorly functioning respiratory system.

The skin

This is the body's largest organ. Every pore eliminates waste and sweat, and the sebaceous glands help to remove toxins. The skin reflects what is happening inside our bodies. If we are stressed, run down, or have over-indulged, this can show up in a dull, lifeless complexion, or as rashes, spots and blemishes. A healthy diet and drinking plenty of water help to promote clear skin.

Below: Clear skin reflects a healthy digestive system.

How to boost your vital organs

Like a car, the body benefits from a regular service to ensure it runs efficiently and has sufficient energy to fight and eliminate toxins. There are a number of simple, common-sense steps that can help to improve the overall functioning of your vital organs.

The digestive system
• Only eat when you are hungry, and do not overeat or eat large meals late in the evening.
• Take time over meals to eat each mouthful properly and slowly.
• Cut down on refined carbohydrates and foods with a high fat content.
• Do not drink too much with meals as this can dilute your digestive juice.
• Start the day with fruit juices or fruit to boost your digestive system.
• Herbal teas, such as chamomile, peppermint or fennel can be soothing.
• Improve the overall condition of the gut by regularly eating low-fat probiotic yogurt.
• Many herbs and spices are an aid to digestion, so use bay, caraway, cardamom, cinnamon, cumin, dill, fennel, ginger, marjoram, mint, parsley and tarragon in cooking.

The liver
• Drink plenty of water – at least 2 litres/ 4 pints/ 8–9 cups a day.
• Eat plenty of fresh fruit and vegetables, in particular apples, citrus fruits, garlic, beetroot (beets), carrots, broccoli, cabbage, globe artichokes, ginger, green leafy vegetables, and bitter leaves, such as dandelion, as well as whole grains, nuts, seeds and beans.
• Avoid processed, salty, sugary, high-fat and very spicy foods.
• Try to eat mainly organic foods.
• Cut down on alcohol and caffeine.
• Exercise regularly.
• Liver-boosting supplements can help to neutralize free radicals that damage cells. Try an antioxidant supplement containing betacarotene, vitamins C and E and selenium.
• Artichoke extract supplements (containing the compound cynarin) claim to help boost a sluggish liver.

The kidneys
• Drink plenty of water.
• Reduce your intake of animal protein foods, such as meat and dairy products, as these can put a strain on the working of the kidneys.
• Cut down on alcohol.
• Dandelion leaves, tea or supplements can be helpful as a diuretic to treat fluid retention and to help to prevent common kidney problems.

The lymphatic system
• Exercise regularly.
• Stimulate the lymphatic system by exfoliating and skin-brushing.
• Have a massage to encourage the efficiency of the lymphatic system.

Left: Citrus fruits stimulate the digestive system and are powerful cleansers. They are also rich in vitamin C.

BREATHING EXERCISE
Use this exercise to check that you are breathing correctly.

1 Lie with your back on the floor, bend your knees and place your feet on the floor a comfortable distance from your buttocks. Rest your hands flat on your stomach, just below the ribs.

2 Breathe in slowly through your nose, filling your lungs. The lower part of your stomach should rise first. If your chest moves first, you are breathing incorrectly and are not using your diaphragm – this is known as shallow-breathing.

3 Exhale slowly though your nostrils, emptying your lungs – notice your abdomen flattening.

The skin
• Drink plenty of water.
• Eat plenty of fresh fruit and vegetables – preferably raw or juiced. They provide betacarotene (the plant form of vitamin A) and vitamin C, both essential for maintaining healthy skin.
• Choose whole grains, lean protein foods and a moderate intake of polyunsaturated essential fatty acids, found in oily fish, vegetable oils and nuts and seeds.
• Ensure that your diet is not lacking in the mineral zinc. Lean meat, skinless poultry, shellfish and nuts are all good sources and yogurt and skimmed milk also supply useful amounts.
• Restrict convenience foods, high in saturated fats.
• Cut down on chocolate, sweets, highly salted snacks and soft drinks.
• Restrict alcohol intake.
• Boost your circulation by exercising and skin-brushing.
• Get plenty of restful sleep.
• Take regular exercise in the fresh air and breathe deeply.

Foods to avoid

Successful detoxing relies on making both dietary and lifestyle changes in order to allow your body to cleanse itself readily and efficiently. Some of the foods that are off-limits during the detox programme are those known to commonly cause digestive problems and other side effects in susceptible individuals. Others are those widely recognized as best limited or avoided in order to promote a healthy body, thus helping you to retrain your eating habits and make healthy food choices for the long term. These restrictions are only suggested for a detox period of up to two weeks to give your body a break and can be reintroduced in moderation afterwards if you like, unless advised otherwise by a doctor or dietician.

Alcohol

Drinking in moderation can be relaxing and sociable and indeed is reputed to help lower the risk of coronary heart disease if it is kept at a 'sensible' level, but you need to give up drinking alcohol completely while following a detox programme.

Below: Alcoholic drinks in excess place unnecessary strain on the liver.

Above: Tea, coffee, cola drinks and chocolate are all high in caffeine.

Alcohol is basically an extremely toxic compound, and although the liver acts as an efficient detoxifier, breaking down alcohol and converting it into harmless components, this process puts unnecessary strain on the liver, which can become damaged with regular or heavy drinking. Alcohol metabolism also depletes many valuable nutrients, particularly essential fatty acids, vitamins A, C and E, thiamin and zinc, and it acts as a diuretic, causing the kidneys to excrete more fluid along with vital minerals, such as calcium and potassium. This has a dehydration effect on the body.

Alcoholic drinks are also loaded with 'empty' calories (nearly twice as many as sugar) and therefore provide little nutritional value. They may also contain various additives. Sulphites and sulphur-based preservatives are commonly added to wines, beers, ciders and ready-mixed cocktail drinks, which can trigger reactions such as asthma in certain people. Colours and artificial sweeteners may also be added, all increasing the toxic load.

Caffeine

Particularly high levels of caffeine are found in coffee (especially ground coffee), but it is also present in tea, chocolate, colas and some fizzy drinks and in some cold and pain relief tablets. Caffeine is a potent substance that stimulates the brain, heart and central nervous system helping to keep us awake, think clearly and feel brighter. It is also a diuretic, causing loss of calcium and an increased risk of osteoporosis. While it is the stimulant effect of caffeine that makes drinks containing it popular, caffeine can also act as a laxative and may cause migraines, insomnia, irritability and palpitations, especially if consumed in excessive amounts. More than six cups a day could give rise to high blood pressure and kidney problems. It is also highly addictive, so to avoid withdrawal symptoms you need to cut back on your intake gradually before starting on a detox programme.

Above: Avoid processed meat products such as sausages.

Meat and meat products

Red meat, and meat products especially, are also generally high in saturated fat, although farmers are now breeding animals to be leaner and modern butchery methods have produced leaner cuts. Meat products, such as burgers and sausages, may also contain additives and may be made with low-quality meat, depending on the manufacturer. Moreover, meat creates extra work for the digestive system, so while detoxing it is advisable to take a break from eating it, then to only eat lean cuts of quality meat in moderation after your detox.

Above: Dairy products can be high in saturated fats.

Dairy products and eggs

Cow's milk and dairy products can be difficult to digest for many people and can often cause excessive production of mucous in the sinuses and nasal passages. Yogurt, however, is usually tolerated by most people and provides a good source of calcium. Low-fat probiotic yohurt has a calming effect on the digestive system and can help to maintain a healthy balance of bacteria in the gut. Dairy products, especially butter, cheese and cream, are also the main source of saturated fats in the diet, which healthy eating guidelines advise most people to cut down on.

Eggs may also cause an allergic reaction in susceptible individuals, in which case all eggs and egg products should be excluded from the diet. However, for the majority of people, eggs (ideally organic) can be eaten occasionally and provide an excellent source of protein as well as a range of valuable minerals and vitamins.

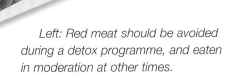

Left: Red meat should be avoided during a detox programme, and eaten in moderation at other times.

Above: Cream is very high in saturated fat and should be eaten sparingly. Eat low-fat probiotic yogurt instead.

Sugar

This is a very concentrated source of energy that is quickly absorbed into the blood stream, however it has little nutritional value and is high in calories. Avoiding sugary foods and added sugar is therefore a relatively easy way of cutting calories without adversely affecting nutrient intake, especially if you are overweight.

Sugar and refined carbohydrates (as found in chocolate and confectionery, cookies, cakes and pastries) can also be responsible for causing tiredness. This is because they provide a sudden surge of energy, as the enzyme insulin is released and the blood sugar level shoots up, before tumbling again soon afterward – with a resulting feeling of tiredness. The key to maintaining maximum energy is to keep your blood sugar levels constant by eating regular, satisfying meals with a good balance of nutrients and to choose healthy snacks such as fruit, nuts or seeds if peckish in between. Learn to enjoy the natural flavours of food without adding sugar and try not to use artificial sweeteners as an alternative.

Below: Cakes and biscuits contain high amounts of fat and refined sugar.

Wheat products

Coeliacs need to avoid all sources of gluten (the protein found in wheat and also present in barley, rye and oats) permanently. Other individuals may be less seriously intolerant of wheat, but still suffer a mild sensitivity, finding it difficult to digest, and experiencing bloating, constipation and/or diarrhoea. Other grains may be consumed without causing problems. Common wheat products include bread, flour, pasta, breakfast cereals, couscous and bulgur wheat. Wheat flour is used for making cakes, pies and puddings and is widely used in the manufacture of many processed foods, such as sauce mixes, soups and stuffings. This can make it quite difficult to cut out, although other grains can be substituted. However, it is important to remember that wheat products, especially wholegrain varieties, are nutritious foods and play an important role in a healthy balanced diet. It should therefore not be eliminated from the diet long-term, unless coeliac disease or a true wheat allergy has been diagnosed.

Above: Wheat flour is used in the manufacture of bread, cakes, cookies and pastries.

Salt

A very small amount of salt is a vital constituent of our diet, but we eat far more than our bodies actually need. Most of the salt that we eat is hidden in processed foods; the rest is either added at the table or during cooking. It's now known that our high salt intake has many potentially adverse effects on our health. It is linked with high blood pressure, kidney disease, strokes, stomach cancer and osteoporosis and may play an aggravating role in asthma. It is not a direct cause of asthma, but a high consumption of salt may make the condition worse. High salt intake also increases fluid retention and the tendency to suffer from bloating and swollen ankles and fingers. Simply restricting salt intake to a much lower level can cause fluid loss of up to 2 litres (4 pints) or 2 kg (4½ lb) in body weight. Lemon juice, garlic and herbs and spices can be used instead.

Above: Fast foods are usually very high in saturated fat.

Processed foods

Foods that are processed are not intrinsically unhealthy. When you cook, you are processing food at home, but much of the manufactured food that we eat includes large amounts of unhealthy saturated and trans fats, sugars, salt, and chemical additives, which may build up and produce harmful effects in the body. Also the more a food is processed, the more likely it is to have lost some of its nutrient value, particularly vitamins and fibre.

While following a detox programme you should aim to choose fresh, natural food, avoid all additives and to eat as much raw food as possible. Some quality canned foods, not including those packed in brine (high in salt) or syrup (high in sugar), are acceptable as well as being very convenient. So are frozen fruits and vegetables, as they are quickly processed at source and can be more nutritious than fresh food that has been transported over a long distance and displayed for days, or that has been treated after harvesting to lengthen its shelf life.

Fatty and fried foods

Fats provide essential fatty acids, which are vital to the body's metabolism. They also provide a concentrated source of energy, make food more palatable and enable the body to make use of the fat-soluble vitamins, A, D, E and K. However most of us eat too much unhealthy saturated fat, which can raise blood cholesterol levels and increase the risk of heart disease. Calorie-rich, high-fat diets can also lead to obesity. While following the detox programme, and for long-term healthy eating, you need to cut down on saturated fat and replace some of it with the healthier unsaturated types. This includes using olive oil (or other vegetable oils high in unsaturates) for cooking, rather than hard fats, and choosing oil-rich fish in preference to red meat. See further information on the different types of fat on page 70.

Below: If you can buy only processed food at work, take in a lunch box instead.

Take-away meals

A take-away (take-out) meal makes an enjoyable treat and occasionally gives you a break from cooking, especially when you are time pressured. However, curries, pizzas, burgers, fried chicken, fish and chips and Chinese dishes are generally loaded with fat and can be difficult to digest. They are also likely to be high in salt, yet lacking in a wide variety of nutrients, especially vitamin C, B group and E, and fibre, and may well contain additives, such as food colours and flavour enhancers that can trigger allergic reactions.

So take a break from these meals while detoxing, although you can still make dishes such as lighter curries and stir-fry dishes, packed with healthy vegetables during the programme, following the recipes in this book. After your detox, take-away meals needn't be banned. Many fast food outlets now offer healthier alternatives, such as grilled chicken salad or chargrilled vegetable kebabs.

Foods to include

You can enjoy a wide variety of foods while following a one- or two-week detox diet, so you should never feel hungry or find the diet difficult to stick to. It is not designed to be a starvation diet, but includes selected foods that help and encourage the detoxification process while providing a healthy balance of nutrients.

Fruit and vegetables

These are an essential part of a healthy, balanced diet, and all types should be included in abundance on a detox diet. They are highly nutritious, packed with antioxidant vitamins A (as betacarotene), C and E, minerals, fibre and other natural plant compounds, called phytochemicals, which together protect against illness and disease. Antioxidants neutralize free radicals that can damage body cells and increase the risk of cancer.

Be sure to buy fresh-looking produce, ideally that is seasonal and that has been grown locally. Always wash fresh produce before using to remove any chemical residues and choose unwaxed citrus fruits – wash in warm water before use if not unwaxed.

Choose a wide variety of different coloured produce to make sure you are getting a range of nutrients. Eat as snacks, in salads or lightly cooked. Limit potatoes and bananas to no more than 3 times a week, as they are high in fast-releasing sugars.

Right: Fresh pineapple aids the digestive system.

Super fruits

Apples Studies have revealed that pectin can help protect against the damaging effects of pollution by helping to remove toxins and purify the system. The malic and tartaric acids in apples also benefit the digestion. Apples – if unpeeled – are also a good source of vitamin C, and fibre.

Berries This group includes strawberries, raspberries, blackberries, blackcurrants, cranberries and blueberries. They are rich sources of vitamin C, which helps to fight infection and boost the immune system. Cranberries and blueberries fight harmful bacteria in the kidneys, bladder and urinary tract.

Citrus fruits All are an excellent source of vitamin C. Lemons have a strong cleansing effect and can help relieve gastric problems.

Melons Their high water content is thought to stimulate the kidneys to work more efficiently. Orange-fleshed cantaloupes have the highest vitamin C and betacarotene content.

Left: Fresh melon has a high water content and can stimulate the kidneys.

Papayas Contain an enzyme called papain, which aids the digestion of proteins and benefits the digestive system. It is rich in fibre, betacarotene, vitamin C and phytochemicals with antioxidant properties.

Pineapples Contain the enzyme bromelain, which aids digestion by breaking down proteins and which also has anti-inflammatory properties, which may help relieve arthritis and speed recovery from injuries. It has also been shown to help to relieve sinus congestion and urinary tract infections. Pineapple must be eaten fresh for its healing powers, as bromelain is destroyed in canned pineapple.

Pomegranates Offer good vitamin C and fibre value, and compounds believed to fight disease. New research suggests that the juice may offer many health benefits.

WAKE-UP DRINK
A glass of warm water with some freshly squeezed lemon juice and sliced fresh root ginger added makes the ideal start to the day.

DRIED FRUITS

Excellent snack foods, dried fruits can also be used for making delicious compotes, or as a cooking ingredient in both sweet and savoury dishes to add sweetness and replace added sugar. Dried fruits provide a concentrated source of valuable nutrients and fibre, although they should not be eaten too freely, as due to their natural sugar content, they are quite high in calories, and if eaten between meals, can increase the risk of tooth decay. There is now a fantastic range to choose from, including common favourites like raisins, sultanas (golden raisins), apricots, prunes, figs and dates as well as cranberries, blueberries, cherries and strawberries and mango, apple, papaya, banana and pineapple pieces. Apricots, in particular, are one of the richest fruit sources of iron, a mineral that is frequently lacking in many women's diets. Prunes are well known for their laxative properties, and can help to relieve constipation.

Much dried fruit is treated with sulphur-based preservatives in order to prevent discolouration and to enhance its colour. Apricots and peaches, for example, are a less attractive brown colour if they are left untreated, but if you want to avoid additives, particularly during a detox, choose unsulphured fruit. It is also important to note that sulphured foods can trigger asthma attacks in susceptible people. Potassium-based preservatives are also sometimes added to ready-to-eat dried fruit (which is partially hydrated to be softer than normal dried fruit) to prevent fungal and bacterial spoilage. The best policy is to always check the ingredients' label, as all additives must be listed.

Right: Carrots are good for the immune system and help to maintain healthy skin and eyes.

Carrots Rich in the antioxidant betacarotene (as evident in their bright orange colour) which is good for the immune system as well as for skin and eye health. Unlike the vitamin and mineral content of many vegetables, the betacarotene is better absorbed if the carrots are cooked.

Celery A good, low-calorie diuretic that helps the kidneys to function efficiently and so hastens the excretion of waste. It may also help to lower cholesterol levels and blood pressure. Use in soups, salads and stir-fries.

Below: Broccoli is packed with goodness and is a powerful antioxidant.

Super vegetables

Beetroot (beet) A powerful blood cleanser and tonic and valued for its value to the digestive system and the liver particularly. It is rich in potassium and provides plenty of folate and iron, essential for the formation of red blood cells and helping to prevent anaemia. It has a reputation for stimulating the immune system and may also help to combat cancer, although this has yet to be proved scientifically. Choose fresh raw or cooked beetroot, but not the type packed in vinegar, because as well as being acidic and therefore an irritant to a sensitive gut, pickling reduces the level of nutrients.

Broccoli A cruciferous vegetable – along with cauliflower, kale cabbage, spring greens (collards), turnips, Brussels sprouts, kale and radishes – rich in carotenoids (phytochemicals), which are powerful antioxidants thought to suppress the formation of free radicals and protect against certain cancers. Broccoli also provides iron and is an excellent source of folate, vitamin C and potassium.

Left: Beetroot contains many beneficial properties that can cleanse the blood and aid the digestive system.

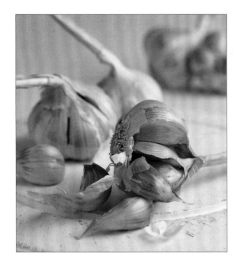

Above: Garlic is one of the most potent natural healers.

Garlic Highly valued for its anti-viral and anti-bacterial properties and many therapeutic benefits. It is a natural decongestant, helps to fight infections and eliminate toxins and may lower cholesterol levels, reduce blood pressure and help to prevent cancer.

Ginger Knobbly-looking, fresh root ginger is valued as an aid to digestion as well as being good for combating colds, stimulating the appetite, improving circulation and helping to alleviate nausea. It's also reputed to help relieve rheumatic pains.

Globe artichokes A substance called cynarin, found in the base of the vegetable leaves, may help liver function and control cholesterol levels.

Onions Like garlic, well known as a cure-all, with an impressive reputation for helping with all kinds of ailments. They have powerful antibiotic properties and are great natural decongestants.

Pumpkin and other squash Supplies a good source of the antioxidants beta-carotene and vitamin E. The flesh is easily digested, and they rarely cause allergies, which makes them an excellent detox food.

FRESH GINGER TEA

Infuse 1 tbsp peeled and grated fresh root ginger in boiling water for 5 minutes. Strain before drinking.

Spinach This and all salad leaves provide antioxidants, vital for healthy immune function. The darker the leaves, the higher their nutrient value.

Tomatoes A rich source of the antioxidant lycopene. Cooking and processing releases this lycopene, so there is even more in tomato products such as tomato purée (paste), passata (bottled strained tomatoes) and canned tomatoes. All can be included on the detox diet, although tomatoes can aggravate eczema and trigger migraine in some people.

Watercress Rich in antioxidant vitamins and minerals and reputed to help speed up the body's detoxification process and purify the blood. It is a natural antibiotic, can help to promote a clear skin and is reputed to help relieve

Above: Watercress is a natural antibiotic and can relieve a number of complaints.

stomach upsets, respiratory problems and urinary tract complaints. Eat in generous portions.

SEA VEGETABLES

Seaweeds, or sea vegetables as they are now known, are highly nutritious. They absorb and concentrate nutrients present in the sea and provide a rich supply of minerals, such as calcium, iodine and iron, and vitamins, including vitamin B12, which is not found in land vegetables. In Japan, where sea vegetables are widely produced in the coastal waters, they are highly valued for the protection they provide against toxic substances, for their intestinal-cleansing qualities, and for helping to combat acidity in the body, which is caused by over-consumption of coffee and alcohol.

Much of the seaweed sold is in a cleaned, dried and packaged form, under its Japanese species name, such as nori, wakame or kombu, but varieties are also harvested in coastal areas around Europe, including Welsh laverbread and Irish carragheen. Dried types are convenient for keeping in the store cupboard (pantry), and

then can be soaked before using (including the soaking water). Nori is most commonly used for making sushi, but sea vegetables generally can be added to soups, stews and salads. They go well with rice and potato dishes and have a special affinity with fish.

Kelp tablets are a convenient way of including some seaweed in the diet. They can be readily bought from most health food stores.

SPROUTS

All sprouts can be eaten fresh and raw in salads and provide a rich source of valuable vitamins and minerals, as well as protein. Bean sprouts, cress and sometimes alfalfa, can be bought quite readily, but it is also quick and easy to grow your own. The best known and easiest to sprout are mung and aduki beans, chick peas, whole lentils, mustard and cress (fine curled cress), fenugreek and alfalfa seeds. Try to buy seeds that have not been treated with pesticides. (See 'How to sprout' on page 44.)

Above: A wide range of nutritious grains provide variety in the diet.

Dried beans, peas and lentils

These are a great source of low-fat, vegetable protein as well as B vitamins and a wide range of minerals, including iron and magnesium. They also have a high fibre value, which helps to prevent and relieve constipation and lower blood cholesterol, reducing the risk of

heart disease and stroke. There is a wide variety of different beans, peas and lentils to choose from, and they can all be included on a detox diet. Dried beans and peas (but not lentils) require soaking overnight. Soak in cold water, then drain, rinse and cook in fresh, unsalted water. Bring to the boil, then boil rapidly for 10 minutes to destroy any toxins, then simmer gently for 1–1½ hours, or as advised on the packet instructions. If using canned varieties, choose those canned in water or with reduced salt and rinse thoroughly before using. They are very versatile and satisfying to eat and present all kinds of delicious detoxing recipe possibilities, including soups, salads, dips and casseroles. They can be mostly interchanged in recipes.

Left: Do not add salt to the water when cooking dried beans, peas and lentils as this prevents them from softening.

Whole grains

These provide slow-releasing carbohydrate for sustained energy and should be eaten regularly. During a detox, it is advised that wheat and wheat products are avoided, but there are many other cereal grains that can be substituted. These can include rye, barley and oats (unless a gluten intolerance is diagnosed), millet, corn, buckwheat or quinoa and rice. Whole grains make the best choice as they have a higher fibre value than refined types, as well as providing a good supply of B and E vitamins, minerals and small amounts of essential oils. Brown rice is particularly efficient at cleansing the digestive system. It is also anti-allergenic and helps to stabilize blood sugar levels. Quinoa is another easily digested cleansing grain that is a good source of protein, B vitamins, minerals and fibre. It has a nutty flavour and can be steamed or boiled and eaten like rice. Corn, millet or buckwheat pastas, or rice noodles can all be substituted for wheat pasta.

Mycoprotein (Quorn)

Quorn is made from mycoprotein, a plant that is related to mushrooms and truffles. It makes a versatile and nourishing alternative to meat that is easily digested, although it is best to choose the mince, pieces or fillets as an ingredient, rather than ready-prepared recipe dishes, while following a detox diet. Quorn is high in quality protein, low in fat and contains no cholesterol, yet provides a good source of fibre, which helps to fill you up. It is quick and easy to use and versatile for a range of dishes from salads to stir-fries. Note that Quorn contains egg albumen, so it is not suitable for people with a true egg allergy.

Tofu

Made from soya bean curd, tofu provides a healthy and versatile rich source of dairy-free, vegetable protein. It contains all eight essential amino acids making it an excellent alternative to meat. It is also low in saturated fat and sodium, cholesterol-free and provides useful amounts of calcium, iron and B-group vitamins. It is a completely natural product and contains no artificial additives. Furthermore, soya products are rich in phytoestrogens, which can help to lower blood cholesterol and relieve menopausal symptoms and may help to prevent breast and prostate cancers and osteoporosis.

Tofu is sold in a variety of forms, the most common of which are chilled firm tofu, and silken tofu, which has a silky, smooth

Above: Nutritious tofu is a wonderfully versatile ingredient.

texture like yogurt or custard. Firm tofu can be sliced or cut into cubes and used for dishes such as salads, kebabs and stir-fries, or blended for soups, dips, dressings, spreads and desserts.

Silken tofu is best suited for making desserts, soups, dressings and smoothies. Tofu has an ability to absorb and enhance whatever flavour or other ingredients it's mixed with. Other forms of tofu are available, including smoked, marinated and deep-fried tofu, but these are best avoided during a detox.

Left: Mycoprotein has a meat-like texture, yet in contrast to animal protein, it contains dietary fibre in addition to high protein levels.

IDEAS FOR USING TOFU

- Mash the tofu and make it into burgers with onion, herbs, spices and garlic.
- Use as a salad dressing: blend with chopped fresh coriander (cilantro) leaves and lemon juice.
- Thread cubes on to skewers with mushrooms, tomatoes and (bell) peppers; marinate in soy sauce and mustard before grilling.
- Whip with fresh herbs and Tabasco sauce as a dip for carrot sticks and other crudités.

- Blend with fresh fruit, such as strawberries or raspberries, to make a fruit fool.
- Stir-fry with Chinese mushrooms, bamboo shoots, pak choi (bok choy) and cashew nuts.
- Poach in a clear broth with seafood and vegetable strips for a simple, light meal.

Nuts

All kinds of unsalted nuts can be included in a detox diet. They are packed with important nutrients that assist detoxification. Nuts provide protein, B vitamins and many minerals and are an excellent source of vitamin E, which helps to support the immune system and protect against heart disease. Almonds are an especially useful source of calcium, walnuts are rich in the essential omega-3 and omega-6 fatty acids and Brazil nuts are a good source of the antioxidant mineral selenium, essential for the proper functioning of the liver, hormone production and healthy hair and skin. However nuts are high in fat, and although this is largely in the healthy form of unsaturated fatty acids, they are high in calories so should only be eaten in moderation.

Seeds

All kinds of seeds are a good source of vitamin E and the B group vitamins, many useful minerals and fibre. They provide antioxidant defence against cancer, help lower cholesterol levels, prevent and relieve constipation as well as soothe digestion. Pumpkin, sunflower, flaxseeds (linseeds) and sesame seeds all make nutritious snacks, eaten in moderation, or can be sprinkled on to soups, salads, muesli (granola) or casseroles, or stirred into smoothies. Sesame seeds are used to make a paste called tahini, which is included in hummus.

Above: Unsalted nuts make a good alternative to animal protein foods.

Poultry

You can include some chicken and turkey on a one- to two-week detox diet, provided it is skinless and simply cooked by a low-fat cooking method. Poultry provides a low-fat source of high-quality protein and is also rich in most of the essential B vitamins. Do not eat duck or goose while following your detox as they have a higher fat content. Organic birds are not fed antibiotics or other drugs so should be free from drug residues.

Below: Trout is a good source of omega-3 fatty acids and tastes delicious baked or grilled.

Fish

Healthy-eating guidelines recommend that we should eat at least one to two portions of fish a week – one of which should be an oil-rich fish, such as sardines, mackerel, herring, salmon or trout. This is to boost levels of omega-3 polyunsaturated fatty acids, which are believed to help provide protection against coronary heart disease, as well as offering many other health benefits. Oily fish is also a good source of the fat-soluble vitamins A and D. White fish, such as cod, haddock and plaice contain low levels of omega-3 fatty acids, but they provide an excellent source of low-fat protein, minerals and vitamins. Shellfish are low in fat and they are also an extremely rich source of minerals.

Fish is easy to digest provided that it is simply cooked using low-fat cooking methods. Canned fish is just as nutritious and provides economical and convenient options. Look out for those packed in natural spring water or oil, rather than brine.

Fish farming in general is often criticized for its use of 'toxic chemicals', but responsible fish farms only use veterinary medicines that are necessary for fish welfare and ensure that their use is strictly monitored and controlled. You can choose to buy wild or organically-farmed fish if you prefer. What is important is that you make sure that you include fish, particularly oily varieties, regularly in your diet. Although there has been an increase in the pollution of sea and river waters, which means that even fresh fish may contain contaminants, it is mainly the longer living fish, such as sharks and swordfish, that are most likely to be affected.

STORAGE

Nuts and seeds can turn rancid fairly easily, so they should be bought in small quantities, stored in a cool dark place in airtight containers and eaten before the 'best before' date. Also, be aware of potential allergies.

Above: Probiotic yogurt can help to restore to the gut healthy bacteria that have been destroyed by antibiotics.

Above: Non-dairy alternatives to cow's milk can be used for drinks and all kinds of recipes.

Non-dairy milk choices

It is important to include an alternative milk in a detox diet because not only will it provide essential calcium and added vitamins, provided the milk is fortified, but it is usually needed to serve with muesli (granola) and porridge and for making low-fat smoothies.

Choose from a wide range of alternative milks, including rice, almond, oat or soya 'milks', readily available in fresh chilled, long-life and organic varieties. These milks are not only free from animal protein and lactose, but they are low in fat and contain no cholesterol. They taste good too, and may be preferred even after detoxing. Soya 'milks' may be unsuitable for people with an allergy to soya.

Yogurt

Although primarily made from milk, yogurt is easier to digest, and can usually be safely consumed by people with a lactose intolerance. Yogurt provides an excellent source of calcium as well as protein and certain B vitamins. Most fresh, chilled yogurt is 'live' (although it may not be labelled as such), which means it contains living bacteria that are helpful to the digestive system. Yogurt labelled as 'bio' or 'probiotic' is particularly beneficial to the digestive system, helping to redress the natural balance of the gut flora frequently upset by poor diet, too much alcohol, stress, food-poisoning bacteria, antibiotics and foreign travel. Evidence suggests that regular consumption of probiotic yogurt,

providing sufficient friendly bacteria to the gut, may help with conditions such as candida, IBS and stomach upsets as well as helping to strengthen the immune system.

Eggs

A very convenient source of protein, eggs also supply many minerals and vitamins, especially vitamin B12, making them an important food, particularly for vegetarians. Choose organic, free-range eggs to be sure that they come from hens that have ample access to land that is free from chemical fertilizers and pesticides and are guaranteed to be free from yolk colorants.

Below: Boiled, poached or cooked as an omelette, eggs provide a nourishing and easy detox meal.

Above: A light oil and vinegar dressing perks up a simple leafy salad without adding masses of fat and calories.

Oils and vinegars

Vegetable oils provide essential fatty aids (omega-6 and omega-3) and are also a good source of vitamin E. They are made from nuts, seeds, beans, peas and lentils, the most common being sunflower, safflower, rapeseed, corn, olive and soya bean, and consist of varying ratios of monounsaturated and polyunsaturated fatty acids. Any of these can be used in small quantities while following a detox diet. Speciality oils, including walnut, sesame and hazelnut oils can also be lightly sprinkled over salads and stir-fries.

Cold-pressed oils, where the oil has been pressed out rather than extracted by heat, retain more vitamin E, but these oils especially must not be kept for long periods, as they do not keep well, lose their vitamin E when exposed to sunlight and are prone to rancidity. Store oils in a cool dark place and buy in small quantities. Also, do not reuse cooking oils because constant reheating sets off a chemical reaction that can create free radicals.

Cider vinegar makes the best choice of vinegar during a detox. It is made from fermented apple juice and is reputed to have many therapeutic properties including helping to ease arthritic pains and stimulating the liver to produce more bile. It may also help the digestion, regulate metabolism, cure gastro-intestinal infections and diarrhoea, and help to relieve chronic fatigue.

Vital water

Drink at least 2 litres/4 pints/8–9 cups of water each day to help flush out toxins and waste products and to avoid fluid retention. Drinking sufficient water also helps to prevent urinary infections, constipation, headaches and bloating and helps to keep your skin clear. It can be drunk as herbal teas or with freshly squeezed fruit or vegetable juice. Drink plenty of fluids throughout the day, but do not drink to excess. There is no benefit in doing so, and it will just be an inconvenience if you need to visit the toilet frequently.

Herbal teas

Also called tisanes or infusions, herbal and fruit teas provide a refreshing, alternative hot drink to coffee, regular black tea and hot chocolate or cocoa, while following a detox diet. These drinks are naturally caffeine-free as well as sugar-free and contain virtually no calories. They are usually enjoyed without milk or added sugar, and are equally good drunk chilled. The myriad of flavours available is a bonus too, ensuring that the taste buds will never be bored, and you can choose various flavours to suit different moods and times of the day, depending on whether you need to perk up or calm down. Some teas are also reputed to help ease common complaints such as a queasy stomach or an aching head.

HEALTH BENEFITS OF HERBAL TEAS

- Chamomile tea is well known for helping to promote a good night's sleep. You could also try adding a chamomile tea bag to your bath to help yourself relax.
- Lemon verbena, peppermint and fennel are all valued for their calming digestive properties, making them ideal as an after-meal soother.
- Mixed fruit, rosehip, cinnamon, ginger and orange blossom offer awakening, revitalizing properties for when you need a pick-me-up.
- Rooibosch (Redbush) tea, made from a South African herb, contains highly beneficial flavonoids and trace minerals and has been scientifically proved to possess both anti-inflammatory and anti-spasmodic properties, offering relief to many allergy sufferers. It may help to relieve both digestive and skin complaints.
- Parsley tea is a great general aid for the kidneys. Infuse fresh parsley in boiling water for 5 minutes.

Below: Herbal teas make a perfect detox drink choice.

Vital nutrients

We need a range of nutrients in the right amounts to be healthy. Choosing a wide variety of foods should ensure that all our nutrient requirements are met, but as detoxing programmes restrict certain foods for a limited period, you need to be sure of obtaining an adequate intake of vital nutrients. Those that may require particular attention are discussed here. Vegetarians and vegans in particular, must keep a careful watch on nutritional balances.

Calcium

Milk and dairy products are the main source of calcium in the diet, so if these foods are avoided while following a detox programme, it's important to ensure that calcium is supplied by other food sources. The mineral calcium is essential for building and strengthening bones and teeth. An adequate intake from infancy and throughout life can help to prevent fractures and the brittle bone disease, osteoporosis, mainly affecting post-menopausal women. Calcium is also needed for normal blood clotting, muscle contraction (including regulating heartbeat) and nerve transmission, as well as for certain digestive processes. Vitamin D, produced by the action of sunlight on the skin, is also needed for the uptake of calcium absorption. Cutting out caffeine and alcohol, and reducing salt while detoxing will all help to prevent loss of calcium.

Main source Milk and dairy products.
Other sources Canned sardines and pilchards (with bones), dark green leafy vegetables, beans, peas, lentils, nuts (especially almonds), sesame and sunflower seeds, soya products and alternative 'milks' that have been fortified with calcium. Yogurt also provides a valuable source while following a detox programme. Yogurt should be a low-fat, natural (plain) probiotic variety. Avoid fruit-flavoured yogurts as they are likely to contain sugar or sweeteners.

Above: Dried fruits make a nutritious snack, but watch the calories.

Iron

This mineral is needed to help the body to convert food into energy and to make haemoglobin, the pigment in red blood cells that carries oxygen around the body in the blood. It is also essential for many other functions, including keeping your immune system in good order. Iron requirements vary depending on your age and sex, and menstruating women in particular should be sure they are getting enough. There are two types of iron in food: haem iron that comes from meat and non-haem iron from plants and grains. Haem iron is better absorbed by the body, but absorption of non-haem iron can be boosted by eating a food or drink rich in vitamin C at the same time as the food containing the non-haem iron. Iron deficiency is the most common cause of anaemia of women of child-bearing age.

Right: Yogurt is a healthy, low-fat source of calcium.

Main source Red meat and offal.
Other sources Sardines, egg yolks, fortified breakfast cereals (ideally wheat-free during a detox diet), oatmeal, beans, peas, lentils, dried fruits, nuts and dark green leafy vegetables, such as Savoy cabbage, spinach, spring greens (collards), chard and kale.

Vitamin B12

There are eight vitamins in the B complex group and they perform similar functions in the body, including the conversion of food into energy; maintaining healthy skin, nerves and heart function and the formation of red blood cells. Many occur together in the same foods, although vitamin B12 is only found in foods of animal origin. Since red meat, offal and dairy products are avoided during a detox, other food sources that will provide this vitamin need to be included.

This could be some white or oily fish, eggs, poultry or yogurt to ensure a good variety of foods, if following the detox diet for two weeks or more. Vegans need to include foods that are fortified with vitamin B12, such as breakfast cereals, yeast extract and non-dairy milk alternatives, or take a regular supplement.

All the B vitamins are water-soluble, so careful cooking will also help to retain their vitamin value.

Main sources Meat, poultry, fish, eggs and dairy products.

Other sources Fortified foods such as soya 'milk', yeast extract and breakfast cereals (ideally wheat-free during a detox diet).

Folate (folic acid)

This B vitamin is essential for the production of red blood cells and is particularly important for women who are pregnant or trying to conceive, to help protect against spina bifida.

Main sources Green leafy vegetables, beetroot (beets), eggs, beans, peas, lentils, whole grains, citrus fruits, bananas and nuts. It is also sometimes used to fortify some breakfast cereals and yeast extract.

Fibre

This is the indigestible cell walls of all plants. It is not present in any animal products. Although fibre contains no nutrients, it is vital for a healthy digestion, helping to create bulky stools and speed the passage of waste products through the body, preventing constipation. There are two types of fibre: soluble and insoluble. Soluble fibre, contained in oats, beans, peas and lentils, and most fruit and vegetables, provides the further benefits of helping to reduce blood cholesterol and slowing down glucose absorption, thus preventing sudden surges in blood sugar levels.

A detox diet should provide plenty of fibre, in fact probably more that you would usually eat, as it includes an abundance of fruit and vegetables, beans, peas, lentils, oats and other grains such as corn, millet and quinoa, rice (particularly brown rice) and nuts.

Avoiding wheat and wheat products during the detox programme should not be a problem, provided other grains are substituted. Wholegrains have a far higher fibre value than refined cereals that have had the outer layers of the grain stripped away during processing. Continuing to eat a high fibre diet, including a wide variety of foods, after following a detox, will help to prevent constipation and many conditions associated with a low-fibre intake, and may help to protect against

Above: Eat apples unpeeled for the maximum fibre value.

bowel cancer. Too much fibre can lead to flatulence and other digestive problems in some people. If your diet is causing any uncomfortable symptoms, consult your family doctor.

Sources of fibre Fruit and vegetables, cereals (especially wholegrain varieties), beans, peas, lentils, nuts and seeds.

Clockwise from right: Flageolet beans, pinto beans, haricot beans, chickpeas and red kidney beans are all high in beneficial fibre.

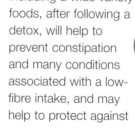

Essential minerals and vitamins

Regular intake of a wide range of minerals and vitamins is essential for general good health, and the vast majority can be found in many different types of food. By regularly eating enough of the correct foods, including at least five portions of fruit and vegetables per day, most people should not need to take additional vitamin or mineral supplements, even during a strict weekend detox, as long as you follow the guidelines and restrict the diet to the specified time limit. Try to ensure that you eat a variety of different types and colours of produce, in particular brightly coloured and dark green fruit and vegetables, to ensure that you are obtaining as wide a range of nutrients and beneficial compounds as possible. This chart describes which foods are the richest sources, the role the mineral or vitamin plays in maintaining good health, and the signs that may suggest a deficiency.

Mineral	Best Sources	Role in Health	Deficiency
Calcium	Canned sardines (with bones), dairy products, green leafy vegetables, sesame seeds, dried figs and almonds.	Essential for building and maintaining strong bones and teeth, muscle function and the nervous system.	Deficiency is characterized by soft and brittle bones, osteoporosis, fractures and muscle weakness.
Chloride	Nuts, whole grains, beans, peas, lentils, tofu and black tea.	Regulates and maintains the balance of fluids in the body.	Deficiency is rare.
Iodine	Seafood, seaweed and iodized salt.	Aids the production of hormones released by the thyroid gland.	Deficiency can lead to sluggish metabolism, and dry skin and hair.
Iron	Meat, offal, sardines, egg yolks, fortified cereals, leafy vegetables, dried apricots, tofu and cocoa.	Essential for healthy blood and muscles.	Deficiency is characterized by anaemia, fatigue and low resistance to infection.
Magnesium	Nuts, seeds, whole grains, beans, peas, lentils, tofu, dried figs and apricots, and green vegetables.	Essential for healthy muscles, bones and teeth, normal growth, and nerves.	Deficiency is characterized by lethargy, weak bones and muscles, depression and irritability.
Manganese	Nuts, whole grains, beans, lentils, brown rice, tofu and black tea.	Essential component of enzymes involved in energy production.	Deficiency is not characterized by any specific symptoms.
Phosphorus	Found in most foods, especially lean meat, poultry, fish, eggs, dairy products and nuts.	Essential for healthy bones and teeth, energy production and the absorption of many nutrients.	Deficiency is rare.
Potassium	Bananas, milk, beans, peas, lentils, nuts, seeds, whole grains, potatoes, fruit and vegetables.	Essential for water balance, regulating blood pressure, and nerve transmission.	Deficiency is characterized by weakness, thirst, fatigue, mental confusion and raised blood pressure.
Selenium	Meat, fish, citrus fruits, avocados, lentils, milk, cheese, Brazil nuts and seaweed.	Essential for protecting against free radical damage and may protect against cancer – an antioxidant.	Deficiency is characterized by reduced antioxidant protection.
Sodium	Found in most foods, but comes mainly from processed foods.	Essential for nerve and muscle function and body fluid regulation.	Deficiency is unlikely but can lead to dehydration and cramps.
Zinc	Lean meat, oysters, peanuts, cheese, whole grains, seeds, beans, peas and lentils.	Essential for a healthy immune system, normal growth, wound healing, and reproduction.	Deficiency is characterized by impaired growth, slow wound healing, and loss of taste and smell.

Vitamin	Best Sources	Role in Health	Deficiency
A (retinol in animal foods, betacarotene in plant foods)	Animal sources: liver, oily fish, milk, butter, cheese, egg yolks and margarine. Plant sources: orange-fleshed and dark green fruit and vegetables.	Essential for vision, bone growth, and skin and tissue repair. Beta carotene acts as an antioxidant and protects the immune system.	Deficiency is characterized by poor night vision, dry skin and lower resistance to infection, especially respiratory disorders.
B1 (thiamin)	Lean meat (especially pork), wholegrain and fortified bread and cereals, brewer's yeast, potatoes, nuts, beans, peas, lentils and milk.	Essential for energy production, the nervous system, muscles, and heart. Promotes growth and boosts mental ability.	Deficiency is characterized by depression, irritability, nervous disorders, loss of memory. Common among alcoholics.
B2 (riboflavin)	Meat (especially liver), dairy, eggs, fortified bread and cereals, yeast extract and almonds.	Essential for energy production and for the functioning of vitamin B6 and niacin, as well as tissue repair.	Deficiency is characterized by lack of energy, dry cracked lips, numbness and itchy eyes.
Niacin (nicotinic acid, also called B3)	Lean meat, fish, beans, peas, lentils, potatoes, fortified breakfast cereals, wheatgerm, nuts, milk, eggs, peas, mushrooms, green leafy vegetables, figs and prunes.	Essential for healthy digestive system, skin and circulation. It is also needed for the release of energy.	Deficiency is unusual, but characterized by lack of energy, depression and scaly skin.
B6 (piridoxine)	Lean meat, fish, eggs, wholegrain cereals, brown rice, nuts and cruciferous vegetables, such as broccoli, cabbage and cauliflower.	Essential for assimilating protein and fat, for making red blood cells, and maintaining a healthy immune system.	Deficiency is characterized by anaemia, dermatitis and depression.
B12 (cyano-cobalamin)	Meat (especially liver), fish, milk, eggs, fortified breakfast cereals, cheese and yeast extract.	Essential for growth, formation of red blood cells and maintaining a healthy nervous system.	Deficiency is characterized by fatigue, increased risk of infection, and anaemia.
Folate (folic acid)	Offal, dark green leafy vegetables, wholegrain and fortified breakfast cereals, bread, nuts, beans, peas, lentils, bananas and yeast extract.	Essential for cell division; especially needed before conception and during pregnancy.	Deficiency is characterized by anaemia and appetite loss. Linked with neural defects in babies.
C (ascorbic acid)	Citrus fruit, melons, strawberries, tomatoes, broccoli, potatoes, (bell) peppers and green vegetables.	Essential for the absorption of iron, healthy skin, teeth and bones. Strengthens the immune system and helps to fight infection.	Deficiency is characterized by increased susceptibility to infection, fatigue, poor sleep and depression.
D (calciferol)	Mainly exposure to sunlight. Also liver, oily fish, eggs, fortified breakfast cereals and fortified dairy produce.	Essential for bone and tooth formation; helps the body to absorb calcium and phosphorus.	Deficiency is characterized by softening of the bones, muscle weakness and anaemia. Shortage in children can cause rickets.
E (tocopherols)	Oily fish, seeds, nuts, vegetable oils, eggs, wholemeal bread, avocados and spinach.	Essential for healthy skin, circulation, and maintaining cells – an antioxidant.	Deficiency is characterized by increased risk of heart attack, strokes and certain cancers.

Herbs and spices for health

Herbs and spices can transform a plain, simple dish into a sensuous eating experience of lively and refreshing flavours that excite the taste buds. They reduce the need for adding salt as a seasoning, can help ease digestion and may also offer natural, curative properties for various common ailments.

The medicinal and cosmetic uses of herbs and spices have a history steeped in tradition, and herbs have been used in these ways throughout the world for thousands of years, as well as for decorative and aromatic purposes. Today, herbs are enjoying a revival, and eaten in abundance, many

varieties can supply a small, yet valuable source of many vitamins and minerals. Use them freely in cooking and for herbal drinks, according to your own personal preferences. Use fresh varieties whenever possible, as they impart the best flavour and beneficial qualities.

Herb/Spice	Good for	Use in
Basil	Aiding digestion and calming nervous system.	Herbal tea, salads, soups, pasta sauces.
Bay	Stimulating the appetite and aiding digestion.	Soups, stews, stocks and marinades.
Black pepper	Stimulating digestive juices, promoting appetite . and relieving constipation. Also improves circulation.	Complements all savoury dishes.
Borage	Rheumatism and respiratory infections.	Hot and cold drinks and salads.
Caraway	Stimulating appetite and digestion and relieving wind. May help relieve menstrual pain.	Cabbage, potato, onion, carrot and bean dishes, casseroles, bread and cakes.
Cardamom	Relieving indigestion and sweetening breath (if chewed). Good for coughs and colds.	Curries, rice, fruit and yogurt dishes.
Chamomile	Relieving anxiety and promoting sound sleep.	Hot herbal tea.
Chillies	Relieving congestion and clearing mucus.	Curries, stir-fries and marinades.
Chives	Cleansing blood, aiding digestion, clearing catarrh, protecting against colds.	Salads, soups, omelettes and dips. Complements egg, cheese, fish, chicken and potato dishes.
Cinnamon	Indigestion and colds, as a nasal decongestant.	Casseroles and curries, sweet and savoury rice dishes, stewed fruits, mulled wine.
Coriander leaf	Stimulating digestion. Both seeds and leaves may help strengthen the urinary tract.	Add to salads, salsas, soups, stews, curries and rice dishes.
Coriander seed	(as above)	Casseroles, curries and chutneys. Complements vegetable and lentil dishes and stewed fruit.
Cumin seed	Helping to relieve indigestion and wind.	Curries and spicy pulse dishes. Complements chicken, lamb, beans, lentils, vegetables and rice dishes.
Dandelion leaf	Fluid retention, blood cleansing and skin disorders, such as eczema.	Salads and herbal teas.
Dill	Wind, hiccups, stomach-ache.	Soups and salads. Complements chicken, fish, egg and vegetable dishes.
Fennel (seed or leaf)	Aiding digestion, and helping to relieve wind, bloating, stomach-ache, nausea, fluid retention and insomnia. The seeds makes an effective breath freshener.	Salads, soups and fish and vegetable dishes. Also complements rice, potatoes, egg and apple dishes. Use for herbal tea.

Herb/Spice	Good for	Use in
Fenugreek seeds	Stimulating digestion, relieving wind and relieving coughing.	Curries and chutneys.
Garlic	Colds, poor circulation, sinusitis. Highly antiseptic and good for purifying and thinning the blood.	Complements meat, poultry, fish, game, rice, pulse and vegetable dishes.
Ginger	Aiding digestion and stimulating the liver to remove toxins from the bloodstream. Helps to relieve colds.	Curries, stews and stir-fries. Complements poultry, Also good for herbal tea.
Horseradish	Stimulating digestion.	Young leaves in salads, grated root in sauces.
Lavender	Soothing headaches, calming nerves and aiding sleep.	The flowers and leaves can be used fresh or dried in herbal teas, salads or to add flavour to custards.
Lemon balm	Relief from chronic bronchial catarrh, feverish colds and headaches.	Herbal teas, cold drinks and savoury or fruit salads.
Marjoram	Aiding digestion, colds and headaches and as a relaxant.	Salads, fish, vegetable, meat, poultry and egg dishes. Infuse as a tea.
Mint	Digestion, upset stomach, colds, influenza and headaches.	Teas and cold drinks, salads, dips and dressings. Complements vegetables, especially peas, tomatoes and new potatoes. Also good with lamb and in yogurt raita.
Nutmeg (and mace)	Helping to alleviate nausea, wind and diarrhoea.	Sweet and savoury dishes including pasta sauces, cheese dishes, cakes and milk puddings.
Oregano	Coughs, nervous headaches and irritability.	Infuse as a relaxing tea and use in the same way as for marjoram.
Parsley and chervil	Stimulating digestion, as a breath freshener and for healthy skin. Good source of vitamin C and iron.	Soups, salads, sauces and casseroles. Complements all kinds of savoury dishes. Chew parsley after eating garlic.
Rosemary	Stimulating circulation and aids in the digestion of fats.	Marinades, vegetable, chicken and oily fish dishes and with roast meats, especially lamb and chicken. Infuse as a tea.
Sage	Aiding digestion of rich food and relieves indigestion. Also antiseptic and antifungal, and can help ease anxiety.	As a flavouring for stuffing, good with vegetable, poultry, cheese and meat dishes, especially pork, game and liver. Infuse as a tea.
Tarragon	Stimulating appetite and digestion and good general tonic.	Soups, salads, fish, chicken and egg dishes, such as omelettes. Also good with raw or cooked tomato dishes.
Thyme	Aiding digestion and can help relieve coughs, colds and sore throats.	Use to make bouquet garni with parsley and bay. Add to stocks, marinades, soups and casseroles. Good with fish, poultry, vegetable and game dishes. Infuse as a tea.
Turmeric	Relieving digestive problems, improves circulation and has antibacterial properties.	Curries, vegetable and rice dishes.

Detox supplements

If following a healthy balanced diet, supplements should not be necessary for most people. However, there are a number of specific supplements, recommended by natural practitioners, that are claimed to help with the detoxification process and that may also be beneficial in helping to relieve certain ailments and conditions.

Aloe vera
Taken as a drink, the juice of this succulent plant is believed to help cleanse and detoxify, boost the immune system and promote greater energy. It also is reputed to be beneficial in helping to relieve a wide range of conditions, including many digestive disorders, allergies, rheumatism and arthritis.

Artichoke extract
Globe artichoke is a member of the milk thistle family. Cynarin, a compound extracted from the artichoke leaves, is thought to help improve liver function, control cholesterol levels and help the gut to break down fats. It is recommended for digestive disorders, helping to relieve indigestion, a bloated feeling and IBS symptoms.

Below: Globe artichokes contain compounds that assist liver function.

Right: Kelp is a form of edible seaweed. It is rich in iodine and can be taken in tablet form, or consumed fresh or dried in soups, salads and dips.

Chlorella and spirulina
These freshwater algae supplements contain a high concentration of chlorophyll and are an excellent source of many essential nutrients, which act as powerful antioxidants. They are claimed to be good blood tonics and cleansers, helping to promote the digestive system by acting as an 'intestinal broom' and removing toxins, boosting the immune system and promoting energy.

Co-enzyme Q10
The full name for this vitamin-like substance is ubiquinol, and it plays an important role in the body's metabolic processes, particularly in the release of energy from food. It is also an excellent antioxidant. It can be made in the body (unlike vitamins that need to be digested) and is found in some foods, but it may not always be synthesized in sufficient quantity, and also levels tend to decline with age. It has been shown to have a stimulating effect on the immune system and may help increase resistance to viral infections, reduce the toxicity of immune-suppressive drugs, alleviate allergic symptoms, help prevent gum disease and help protect against arthritis and other degenerative diseases. It may also help to maintain healthy blood pressure and strengthen the heart and may be prescribed for people with high cholesterol or who are obese or lacking in energy.

Dandelion
Recommended for helping to relieve poor digestion and water retention, and it may also help to cleanse the blood and treat skin disorders, such as eczema. Bitter compounds in the leaves and root act as a general stimulant to the digestive system, especially the urinary organs. It is well known as a traditional diuretic, but with the benefit of not causing potassium depletion, since the dandelion's own potassium content replaces that which may be lost in the urine. Dandelion can also help to increase bile production in the gall bladder and bile flow from the liver, which helps to improve fat (including cholesterol) metabolism. It is a great tonic for sluggish liver function, resulting from poor diet and excess alcohol consumption. You can take dandelion root capsules or add young leaves, gathered from the countryside, to salads. The leaves contain betacarotene and calcium, as well as potassium and more iron than spinach.

Ginkgo biloba
This is excellent for the circulation and is thought to be good for boosting memory as it aids the blood flow to the brain.

Kelp
This form of marine algae is best known for its high iodine content, a mineral that is needed for the thyroid gland to function normally. Kelp tablets (and fresh and dried seaweeds) have long been used in traditional medicine to help treat colds, constipation, arthritis and rheumatism.

Liquorice

This root has a mild anti-inflammatory effect and can help relieve the symptoms of most allergies. However, it should not be used alongside steroid medication or by anyone who suffers from high blood pressure, as it can cause the retention of sodium and the depletion of potassium. Liquorice is available as a root from most health food stores. Grind the root with a mortar and pestle or buy pure powdered root.

Milk thistle

This herb is often recommended to counter-balance the effects of a modern lifestyle, stress, pollution and over-consumption of rich 'junk' foods. It is a powerful liver detoxifier and antioxidant, helping to protect and regenerate liver cells. As well as helping the liver to work more efficiently, this herb increases the secretion and flow of bile from the gall bladder, increasing the body's ability to digest heavy fatty foods. Health conditions where milk thistle is useful include liver problems, such as hepatitis and cirrhosis, over-burden from drugs and hormones, skin conditions such as psoriasis and gall bladder problems.

Probiotics

These are live, beneficial bacteria essential for the healthy functioning of the gut. In a healthy body they are present naturally, but frequently the stores are depleted by the use of antibiotics, illness or by eating a diet high in refined sugars. To help restore a good balance, you should eat live probiotic yogurt regularly or you can take tablet supplements.

Psyllium husks

These are the crushed seeds of the herb plant, plantain, and as a supplement, should be taken with plenty of water. They are rich in soluble fibre, which is good for cleansing the colon, speeding up the passage of waste materials and acting as a gentle laxative. They are also effective in helping to lower blood cholesterol levels and reducing the risk of heart disease.

Rosehip

The reddish-orange fruit of the wild rose (dog rose) has extremely high levels of vitamin C. Fresh hedgerow rosehips can be stewed then strained, to use in drinks. Alternatively, you can buy rosehip tea or tablets. Avoid rosehip syrup as it is very high in sugar.

Wheatgrass

This is a widely used, popular supplement that is available in tablet form, but that can also be bought fresh, from health food stores or home-grown, to use for juicing. It is another potent detoxifier and cleanser, due to its high

Left: Rosehips appear around late summer/early autumn and can be found growing wild in many hedgerows. Use them to make drinks high in vitamin C.

chlorophyll and nutrient content, providing a rich source of B vitamins, plus vitamins A, C and E, as well as many minerals. It is reputed to have many healing properties. Despite being sprouted from grain plants and called wheatgrass, it is gluten-free.

Left: Wheatgrass, rich in chlorophyll (known as nature's healer) is a powerful detoxifier and cleanser.

GUIDELINES

- Always read the label and follow the recommended dosage and guidelines, especially if you are pregnant or have a medical condition. Supplements can be dangerous if the dose is exceeded or the guidlines not adhered to.
- Buy supplements that are as natural as possible, ideally without artificial colourings or flavourings, gelatin coatings or fillers.
- Generally supplements are best absorbed if eaten with food or just after a meal, but follow the instructions on the pack.
- If in doubt about taking any supplement, take advice from a qualified naturopath, a pharmacist or your family doctor, especially if taking medication for a condition. Supplements can interfere with other drugs and supplements, so always seek medical advice.
- Store all supplements in a cool, dry place and safely out of the reach of children.
- Follow the 'use by' date.

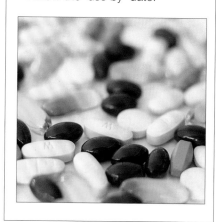

Healthy shopping

Large-scale farming and food production has led to the widespread use of fertilizers, pesticides and other chemicals being added to our food. There is also increasing concern about irradiation and genetically modified food. Choosing carefully where to shop and what you buy can help to reduce your consumption of chemical toxins.

Choose seasonal and locally grown

Although most fresh ingredients are now available all year round, they are at their best nutritionally, and taste infinitely superior, when they are eaten in season.

Moreover, fresh seasonal produce is more likely to be locally grown and not to have been transported thousands of miles, sprayed with preservatives or stored in a controlled-atmosphere container. In order to try and reduce the quantity of toxins consumed, it is essential to return to choosing foods that nature intended for us to eat and to eat them as close as possible to their natural state, free from chemicals. That means choosing food that is seasonal, freshly produced and processed as little as possible. Welcome irregular shapes and sizes, as this is how food looks naturally.

Below: Look out for home-grown fruit at farmers' markets.

Above: Join in a farm-box scheme for the best seasonal produce.

Benefits of organic

Organic agriculture is a method of farming that avoids the use of pesticides and fertilizers for growing crops, and the routine use of drugs and antibiotics for rearing animals. Strict laws and regulations ensure that these conditions are complied with, and organic producers must be certified by a recognized organization responsible for checking that standards are followed. Organic symbols on food labels guarantee it is genuine.

Organic farming is more labour intensive so organic produce tends to cost a little more. However, it does not contain many of the chemical residues found in intensively farmed produce, it tends to be higher in vitamins and minerals, and it also contains higher levels of micro-nutrients believed to offer protection from diseases such as cancer. It may also taste better.

Due to increased demand for organics, led by environmental and health concerns, there is now a wide range of organic produce widely available from supermarkets, local stores and farm-box delivery schemes. However, while it makes sense to choose organic whenever possible, and especially while detoxing, just eating plenty of fruit and vegetables is the most important thing. Everything should be well washed or peeled before eating.

Below: Fresh pears make a juicy autumnal snack or dessert.

Farmers' markets

These are now held frequently around the country and as well as providing an opportunity for farmers and small producers to sell directly to the public, they offer a great way to buy quality, wholesome, local food products. All products must have been grown, reared, caught, brewed, pickled, baked, smoked or produced by the stallholder; and you, the customer, can be confident of the origins of the food and how it has been produced.

Many farms and organic producers run farm-box schemes. Each week they will deliver a box of seasonal produce to your door, providing a bounty of fruit and vegetables, freshly harvested and bursting with optimum nutritional value. Also, look out for signs at farm gates, offering home-grown produce for sale.

Right: Food bought from farmers' markets is usually fresher than that found in supermarkets.

SHOPPING TIPS

• Choose to shop where you know the food is of a good quality. Independent shops generally sell fresh produce supplied by local growers and producers.

• Shop selectively and plan what you need. Look at your menus and recipes for the week (see meal

planners) and make a note of what ingredients you will need to buy.

• Take a list and do not shop when you are hungry, so that you're less likely to be tempted to buy foods that should be avoided while following the detox programme. The shopping list does not need to be too specific, as you will want to be flexible and buy what looks fresh and appealing. So for example, you could just list ' fruit for fruit salad', then decide what to buy when you see what looks good.

• Do not buy ready-prepared fruit, vegetables and salads. Not only will you pay a premium price, but because they are already cut up, they will have lost some vitamin value.

• Buy fresh herbs freely, unless of course you are able to use home-grown. Depending on where you live, there may be a herb farm close by that you can buy from directly.

• Buy fresh foods on a regular basis rather than storing for long periods.

• Stock up on staples, like rice, beans, whole grains, dried fruits, nuts, seeds and good quality canned foods so that you always have ingredients ready to hand for making a satisfying and nutritious detox meal. Wholefood stores or co-operatives are a good place to buy a wide variety of dry goods that are of good quality and reasonably priced.

• Store dry goods in airtight containers to keep them in peak condition and use them before their 'best before' date.

• Don't buy anything that is high in sugar, saturated fat, salt or artificial additives. Always read labels carefully if you are unsure.

• Don't be taken in by terms like 'natural', 'country' or 'traditional' as they mean very little when used on processed foods.

• Take durable shopping bags with you; reuse paper and plastic bags rather than using a new one each time.

Healthy cooking

While following a detox, you need to ensure that you get the maximum nutrient value from your food. However, certain vitamins and minerals are destroyed by heat and are water-soluble, so it is essential that such losses are reduced by thoughtful preparation and cooking.

Raw food

Fruit and vegetables are an excellent source of many vitamins and minerals, yet some of these nutrients are lost during even the most careful cooking. B group vitamins and vitamin C are water-soluble and also destroyed by prolonged heating so eat plenty of raw produce, provided that it can be easily digested. Always wash thoroughly or peel, use a sharp knife to cut with and prepare shortly before eating. Here are some ideas:

• Raw vegetable crudités with dips.
• Plenty of main meal and side salads.
• Use sprouted seeds in salads.
• Enjoy fruit at any time as a quick snack or dessert.
• Add a variety of chopped fresh fruit to probiotic yogurt.
• Make a chilled soup, like Gazpacho.

Below: Raw carrots, red peppers and small florets of broccoli make ideal crudités for dips.

Above: Peel non-organic produce to remove any chemical residues.

Juicing

This is a quick and convenient way of enjoying raw fruit and vegetables, increasing your intake and benefiting from the many nutrients they contain. Juices are easy to digest and help flush out the digestive system, encouraging the elimination of toxins. You can also boost their value by adding a few drops of flaxseed (linseed) oil, a rich source of omega-3 essential fatty acids.

Most fruit and vegetables can be juiced, although some are particularly well suited. A blender or food processor is suitable for juicing tender produce, such as berries, mangoes, melons and bananas, but for firmer-fleshed raw fruit and vegetables, such as apples, pears, carrots, celery and beetroot (beets), you will need a proper juicer, specifically designed for the job.

Juices make super-nourishing drinks, ideal for breakfast or to enjoy as a snack, although remember that only one juice daily counts towards your 'Five a day' intake, and juices should not replace eating a good selection of whole fruit and vegetables.

Juices are best drunk freshly made, because their vitamin content soon begins to diminish, but if made ahead, be sure to keep in an airtight container in the fridge and drink within 24 hours.

You can also now buy many good quality fresh juices and fruit smoothies (not those made from concentrate) that are convenient when you are out and about or if you don't have the time or right equipment to make your own.

HOW TO SPROUT

Beans, peas and lentils are not only nutritious, but they are also easy to grow. This technique is suitable for mung and aduki beans, chickpeas, whole lentils, mustard, fenugreek and alfalfa seeds.

1 First pick over the beans or seeds, removing any tiny stems or stones, and rinse them in a sieve (strainer) under cold running water. Then put about 2 tbsp in a large, wide-necked jar (they should fill about one quarter of the jar) and soak them in plenty of warm water overnight (to encourage quick germination).

2 The next day, drain off the water, cover the jar with a piece of muslin and fasten with string or an elastic band. Lay the jar on its side in a warm, well-ventilated place, out of direct sunlight.

3 Every night and morning, uncover the jar, fill with warm water, swirl around, then cover again and drain off the water completely through the muslin. The jar must be properly drained to prevent mould. Seeds should start to sprout after 2–3 days; beans and lentils will take 5–7 days. When the sprouts have grown to 1–2cm (½–¾in) long, they are ready to eat. Rinse again before using.

Above: Heat the wok or frying pan over a high heat before adding the vegetables, and keep the food moving all the time.

Stir-frying

Being quick and using the minimum liquid and fat, this is an excellent method for preserving maximum nutrients. Peel, chop and slice all the ingredients into bite-size pieces before you start cooking so that they are ready for use and they cook quickly and evenly. Place them in individual piles so that you can add them to the wok in the order of their cooking time – crunchy vegetables like carrots and baby corn first, then quick-cooking vegetables like peppers and mangetouts (snowpeas), and finally delicate leafy vegetables.

The best technique is to place the wok or frying pan over the heat without any oil. When the pan is hot, dribble drops of oil, necklace fashion, on to the inner surface just below the rim. As the drips slither down into the pan, they coat the sides, then puddle in the base. You can get away with using just about a teaspoon of oil if you follow this method. Add the food to be cooked when the oil is very hot, and keep it moving using two spatulas or spoons, as when tossing a salad.

Steaming

This method of cooking is nutritionally excellent as the food does not come in to direct contact with the water, so few soluble nutrients are lost and the flavour and texture of the food is retained. Also, no oil or fat is needed. There are many types of steamer available, including electrical tiered steamers, insert pans with a stepped base that will fit on top of any pan, or Chinese-style bamboo or expanding steamer baskets, which are placed above a pan of simmering water. You can even improvise with a foil-covered wire sieve (strainer) set over a pan of simmering water if you do not own a steamer or do not have space for an electric steamer. Steaming is the ideal way to prepare fish, as the delicate flesh requires only the gentlest cooking.

HOME-MADE VEGETABLE STOCK

Vegetable stock is often used to add extra flavour to soups and stews. However, bought stock (bouillon) cubes, and powder and chilled stocks from the supermarket are often high in salt and may contain flavour enhancers and other artificial additives. The best option, therefore, especially when detoxing, is to make your own stock so you can be sure of what goes into it. It is easy to make using a selection of vegetables, with fresh herbs added for flavour and black pepper for seasoning.

Makes 1 litre/1¾ pints/4¼ cups

750g /1lb 10oz vegetables (such as onions, leeks, celery, carrots, fennel, swede (rutabaga), turnip, squash, broccoli and mushrooms), trimmed, peeled if necessary, and roughly chopped
bunch of fresh herbs (such as bay leaf, thyme, oregano, rosemary, tarragon or parsley stalks)
large strip of lemon zest
6 black peppercorns

Above: Steam fresh vegetables by slotting this basket inside a pan.

Boiling

Always plunge vegetables into boiling water, use the minimum amount of liquid and cook them for the shortest time needed to make them tender. Vegetables cooked in soups and stews retain water-soluble vitamins in their cooking liquid.

1 Put all the ingredients in a large pan and pour over 1.5 litres/2½ pints/6¼ cups of cold water. Bring to the boil, then reduce the heat, partially cover the pan and simmer gently for about 40 minutes.

2 Remove from the heat, strain the stock through a sieve (strainer) or colander and discard the vegetables.

3 Leave to cool, then pour into a plastic container. Keep chilled in the refrigerator and use within 4 days, or store in the freezer for up to 6 months. Thaw in a microwave or slowly in a pan, before using.

Exercise for body and mind

Although making changes to your diet is the most effective way of eliminating toxins, any diet should also incorporate regular exercise to be really beneficial. Also build in some complementary therapies and relaxation techniques, which are therapeutic and make the diet all the more enjoyable.

The importance of exercise

Regular gentle exercise is essential for promoting a healthy body, mind and spirit. It is vital to living a healthy lifestyle and a valuable part of a detox as it stimulates the metabolism and the lymphatic system as well as improving circulation – efficiently transporting oxygen and nutrients to cells while removing waste. It also provides an opportunity to unwind and reflect.

KEY BENEFITS

• Speeds up the metabolism.
• Helps to burn fat and control cholesterol levels.
• Muscular movement enables your body's systems to work more efficiently, removing toxins.
• Stimulates the heart and lungs, improves circulation and helps to reduce blood pressure.
• Helps to combat fatigue and boost energy levels.
• Boosts the immune system.
• Helps to keep bones strong and healthy.
• Improves strength, stamina and suppleness of the major muscles and helps to prevent back pain.
• Promotes deep breathing which is key to relaxation.
• Triggers the release of endorphins – chemicals in the brain that lift your spirits and reduce anxiety, and make you feel calmer and more clear-headed.
• Improves self esteem.
• Aids a good night's sleep.
• Helps to prevent a variety of health problems.

Above: Gentle jogging, especially through water, is a great way to keep fit.

Exercise shouldn't be anything too strenuous or demanding, especially if you are not used to taking much exercise, but should be something you enjoy and can easily fit into your life. Aim to exercise at least three times a week for a minimum of 20 minutes, choose different types of exercise and if you lack motivation, get a friend to exercise or join a class with you. Generally, be as active as you can, walking whenever possible rather than taking the car or using public transport.

The following forms of exercise are excellent at all times, and particularly while you are following one of the detox programmes:
• Brisk walking or jogging
• Rowing
• Swimming
• Cycling
• Skipping
• Dancing
• Golf
• Tennis
• Exercise class
• Gardening
• Yoga
• Pilates

Above: Gardening is therapeutic as well as good, gentle exercise.

Above: Cycle with a friend for added enjoyment and motivation.

Relax your mind

Relaxation, de-stressing and clearing the mind of negativity are just as important as physical exercise and diet during a detox. Body and mind are fully integrated, and stress, anger, fear and negative thoughts can be damaging to the system, reducing its ability to eliminate toxins.

Stress can wear you down making you more susceptible to infections and disease. As well as affecting your health, prolonged stress will make you tired, depressed, irritable and affect your concentration. In a stressful situation, the body produces the hormone adrenalin, which induces a 'ready for action' state in the body.

When there is no outlet for this, it can affect the internal organs, manifesting itself as a headache or causing tense shoulders, indigestion or skin problems. Deep relaxation will therefore benefit not just your mental state, but your body too. There are many kinds of relaxation techniques such as massage and meditation. These are discussed in detail in the following pages.

WAYS TO REDUCE STRESS

• Take time out from work and the pressures of daily life at least once a week.
• Delegate to ease the burden of everyday tasks.
• Share problems with a partner or friend, or talk to a professional counsellor.
• Face up to problems and do something to resolve them.
• Plan a holiday or outing so that you have things to look forward to.
• Eat regular and healthy meals.
• Build regular physical exercise into your life.
• Put on some calming music and sit back with a good book.
• Watch a comedy film, that makes you laugh and smile.
• Treat yourself to a massage, facial, manicure or pedicure.
• Learn, practise and master different relaxation techniques.

Below: Make sure you take time out to relax regularly.

Above: Sleep is a great antidote to daily stresses and strains.

How to get a good night's sleep

Diet can play an important role in affecting your sleep. During a detox, you should find that you sleep better anyway, as caffeine drinks, chocolate and alcohol are eliminated from your diet, and hopefully you will not be smoking. All of these are stimulants (except alcohol which is a depressant), and can keep you awake and interfere with sleep patterns.

• Anxiety, stress and depression can all cause insomnia. Find ways to reduce or cope with stress.
• Never go to bed hungry, and never go to bed on an over-full stomach. Detox meals are not heavy or rich and include complex carbohydrates that have a calming effect on the brain.
• Chamomile tea and valerian are the best herbal teas to help promote sleep and can act as mild sedatives. Stir in a little honey, if liked.
• Regular exercise will promote deeper sleep, but avoid anything too strenuous late in the evening.
• Don't over-stimulate your mind before bedtime. Instead of watching television, try listening to some gentle music or read a book (not one related to work).
• Relaxation therapies, including a soothing bath, will help you sleep well.
• Love-making is also conducive to good sleep.

Complementary therapies and relaxation techniques

Complementary therapies have become increasingly popular and are now widely available in holistic therapy practices, beauty salons, health clinics, and sports and fitness centres. Not only can these help with the detox process, but because they aim to treat the body as a whole, they are beneficial for correcting your emotional, mental and spiritual state and inducing a state of balance and harmony in the body. Aim to treat yourself to at least one complementary therapy during your detox.

Massage

Not only is a massage pleasurable and relaxing, but it can offer a great many physiological and psychological benefits. These include:

• Stimulating the lymphatic system helping to reduce fluid retention and eliminate toxins.
• Increasing the oxygen and nutrient supply to the tissues by increasing the blood circulation.
• Helping to restore balance and to regulate hormone production in the body.
• Stimulating the body's natural immune system.
• Reducing bodily tensions and easing stiff, tight muscles that can result from being stressed.
• Helping to increase energy levels.
• Promoting a general state of happiness and well-being.
• Calming and soothing the mind.

Massage can also be helpful for conditions such as asthma, depression, neck and back pain, insomnia and immune-deficiency disorders.

There are many kinds of massage, including Swedish, therapeutic, aromatherapy and acupressure, but they all apply the same technique of using the hands to perform stroking, kneading and pummelling movements, usually directly on the skin, to promote relaxation, healing and well-being.

LYMPHATIC DRAINAGE MASSAGE

One of the most gentle forms of massage is lymphatic drainage massage. It works on the lymphatic system (the body's drainage system, which carries nutrients into cells and removes waste products), and since lymph vessels are positioned close to the surface of the skin there is no need for heavy pressure.

The lymphatic system of the body is a secondary circulation system, which supports the work of the blood circulation. The lymphatic system has no heart to help pump the fluid around the vessels, and therefore it must rely on the activity of the muscles to aid movement.

Lymphatic massage involves using sweeping, squeezing movements along the skin. The action is always directed towards the nearest lymph node. The main nodes used when treating the foot are located in the hollow behind the knee.

Lymphatic drainage massage is hugely beneficial in helping to eliminate waste and strengthen the body's immune system and leaves you feeling wonderfully relaxed.

1 To improve lymphatic drainage to the feet and legs, try a daily skin "brush" using your fingertips. Begin by working on the thigh. This clears the lymphatic channels in this region so that it is ready to receive the lymph flood from the lower legs. Briskly brush all over the thigh from knee to top, three or four times.

2 Work on the lower leg in a similar way. Brush either side of the leg from ankle to knee, then treat the back of the leg. Follow this by brushing along the top of the foot, continuing up the front of the leg to the knee. Brush over each area twice more, making three times in total.

This facilitates the flow of blood and lymphatic fluid and relaxes the muscles. Massage strokes are light and move rhythmically towards the heart. A light oil, lotion or talcum powder is used so that the hands can glide smoothly and easily over the skin. For an aromatherapy massage, blends of specially selected essential oils are used. Treatments that involve a whole body massage usually take about one hour and should only be performed by a qualified practitioner.

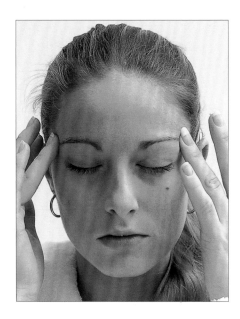

Right: Performing a simple head massage can help to reduce the tension that can lead to headaches.

SIMPLE SHOULDER MASSAGE

If you are unable to visit a practitioner for a full body massage, a simple shoulder massage is easy to perform with a partner, either sitting on an ordinary kitchen chair or lying face-down on a bed, with your partner standing behind or at the side of the bed. Place your hands on his or her shoulders, close to the neck. Your fingers should be to the front over the top of the shoulders. Using your thumbs, press down and firmly roll the flesh upwards, working outwards across the shoulders and taking great care not to dig in with your fingernails. A massage should be relaxing and pleasurable, not painful.

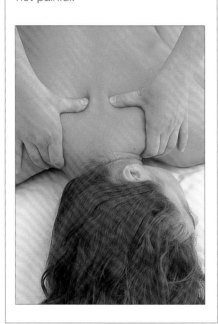

Reflexology and shiatsu

This treatment, also sometimes called 'zone therapy', massages the acupressure points on the feet, and sometimes the hands, and has been shown to help remove blockages and eliminate toxins, and to rebalance the body. Reflexology is based on the belief that there are reflex areas on the feet (and hands) corresponding to all the parts of the body, including major organs. The therapist stimulates and

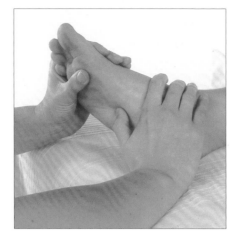

Above: Foot massage stimulates the body's natural healing powers.

works these organs and systems through the reflexes, applying pressure to the feet with thumb and fingers.

Not only is reflexology a very relaxing therapy, but it can also help with digestive disorders, asthma, migraine, sinus problems, hormone imbalances (including menstrual and menopausal problems), poor circulation and muscular pains, and relieving tension and stress. With regular treatments, many conditions can be alleviated without the need for medication.

Shiatsu is based on similar principles to those of reflexology but incorporates the whole body and uses pressure, stretching and manipulation to stimulate the healing process and restore a sense of well-being.

Aromatherapy

Aromatherapists use the purest plant essences in the form of organic essential oils extracted from plants, fruits, flowers, leaves, berries and roots. These aromatic oils contain powerful, complex natural chemicals with therapeutic properties that can be used to treat a wide range of ailments and conditions. Based on individual consultation, a qualified aromatherapist will select the most appropriate essential oils for each client. These oils are quite potent and should not be used directly on the skin, but are blended with a carrier/base massage oil – sweet almond or grapeseed oil are commonly used. This aromatherapy blend is usually applied to the skin with traditional body massage, then penetrates the skin and travels round the body via the bloodstream and lymph vessels. Lightly warming the oil increases absorption.

A few drops of diluted essential oil can also be added to your bath water, sprinkled on a pillow to help promote a good night's sleep (lavender is particularly good), used in an oil burner or vaporizer as an air freshener, or added to a bowl of hot water for steam inhalation. Lean your face over a bowl, drape a towel over your head to completely enclose the bowl, then breathe in the steam deeply and slowly for 3–4 minutes.

Book an appointment with a practitioner for an aromatherapy massage or for advice on choosing aromatherapy oils.

Left: Essential oils should be used sparingly and must be diluted.

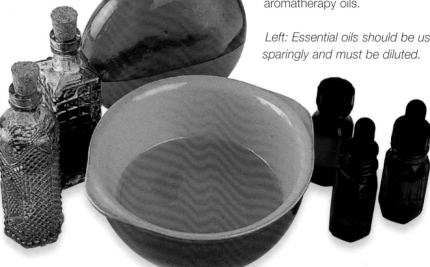

Right: Moisturizing your skin straight after a warm bath leaves it soft and supple.

Hydrotherapy

Water therapy is not only relaxing but boosts the circulation, opens and unblocks the pores and encourages the removal of toxins. A bath or sauna taken before a massage will help to relax the muscles and encourage further elimination of toxins.

Aromatherapy bath Run a warm bath and add drops of your chosen essential oil or oil blend, stirring the oil into the water to disperse it. Calming oils include chamomile, myrrh, lavender, sandalwood, frankincense, patchouli and ylang-ylang. Stimulating oils include rosemary, geranium, rose, lemon and juniper. (Note that many oils are not suitable for use during pregnancy.)

Epsom salts bath This encourages the elimination of toxins through your skin. The salts are high in magnesium, which is good for tired muscles. Pour 450g/1lb Epsom salts into a warm bath and lie back for 20 minutes, adding more hot water if the bath becomes cool. Afterwards, pat yourself dry, wrap yourself in a warm towel and go to bed or relax for an hour. You may sweat during the night, so drink plenty of water before you retire. In the morning, have a bath or shower to remove any salty residues.

Sitz bath Spend a few minutes in a warm bath, then have a very brief icy-cold shower, or dip into cold water. The temperature change stimulates the circulation and internal organs, encouraging the removal of toxins.

Sauna and steam (Turkish) baths These encourage sweating and boost the circulation, which aids the removal of toxins. Spend 5-10 minutes in the sauna or steam room at a time, taking a cold shower or swim in between. Finish with a cold shower. Relax for 30 minutes to allow your body to adjust to its normal temperature.

Note If you suffer from heart problems, avoid any of these baths. If you suffer from eczema or high blood pressure, avoid the Epsom salts bath.

SKIN BRUSHING

Dry skin brushing, using a natural bristle brush or loofah, is a wonderful way to boost your circulation. It makes your skin smooth and soft and helps to get rid of cellulite, because it encourages the lymphatic system and the expulsion of toxins through the skin. The whole process should take less than 10 minutes and it is a great way to start a detox day before

taking a bath or shower. It also increases the effectiveness of an aromatherapy bath.

1 Start at your feet and toes, brushing up the front and back of your legs using long, firm strokes (always brush towards your heart to encourage blood flow). Move up to your thighs and groin area.

2 Brush over your buttocks, up to the lower back. Now brush your hands and arms, moving towards the heart, using long, smooth strokes.

3 Brush your stomach using circular, clockwise movements.

4 Move across your shoulders, down over your chest, then down your back, towards your heart.

Meditation

This uses the same technique as visualization, by focusing the mind on a word or phrase (a mantra), and on an object, or a visual symbol, which has a special meaning for you. Your mantra can be any calming word you choose, such as 'peace', 'love' or 'joy'; an object could perhaps be a flower or a candle; the visual symbol could be a memory of a particularly happy time in your life. Choose a quiet place to meditate where you will not be disturbed, close your eyes and breathe slowly and deeply. If distracting thoughts arise, bring your attention back to what you are meditating on. To begin with, you will find that your mind constantly wanders, but the more you practise, the easier it becomes. During the day, whenever you feel stress building, simply contemplate your word, object or symbol – this will help your mind to relax.

Below: Ensure you are not going to be disturbed, wear comfortable clothes and sit in an airy room when meditating.

Deep breathing

Learn to breathe slowly and deeply, through your nose rather than your mouth, and you will immediately feel more relaxed. All too often, and especially when stressed, breathing tends to be shallow, and if you don't take in enough oxygen, it is harder for the lungs to expel waste products and harmful toxins.

This exercise costs nothing and will help your body to detox as well as to reduce blood pressure, levels of stress hormones and tiredness.

CALMING VISUALIZATION

This is a very simple and effective relaxation technique, which will have the added bonus of heightening your senses.

1 Lie or sit down in a quiet place and close your eyes. Try to clear your mind and relax your muscles.

2 Imagine yourself in an idyllic, peaceful place, where you feel comfortable and safe, such as a sandy beach or the countryside. Use your senses to visualize the colours, smells, sounds and feel.

3 Think of a short and positive statement such as 'I am calm and relaxed' and repeat it a few times. You can escape to this favourite place whenever you feel stressed.

Preparing to detox

Following a detox diet should be a relaxing and rejuvenating experience, so it is essential that you are in a positive, stress-free state of mind. However, before starting, you should be fully prepared as this is the key to a successful detox. Here are some tips and guidelines for things you need to plan and think about before you embark on a detox diet.

Timing

You can detox at any time of the year, although popular times tend to be at the start of spring or summer, after the Christmas and New Year excesses, or in preparation for a holiday or a special occasion. There is nothing like a big incentive to spur you on, but the most important factor is to start with a positive attitude.

Choose a time when you are not too busy and can allow yourself plenty of time to relax. Delegate as many tasks as you can to others so that you do not feel pressured. A short weekend detox should be relatively easy to plan, but if you are planning to follow the detox programme for one or two weeks, you will want to make sure there are no important dates like dinner parties or holidays that could make it difficult to stick to a prescribed eating plan.

It is also not a good time to detox if you are going through any kind of particularly stressful major life change, such as moving house, changing your job, or divorce or separation. Wait until your life is calmer, when a detox may be just what you need for a new lease of life following a particularly demanding or worrying occasion or point in time.

WHEN NOT TO DETOX

As long as you are fit and healthy, it is safe for you to follow a detox programme. However, if you have any concerns, you must check with your family doctor first. Do not embark on a detox if any of the following conditions apply to you:
• If you are pregnant, breast-feeding or trying to become pregnant.
• If you are diabetic or following a special diet for any other medical condition.
• If you have recently been ill, or are recovering from an illness. Wait until you feel completely better.
• If you are under 18 years of age or over 65 years of age.
• If you are taking any kind of medication, you must first consult your family doctor.

Clear away temptations

Remove from your kitchen cupboards items of food that should be avoided during a detox, such as processed and refined foods, and particularly sweet or salty snack foods that you might be tempted to grab in a weak moment. Pack away and certainly do not buy any biscuits, crisps or chocolate. Out of sight, out of mind is the best policy, which will make it so much easier for you to stick to the diet. Then restock your cupboards with the healthy choices you plan to eat.

Fill bowls with fresh fruit and place them on a sideboard in the living room, on the kitchen work surface and/or on a desk at work, to be readily available for healthy snacks.

Fill a jar with a selection of herbal tea bags and place it next to the electric kettle, ready for making refreshing hot drinks whenever you like.

Left: Making an action checklist and planning your detox in advance will help you to be much better prepared and to achieve your goals.

Kitchen essentials

Clear kitchen work surfaces of all equipment and gadgets that you will not be needing, such as toasters, coffee-makers and sandwich toasters. This will give you more space to create healthy dishes that are suitable for a detox regime, and will also help you to resist the temptation of a piece of toast or a cup of coffee.

Put out on display all types of equipment that will be useful, such as chopping boards, knives, peelers, graters, weighing scales, a blender, a food processor and a juicer or smoothie-maker. This will encourage you to use the time during a detox to experiment with dishes and equipment that you have not tried before, or that you do not use very often.

You should also make sure that you have plenty of airtight containers in which to keep dried foods – such as dried beans, peas and lentils – and to transport suitable lunchtime foods to work. It is recommended that you

buy a water-filter jug and a steamer for cooking vegetables, if you do not have these already. A wok and/or griddle pan are useful but not essential pieces of equipment – you can use a large non-stick frying pan in place of both.

Use the detox as an opportunity to have a good spring-clean in the kitchen, and clear the refrigerator of any foods that are not appropriate so that it is ready to be stocked up with all the foods that are suitable for the detox regime.

Left and below: A blender or food processor is ideal for making soups and smoothies using fresh fruit and vegetables, and a juicer is useful for making a wake-up drink of warm water and freshly squeezed lemon juice.

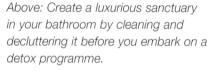

Above: Create a luxurious sanctuary in your bathroom by cleaning and decluttering it before you embark on a detox programme.

Bathroom essentials

Clean, clear and tidy the bathroom, giving yourself a relaxing and calming environment where you can retreat for some time to pamper yourself each day, and where you will be able to relax in undisturbed peace.

Stock up with bathroom beauty products, such as luxurious bubble bath, moisturizing cream, exfoliating scrub, face masks, hair treatments and a new loofah or flannel mitt (towelling or natural fibre). Try to choose pure, natural skin care products and treat yourself to some good quality aromatherapy oils.

Position some scented candles around the bathroom so that you can enjoy their warm and scented glow while you are in the bath. Select large, thick cotton bath towels and a soft and cosy bathrobe to wrap yourself up in when you get out of the bath. In fact, why not use the opportunity to treat yourself to something new? It is all about pampering yourself without the expense of booking into a health farm.

Setting the Mood

Clear out clutter Physical disarray adds to the tension of life, so have a good tidy up and either put away or give away what you don't need. Clearing clutter is an orderly way to help you feel calm. Also, you do not want to spoil your detox time by having to do very much housework.

Buy fresh flowers Studies have shown that fresh flowers can help to relieve stress, soothe away anxieties and help trigger feelings of happiness. So choose some pretty favourite blooms to enhance your living and working environment.

Choose greenery Plants pour oxygen into the environment and soak up carbon dioxide and pollutants. Keep plants where you work, live and sleep and you will enjoy more oxygen, allowing you to breathe better.

Bring in fresh air Open at least two windows in two different rooms to let fresh air sweep away any stale air in your rooms, particularly if the air is polluted with cigarette smoke. If you live on a busy road, open windows at the back of the house or at a time when there is the least traffic. Do not use air fresheners, although pot pourri and incense can be a pleasant, non-toxic way of scenting the air.

Turn down the lights Electric lighting can be harsh and cold, so although bright lights are frequently needed for many daily activities, candles can provide a more soothing glow for when you want to wind down and relax, especially after a hectic day. Choose from a range of scents to suit your mood.

Music therapy Music is also brilliant for helping you to relax and unwind.

It can produce a sense of well-being and stimulate the production of endorphins, the body's natural painkillers. During a detox, calming music is likely to be the best choice. You may wish to buy or borrow some suitable cassette tapes or CD's, such as some of the New-Age music styles especially suited to meditation, yoga, relaxation, massage and reiki.

Reading material Since you are unlikely to be going out wining and dining or partying and will have time to relax more at home, collect some good books and magazines for leisurely reading.

Miscellanious Buy a notepad and pen for creative writing or artist's materials for drawing or painting.

Below: Enhance your bedroom environment with fresh linen, and declutter.

Detox your home

Give your home a quick detox and improve your environment.

- Open windows regularly.
- Turn the central heating down by a few degrees.
- Put water-filled bowls on windowsills or next to fireplaces.
- Don't overuse appliances like computers and mobile phones.
- Choose natural fabrics and materials.
- Buy some pot plants. They are natural air filters and can effectively enhance and freshen air quality.
- Keep pet allergens at a minimum by making certain rooms, such as the bedroom, a pet-free zone, and remember to wash and groom pets regularly to prevent shedding.
- Use a vacuum cleaner that has a high efficiency filter. Dusting with a damp cloth will reduce air-borne particles, and use a natural beeswax type polish rather than aerosol sprays.
- Have your boiler and any gas fires checked regularly.
- Filter your tap water if you are concerned about the quality.

Below: Houseplants can detox and freshen stuffy air.

Above: Enlist friends and family for motivation and support.

Light up your life

Your detox living space should ideally be light and airy. Light makes you feel happy and energized, whereas dark rooms and a lack of natural sunlight can make you feel depressed. So make sure that your windows are sparkling clean, do not block out natural light with fussy window dressings and make the most of mirrors, especially opposite windows, to reflect light.

Colour too can affect your mood. For detoxing, light shades of blue are calming and relaxing, and pale green can make us feel cooler and more comfortable. Pastel shades are ideal for a tranquil bedroom atmosphere, and the tones of the sea work well in a bathroom for a feeling of freshness and cleanliness.

Gather support

Tell friends and family that you are setting aside some time to detox. With their support in helping to share healthy meals, helping with household chores and not making demands on your time, it will be so much easier to stick to the programme. Real enthusiasts may even like to join you, and following any kind of diet is so much more enjoyable with support than attempting it alone.

Easing in gently

In the weeks preceding a detox, choose healthy meals, avoid junk food, wean yourself off alcohol and cut back on tea, coffee and fizzy drinks, gradually substituting with decaffeinated coffee or tea, or herbal infusions .

If you're a smoker, certainly cut back, and if possible, think about trying to give up completely. Speak to your doctor for advice or investigate the various alternative methods such as acupuncture and hypnosis.

Take some regular gentle exercise, such as a brisk 15–20 minute walk at least three times a week, to stimulate the circulation and metabolism.

Book any complementary treatments. See what's available in your area and treat yourself.

Following the detox programme

Whether you wish to follow a one- or two-week programme or experience a reviving weekend, you will need to incorporate the programme into your lifestyle so that the changes to your diet are relatively easy to make and adhere to. Plan for all eventualities so your detox runs as smoothly as possible.

How long for?

You can choose to follow either a strict weekend detox programme based on fruit and vegetable dishes, or a one- to two-week detox diet that allows you to eat a wide variety of foods. You will feel the benefit after one week or just after a weekend detox, but if you are able to continue for two weeks, this will reward you with an even greater boost to your health and general well-being.

The two week detox diet is based on a programme of light and healthy eating, incorporating wholefoods and a wide variety of fruit and vegetables, and avoiding foods that commonly cause sensitivities. Some light fish, poultry and egg dishes have been included to ensure that you obtain all the nutrients you need while encouraging your body to flush out toxins.

It is not advisable to follow a detox diet for longer than the time specified. This is because certain food groups are restricted and a healthy diet should include a wide variety of foods, unless you have sound medical reasons for excluding a particular food.

Detoxing should not be viewed as a time of deprivation, but rather as an opportunity to spring-clean your body and to restore balance. Do not worry too much if you lapse on occasional days. Simply resolve to get back on track the following day.

Once you have completed your detox regime, try not to slip back into unhealthy habits. Gradually reintroduce the foods and drinks that were temporarily restricted, while continuing to eat healthily and exercise regularly, in order to maintain the benefits gained by following the healthy-eating guidelines.

Above: Detox dieting encourages you to freely eat a wide range of fresh fruit and vegetables, and is a good way to experiment with produce you have not tried before.

Flexible Eating

Menu plans are suggested in this book, although you can vary the recipes, swap meals around and substitute ingredients to suit your own food preferences and according to availablity and what is in season. However, be sure to choose a wide variety of foods, within the detox guidelines, to ensure that you get a balance of food groups and do not get bored.

Eat in abundance A wide range of all fresh fruit and vegetables.

Eat in moderation Rice, beans, peas, lentils, grains and grain products (including oats, barley, rye, millet, buckwheat, corn and quinoa), nuts and seeds, tofu, low-fat probiotic yogurt, fish, skinless poultry and eggs.

Avoid Red meat and meat products, dairy products, wheat products, processed and refined foods, ready meals and fast food, crisps (potato chips) and savoury snacks, chocolate and sweets (candies), sauces and pickles, caffeine drinks and alcohol.

Plan meal times

Eat three meals a day – breakfast, lunch and dinner. Do not skip any meals and make time for breakfast. Even if you do not feel hungry in the morning and do not usually eat a breakfast, get into the habit of doing so. There are lots of delicious choices suggested in the chapter on 'Juices, smoothies and breakfast ideas'. Breakfast kick-starts the metabolism after resting overnight and the body needs fuel for energy so that you do not feel tired and unable to concentrate. Eating regularly also helps to keep your blood sugar levels stable and helps prevent binge eating or snacking between meals. Aim to have breakfast before 9am, lunch between midday and 2pm and dinner before 8pm, allowing a reasonable time between meals for comfortable digestion. If you have a busy work schedule, try to arrange your appointments around meal-times rather than letting your diary rule when you have time to eat.

Above: Canned beans in water are healthy, versatile and convenient.

Be prepared

Keep the kitchen cupboards well stocked with staples like rice, beans, lentils, canned tomatoes, nuts and dried fruit, so that you always have the basics to hand for making a healthy detox meal. Also keep a selection of frozen fruit and vegetables, fresh home-made stock and fish and chicken in the freezer. Read through the recipes and buy ingredients that keep well so that you are prepared if you don't have much time to shop.

Coping with family meals

All of the recipes in this book make healthy choices and can be enjoyed by everyone, but a detox diet is not suitable for children or certain other members of the family, as discussed under 'When not to detox' on page 52. If you can follow a detox with a partner so much the better, as this will make food shopping and meal preparation easier, plus you will be able to support and encourage each other. Most of the recipes serve four, but quantities can easily be halved if just cooking for two.

For children or other members of the family who are not detoxing, you can remove your portion from the pan or dish and then simply add bread, pasta, meat and dairy products to their portions. The recipes in this book can be useful for helping all of the family to follow a healthier diet. They encourage the use of a wide range of different fruits and vegetables, whole grains and oily fish, in preference to highly processed and refined foods, which are usually loaded with unhealthy fats, sugar, salt and chemical additives as well as being low in fibre. Try to sit down for a social and structured meal rather than grabbing food on the move.

Below: Make meal times an occasion for talking and relaxing.

Eating out

You should not eat out while following a weekend detox diet, and if you can you should avoid it while following a longer-term programme as it will be harder to control exactly what goes into the food. Should you for some reason have to dine out, here are some suggestions for dishes that you could choose:

• Tzatziki, guacamole, salsa or hummus with raw vegetable crudités.
• Vegetable soups (non-creamy).
• A simple bean and young vegetable salad, without any mayonnaise.
• Grilled, baked or steamed fish or chicken with plain boiled rice or new potatoes and a large green leafy salad on the side.
• Jacket potato, without any butter, topped with beans, hummus, tuna or mixed salad.
• Vegetable, chicken or tofu stir-fries with rice or rice noodles.
• Casseroles made with vegetables, beans or chicken.
• Lentil or vegetable curry with plain basmati rice.
• Plain or herb omelette with salad.
• Fresh fruit or fruit salad.

Above: Spring Vegetable Omelette would be an ideal light meal in a restaurant. Order with a large serving of fresh salad on the side.

Below: Butternut Squash Soup with Tomato Salsa is quick and easy to make and perfect for a working lunch.

Working lunches

If you are out at work or away from home during a one- or two-week detox, you will need to take a packed lunch with you so that you have something suitable to eat and do not end up resorting to a food that should be avoided. Sandwiches made with wheat bread will be off the menu during a detox, although you can make sandwiches with rye bread, or add toppings to rye crispbreads, rice cakes or oatcakes. Good detox lunch choices include:

• Soups (home-made or good-quality fresh store-bought soup). Pack in a vacuum flask.
• Salads (large, mixed or a selection of simple salads).
• Dips with vegetable crudités.
• Slice of Spanish omelette made with vegetables, with side salad.
• Half an avocado filled with tuna or prawns and salad.
• Chopped fresh fruit and low-fat probiotic yogurt.
• Falafel (spiced chickpea patties) with salad and yogurt raita.

IDEAS FOR HEALTHY SNACKS

On the detox diet you should never feel hungry if you eat regular meals. This is because the meals are packed with fruit, vegetables, whole grains and beans, which are high in dietary fibre, so they are filling and satisfying. However, if you are ever peckish between meals, or need to eat something quick on the run, here are some ideas for healthy snacks to keep you going. Ensure that you do not snack to excess. Nuts, seeds and dried fruit especially are high in calories, and eating them too frequently or in large quantities can easily lead to weight gain.

• Small handful of sunflower or pumpkin seeds.
• Piece of fresh fruit or a handful of raw vegetable crudités.
• Oat cakes or rice cakes spread with Hummus or Pea Guacamole.
• Small handful of unsalted nuts or dried fruit.
• Small pot of low-fat probiotic or soya yogurt (preferably unsweetened if possible).
• Home-made unsweetened fruit or vegetable juice or smoothie (or choose good quality fresh, chilled store-bought varieties).
• Handful of olives (rinsed if packed in brine).

Above: Herbal tea makes a caffeine-free alternative hot drink.

Possible side effects

While detoxing, your health should gradually start to improve, but you may experience temporary side effects, known as 'healing or cleansing crises'. Symptoms may include headaches, tiredness, nausea, feeling cold, spots on the skin, bad breath, a furry tongue or irritability. Do not be concerned or think about giving up the diet. This is perfectly normal and a positive sign that the body is getting rid of accumulated toxins that were previously stored. The severity of any symptoms you experience will depend on the level of toxins present in your system, and on how strictly and for how long you follow a detox programme. These symptoms may also be a reaction to withdrawing foods, such as coffee or alcohol, to which you may be allergic or dependent on.

There is no need to take painkillers or other medicines, as the symptoms will soon pass. Painkillers can also be detrimental to detoxing. Simply drink plenty of water or herbal teas to flush the toxins out, and get plenty of rest.

You may also lose weight on a detox because you've cut out eating fatty and sugary foods and alcohol, all of which are high in calories, as well as removing foods that have encouraged water retention. Weight loss is not the main aim of a detox, but if you are overweight, it can be an added benefit.

A well-balanced diet is vital for good health. Detox diets are restrictive and should only be followed occasionally and for no longer than the maximum time recommended.

CAFFEINE WITHDRAWAL

Sudden removal of caffeine can cause the same symptoms as regularly drinking too many caffeine drinks. If you regularly drink six or more cups a day, cut down gradually over a couple of weeks to avoid withdrawal headaches and irritability.

A weekend detox

A weekend detox is an excellent introduction to detoxing and provides an opportunity to take some time out of a hectic lifestyle just to concentrate on your own well-being. Use this programme either as a short refresher to relax and give your health a boost, or as a lead-in to a less strict one- or two-week detox plan. This weekend detox is a strict regime based on fruit and vegetable dishes and juices, so it should only be followed for two days and no longer. For a longer detox, follow the menu planners provided

A weekend detox programme is designed to give your digestive system a rest, allowing it to concentrate on eliminating stored toxins. It is based on three light meals a day – breakfast, lunch and dinner, but you can also have fruit and raw vegetable snacks during the day. It is essential to drink plenty of water, as well as vitamin-rich juices and herbal teas. Raw fruit and vegetables have a powerful cleansing effect on the body and also supply plenty of vitamins, minerals and fibre.

Above: Give your body a boost before you start the weekend detox by enjoying a delicious nutrient-packed drink, such as Banana and Mango Smoothie.

Below: Cut down on chocolate before starting a detox programme.

Timing
Choose a weekend when you are free to completely rest and relax. You will gain the greatest benefit from your detox if you can fully devote yourself to the regime without distractions and not feel under pressure from anyone.

Preparation
• Prepare for your detox by gradually cutting down on all the 'Foods to avoid' up to one week before. This will help your body to adjust more easily to the restricted eating plan and also help to prevent withdrawal symptoms from reducing or cutting out addictive food and drinks, like chocolate and coffee.
• Follow the detailed guidelines for 'Preparing to detox' and 'Following the programme', discussed in the previous pages.

• Let friends and family know about your detox plans, not only so they can help out with household jobs or perhaps looking after children, but also so that you have company for your planned activities and choice of exercises. They can also provide you with motivation and support.

Above: Reduce your intake of caffeine gradually before a detox to avoid withdrawal symptoms.

Friday

Make sure that your diary is free and that you have no urgent work or household chores that need doing or that will prevent you from relaxing. Avoid subjecting yourself to stressful situations that may cause anxiety. Shop for all of food that you will need over the course of the weekend and cook a healthy light meal for the Friday evening that will be easy to digest. A vegetable soup or a stir-fry would be ideal.

Dinner Here are some suitable recipe ideas – but you can choose something else, if you prefer, from the selection of recipes in this book.

- Spicy Pumpkin Soup
- Citrus Fruit Salad with Avocado
- Mushroom Rice with Cashew Nuts
- Spring Vegetable Stir-fry
- Harvest Vegetable and Lentil Casserole
- Barley Risotto with Roasted Squash and Leeks
- Fresh Fruit with Mango Coulis

Below: An exotic fruit salad is delicious and packed with vitamin power.

Above: A warm bath is relaxing and helps to improve circulation.

TOP TIPS

Do not drink any alcohol and try to avoid smoking to ensure that you have a good night's sleep. Soak in a relaxing aromatherapy bath before retiring, then go to bed early with a good book or perhaps listen to a story on the radio.

Below: Barley Risotto makes a tasty, light and nutritious main meal.

Saturday

Morning Rise and shine with a cup of warm water flavoured with the juice of half a lemon. This will give a kick-start to the liver. Do some simple stretching exercise to stimulate the lymphatic system. Give yourself a dry skin brush to stimulate your circulation, then take a shower or warm bath.

Breakfast Fragrant Fruit Salad, or any other alternative fruit salad or smoothie.

Morning Exercise Take a brisk walk, go cycling or do any other form of exercise you enjoy. Sip water at regular intervals. When you have finished, eat some fresh or dried fruit or raw vegetable crudités, and drink a herbal tea. You could also have some unsalted nuts or seeds, if you are feeling hungry.

Morning Activity Choose from the list of ideas on page 61.

Lunch Choose a chilled tomato or vegetable juice or a juice from the recipe section, followed by a large salad with a light dressing. If it is a cold day, choose a vegetable soup instead. Good choices might include:
• Carrot and Celery Juice
• Red Pepper and Sprout Salad with Cashew Cream Dressing
• Borlotti Bean and Vegetable Soup

Above: Borlotti Bean and Vegetable Soup is served ladled over spinach.

Afternoon Relax with a book or a complementary therapy such as a massage or reflexology treatment. Follow with some free time to put your feet up to enjoy a good book, watch a film or listen to relaxing music. Drink a herbal tea or a refreshing juice. Good choices might include:
• Lime and Watermelon Tonic
• Blueberry Tonic

Dinner Between 6 and 8pm have your evening meal. This should be a lightly cooked vegetable dish served with wholegrain rice to be satisfying. Follow this with a fresh fruit salad, topped with low-fat probiotic yogurt. Good recipe choices might include:
• Stir-fried Vegetables with Cashew Nuts
• Stir-fried Rice and Vegetables
• Spanish-style Vegetables with Thyme

Left: Cinnamon and Squash Smoothie is made with vitamin-rich butternut squash and is as filling as it is delicious.

Evening

Practise a relaxation technique such as meditation or visualization. Pamper yourself with a manicure or pedicure. Have an Epsom salts bath, then relax with a book or calming music and a drink of chamomile or peppermint tea.

Below: Meditation is a great way to relax your mind.

Thursday	**Friday**	**Saturday**	**Sunday**
• ½ fresh grapefruit • Porridge made with water or non-dairy milk	• Fresh chilled unsweetened apple juice • Granola with non-dairy milk or probiotic yogurt	• Tropical Scented Fruit Salad • Scrambled egg with red pepper and fresh basil	• Mango and Lime Lassi • Porridge with Dates and Pistachio Nuts

• Country Mushroom, Bean and Barley Soup • Rye or pumpernickel bread • Handful of dried fruits	• Date, Orange and Carrot Salad • Oatcakes and cherry tomatoes	• American Red Bean Soup with Guacamole Salsa • Minted Pomegranate Yogurt with Grapefruit Salad	• Pan-fried Chicken with Pesto • Roasted Plum Tomatoes with Garlic • New potatoes • Strawberry and Lavender Sorbet

• Seared Tuna Steaks with Tomato Salsa • Wild Rocket and Cos Lettuce Salad with Herbs • Poached Pears in Scented Honey Syrup	• Rice Noodles with Vegetable Chilli Sauce • Fresh Fruit with Mango Coulis	• Teriyaki Salmon • Herby Rice Pilaf or basmati rice • Steamed broccoli • Nectarines baked with Nuts	• Stir-fried Vegetables and Seeds • Exotic Fruit Platter with Ginger

WEEK 2	Monday	Tuesday	Wednesday
Breakfast	• Apricot and Ginger Smoothie • Handful of mixed unsalted nuts and seeds 	• Figs and Pears in Honey • Boiled egg with rye crispbread, spread with yeast extract or nut butter 	• Strawberry and Tofu Smoothie
Lunch	• Baked jacket potato topped with stir-fried vegetables • Orange or satsuma 	• Carrot and Orange Soup • Warm Chicken and Tomato Salad with Hazelnut Dressing 	• New Spring Vegetable Salad • Fresh seasonal fruit salad or piece of fruit
Evening Meal	• Spanish-style Vegetables with Thyme • Wholegrain rice • Strawberries with Passion Fruit Sauce 	• Roasted Cod with Fresh Tomato Sauce • Green beans and new potatoes • Papaya and Green Grapes with Mint Sauce 	• Brown Rice Risotto with Mushrooms • Mixed Green Leaf and Herb Salad • Baked Apples with Figs and Walnuts

Thursday	Friday	Saturday	Sunday
• Lime and Watermelon Tonic • Porridge made with water or non-dairy milk	• Fresh raspberries layered with low-fat probiotic yogurt and sprinkled with granola	• Fragrant Fruit Salad • Luxury Muesli with non-dairy milk	• Summer Fruit Smoothie • Mushroom omelette with grilled tomatoes

• Salad Niçoise • Oatcakes or rice cakes • Grapes or other fresh fruit	• Avocado, Red Onion and Spinach Salad with Polenta Crôutons • Summer Berry Frozen Yogurt	• Artichoke and Cumin Dip with vegetable crudités • Roasted Peppers with Sweet Cicely • Grilled Fennel Salad with Niçoise Olives	• Thai Vegetable Curry with fragrant jasmine rice • Lemon Grass Skewers

• Penne with Green Vegetable Sauce • Rose Water-scented Oranges with Pistachio Nuts	• Griddled Chicken with Tomato Salsa • Minty Broad Beans with Lemon • Baked Peaches	• Chinese-style Steamed Trout • Stir-fried Broccoli with Sesame Seeds • Orange Granita with Strawberries	• Warm Mixed Seafood and Fresh Herb Salad • Baked potato topped with a spoonful of low-fat probiotic yogurt

Long-term healthy eating

Now that you have completed your detox, you will want to maintain and improve on all the benefits you have experienced, and this means continuing with a healthy diet. Foods that were avoided during your detox can now be gradually reintroduced, unless you have specific food allergies or have been advised to follow a special diet by your family doctor or dietician. But do not slip back into bad habits. Healthy eating, combined with regular exercise, sensible drinking and not smoking are the most important ways in which you can help yourself to look and feel well, and avoid many of the chronic ailments and diseases associated with a modern lifestyle.

A healthy balance

Healthy eating does not mean banning favourite foods or worrying about what you eat. It simply means choosing a wide variety of foods and getting the balance right. Choose plenty of starchy (complex) carbohydrates, all kinds of fruit and vegetables regularly and moderate amounts of meat, fish and alternative protein foods, and milk and dairy foods. Choose lower-fat foods whenever you can and particularly try to cut down on saturated fats. Also try to restrict foods that are high in salt, sugar and additives.

If you notice any uncomfortable symptoms returning, like bloating or headaches, then cut back on those foods that you think may be responsible. If you suspect that you may be suffering from a food allergy or intolerance, keep a food diary and discuss your symptoms with your family doctor or a dietician, before restricting your diet.

All of the recipes in this book meet the criteria for healthy eating. Simply reintroduce foods such as different types of bread and pasta, wholegrain breakfast cereals and couscous, and lean meat and dairy products occasionally, to make sure that your diet is varied and above all, enjoyable.

Starchy foods

Foods such as bread, pasta, rice, grains, beans and lentils, breakfast cereals and potatoes (and other starchy vegetables such as parsnips and yams), are all complex carbohydrate foods, rich in starch, which provide the body with energy. They also provide valuable vitamins and minerals and can be good sources of fibre, particularly wholegrain, wholemeal or brown varieties. Fibre in wholegrain cereal foods helps to prevent constipation and may help protect against bowel disease, heart disease and many other health problems. Soluble fibre – the type found in beans, lentils, chickpeas and oats – can also help to reduce high blood cholesterol levels and control blood sugar levels. Wholegrain carbohydrate foods also provide higher levels of nutrients than refined carbohydrates and are more satisfying to eat, providing a sustained source of low-fat energy.

Above: Brown rice, wholewheat pasta and beans are all good sources of fibre.

Healthy-eating guidelines recommend that we should eat plenty of these starchy foods. They are not stodgy, fattening or high in calories, provided they are not cooked or served with a lot of fat or sugar.

Go for a wide selection of beans, lentils and preferably wholemeal, wholegrain (whole-wheat) or brown forms of other complex carbohydrates.

Restrict fried starchy foods such as crisps (potato chips) and chips (French fries); rich creamy sauces with pasta; thickly spread butter/margarine on bread; store-bought sandwiches containing a lot of mayonnaise; butter, sour cream and mayonnaise toppings on baked potatoes; refined breakfast cereals with added sugar or salt; cakes, biscuits, pastries and puddings made from white flour and high in fat and sugar.

Fruit and vegetables

Essential for a healthy diet and helping to remove harmful wastes from the body, everyone should aim to eat at least five portions (about 400g/14oz) of different fruit and vegetables each day. Fresh and frozen are ideal, but canned (in natural juice or water rather than sugar syrup) and dried are good too. Fruit and vegetables are packed with fibre, essential for a healthy digestive system, and provide essential antioxidant vitamins betacarotene (converted by the body into vitamin A), C and E, minerals and natural plant compounds called phytochemicals, believed to help protect against disease. These nutrients vary depending on the type of produce, so for the greatest benefit choose a wide variety. For example:

• Citrus fruits, strawberries, kiwi fruit, pomegranates, blackcurrants, tomatoes, peppers and broccoli are especially rich in vitamin C.

• Brightly coloured fruit and vegetables such as carrots, red peppers, sweet potatoes, mangoes, papaya and apricots are also rich in betacarotene, a powerful antioxidant that is thought to help fight against cancer, heart disease, cataracts, arthritis, general ageing and damage to sperm.

• Dark green, leafy vegetables, such as spinach, broccoli, Brussels sprouts and cabbage are also an excellent source of betacarotene and other beneficial phytochemicals.

• Fresh tomatoes and tomato products, such as canned tomatoes, are rich in the phytochemical lycopene, another powerful antioxidant that is believed to help protect against certain types of cancer.

• Onions, garlic and other members of the onion family contain the phytochemical, allicin, which is believed to help lower blood cholesterol and stimulate the immune system.

Right: A wide variety of fruit and vegetables should form the backbone of a healthy diet. Choose a mixture of different-coloured produce.

Ways to boost your intake of fruit and vegetables

• Chop your favourite fresh fruit into low-fat probiotic yogurt.

• Add a selection of fresh or dried fruit to breakfast cereals.

• Make a smoothie containing several different types of fruit to have for breakfast or throughout the day.

• Fill sandwiches and wraps with plenty of crisp salad.

• Make a habit of taking chopped raw carrots and celery to work or school to eat as a snack.

• Add canned tomatoes and plenty of fresh seasonal vegetables to a home-made casserole.

• Add finely chopped vegetables such as celery, courgettes (zucchini), (bell) peppers or mushrooms to a pasta sauce or pasta bake.

• Make home-made pizza and scatter vegetables like onions, mushrooms, peppers, corn or canned pineapple on top.

• Stir-fry a selection of fresh vegetables with garlic and ginger for extra flavour.

• Serve at least two types of vegetables or a side salad with your dinner.

• Always order a vegetable side dish with a take-away or follow with fresh fruit or a fruit salad.

WHAT IS A PORTION?

There are so many tempting choices that it should not be difficult to eat your daily essential five portions, and preferably more. The following is a general guide to portions:

• 1 small glass of pure fruit or vegetable juice or a smoothie (Juice counts as one portion per day, no matter how much you drink.)

• 1 medium-size piece of fruit, such as an apple, orange, peach or banana

• 2 small fruits, such as plums or satsumas

• a handful of very small fruits such as cherries, grapes, berries or cherry tomatoes

• 3 dried fruits such as apricots or figs

• 1 large slice of melon

• 6 tbsp canned fruit (in natural juice or water)

• 3 tbsp cooked vegetables or corn

• cereal bowl of mixed salad

Note: Potatoes, tomato ketchup, fruit yogurts, jams and fruit squash drinks do not count.

TYPES OF CHEESE

Cheeses are all made from milk and are nourishing, but the fat content can vary from low to high. Here is a guide to popular varieties:

Cheddar Ranges in flavour from mild to extra mature. All varieties are high in fat. For cooking, it is better to use a small quantity of a strongly flavoured variety.

Cottage cheese Made from skimmed milk and therefore low in fat, it has a creamy flavour. Ideal for use in salads.

Feta Originally from Greece, this cheese has a crumbly texture and a sharp tangy flavour. It has a medium fat value. Good in salads or stuffed vegetables.

Goat's cheese It has a distinct flavour and a medium fat content. Ideal for a cheeseboard, salads or for cooking.

Mozzarella This fairly bland soft cheese is not too high in fat and has a characteristic stringy texture when melted. It is commonly used for pizzas or salads.

Parmesan High in fat but strongly flavoured so only a small amount is needed. For the best flavour, buy a piece and grate or shave as required.

Quark A low-fat, mild cheese that can be used instead of cream.

Ricotta A bland, unsalted Italian soft cheese with a relatively low fat content. It can be used as a substitute for cream cheese.

Milk and dairy foods

These foods, which include milk, yogurt, cheese and fromage frais, are an excellent source of easily absorbed calcium, needed for strong bones and teeth and a healthy nervous system. They also provide protein and a range of other minerals and vitamins.

Dairy products, particularly cheese and cream, can be high in saturated fat so only eat them occasionally and go for reduced-fat versions whenever possible. (The exception to this is children under the age of two, who should always eat full-fat versions, as they need the calories.)

Aim to include two to three portions of dairy foods per day. A portion could include semi-skimmed milk poured on breakfast cereal, a small pot of yogurt or a

Above: Semi-skimmed milk, reduced-fat cheese and low-fat probiotic yogurt are all excellent sources of calcium and protein after you have finished detoxing.

little Parmesan or other mature-flavoured cheese lightly sprinkled over pasta dishes.

Go for skimmed or semi-skimmed milk, low-fat probiotic yogurt and lower-fat cheeses.

Restrict full-fat milk, butter, cream and cream cakes and desserts, and hard cheeses.

Right: Use naturally low-fat dairy products, such as cottage cheese, quark, ricotta and yogurt.

Meat, fish, shellfish and vegetarian alternatives

Meat, poultry, fish, eggs, beans, lentils, nuts, soya, tofu, and vegetarian 'meat' alternatives, such as TVP (textured vegetable protein) and mycoprotein (Quorn), are all good sources of protein, which is essential for building, maintaining and repairing our cells. They also provide useful amounts of B vitamins (vitamin B12 is only found in foods of animal origin), and minerals, such as iron.

The quality of a protein depends upon its composition and whether it is able to supply the building blocks that the body needs. As a general rule, proteins from animal or fish sources supply all of these building blocks in one food. Vegetable sources have to be combined or eaten together on the same day to provide them all. Soya and its products, such as tofu, is the exception, as it has a similar protein

Right: (clockwise from top) Pressed, silken and firm tofu. All of these are very good low-fat sources of protein and make ideal alternatives to meat and fish.

quality to animal protein; this is an excellent vegetarian alternative. Beans, peas and lentils also contribute fibre to the diet.

The body does not require a huge amount of protein, and in the Western world we tend to eat too much, which increases the amount of saturated fat in the diet – especially if the main source is red meat (and cheese). For optimum health, you should aim to eat some protein every day, but make sure that it derives from a wide variety of animal and vegetable sources.

Eat fish twice a week or more – at least one portion should be an oily fish, such as sardines, salmon, mackerel, trout or fresh tuna. Oily fish are rich in omega-3 essential fatty acids, which are thought to help reduce the risk of heart disease. **Go for** lean meat, trimmed of fat, skinless poultry and all fish and shellfish. **Restrict** meat pies, sausages and burgers, battered and deep-fried fish.

Below: Animal and fish sources of protein provide the nutrition we need to build, maintain and repair the body's cells.

Foods containing fats

A small amount of fat in the diet is essential for health and to make foods more pleasant to eat. However, most people eat far too much fat and particularly too much of the saturated type. Fat is also very high in calories, providing more than twice as many calories as the equivalent weight of carbohydrate or protein, so eating too much can easily lead to weight gain. Fats can be divided into three primary categories:

• Saturated fats are found mainly in meat and dairy foods and are usually solid at room temperature. A high intake of these fats is known to increase the level of cholesterol in the blood, raising the risk of heart disease and some cancers. Intake of these fats should be kept to a minimum.

• Unsaturated fats includes two types: monounsaturated – found in nuts, avocados and olive oil, for example; and polyunsaturated – found in foods such as oily fish and vegetable oils. The difference lies in their chemical make-up, and the different vegetable oils and margarines available simply vary in the proportions of these fats that they contain.

Right: Butter and solid margarine should be kept to a minimum.

Polyunsaturates are important in the diet because they provide essential omega-3 and omega-6 fatty acids that the body cannot manufacture itself and that are essential for controlling many functions, including blood flow and inflammation.

• Trans fats are artificially produced, usually when vegetable oils are hydrogenated to make solid margarine and reduced-fat spreads. They are widely used in processed foods such as cakes, biscuits and pies, and carry the same health risks as saturated fats. They should be kept to a minimum.

Go for vegetable oils in place of hard fats for cooking and margarines labelled 'high in polyunsaturates' or 'high in monounsaturates' as spreads.

Restrict hard fats like butter and cheese, hidden fats in processed and baked foods like pastries, cakes, puddings and savoury snacks, chocolate and deep-fried foods.

Below: Oils provide a number of health benefits, but should be used in moderation as part of a healthy diet.

LOW-FAT SNACKS
• Wholemeal pitta bread with hummus or tzatziki
• Raw vegetable crudités with tomato salsa, guacamole or other vegetable dip
• Sesame breadsticks, rice cakes, oatcakes or plain popcorn
• Handful of unsalted nuts or trail mix (dried fruit, nuts and seeds)
• Slice of fruit loaf
• Smoothie or milk shake made with skimmed or semi-skimmed milk or yogurt
• Wholemeal sandwich spread with mashed banana

Above: There are now many reduced-salt foods available in supermarkets and health food stores, so buy these to gradually wean yourself off salt.

The question of salt

Although a small amount of salt is needed for healthy body function, most of us consume far too much, which increases the risk of high blood pressure, heart disease and having a stroke. Processed foods, fast foods, ready-made foods, and habitually adding salt to food in cooking and at the table are the main culprits that cause over-consumption of salt. Many everyday foods, including bread, cheese, cured meats, such as ham and bacon, and smoked fish, also contribute 'hidden' salt, as it is used as a preservative as well as for seasoning. Other high-salt foods include sauces, condiments and foods canned in brine.

Go for fresh foods, use herbs and spices to replace or reduce the need for salt in cooking. Always taste first before routinely adding salt.

Restrict convenience meals, bacon, cheese, pickles, smoked fish and crisps (potato chips).

Foods containing sugar

Sugar is a simple carbohydrate that provides the body with an almost immediate source of energy but few useful nutrients, so the energy provided is often referred to as 'empty calories'. Not only can this easily lead to weight gain, but if sugar intake is high, this can cause yo-yoing blood sugar levels and a condition known as the 'sugar trap'. This happens if there is a high intake of sugar, as excessive amounts of the hormone insulin are then released into the blood stream to mop it up. The blood sugar levels then drop again to lower than they were before you ate, causing tiredness and a lack of energy and the desire to eat more sugar to provide another quick energy fix. By choosing complex carbohydrates, which are more slowly digested, blood sugar levels are kept on an even keel, providing sustained energy.

A small amount of sugar adds to the enjoyment of food, but you should avoid eating sugary foods regularly or as snacks between meals, in place of more nourishing and satisfying foods. Eating sugary foods is also the main cause of tooth decay.

Go for naturally sweet foods such as fresh and dried fruits, honey and reduced-sugar preserves with a high fruit content.

Restrict cakes, cookies, sugary breakfast cereals, chocolate, sweets (candies) and sugary drinks, such as cola or cordials.

Water and other drinks

Drinking plenty of liquid each day is essential for healthy body function, including flushing out toxins and waste products. You should aim to drink at least 2 litres/4 pints /8½ cups (6–8 glasses) of non-alcoholic liquid each day. Water is the best choice, although fruit and herbal teas, juices and skimmed or semi-skimmed milk are also good options.

Tea, coffee and cola drinks are natural diuretics that cause the body to lose fluids, taking useful nutrients such as calcium with them. It is therefore advisable not to drink too much of these, especially as they are also high in caffeine.

Drinking moderate amounts of alcohol has been linked to a reduced risk of heart disease and stroke, although drinking in excess can be detrimental to health. If you enjoy an alcoholic drink, drink small amounts with food, avoid getting drunk, and make sure that you have a few alcohol-free days each week.

Go for water, herbal teas and fresh fruit and vegetable juices.

Restrict alcohol and sugary drinks.

Below: Chocolate, cookies, sweets (candy), cakes, jams and fizzy drinks contain high levels of sugar and should only be eaten as occasional treats.

Safe drinking

A small amount of alcohol does you no harm, can be enjoyable and may even do you some good. However, alcohol does put strain on the liver, the body's main detoxifier, so it is wise to know how best to enjoy the pleasures of social drinking without putting your health at risk.

What happens when you drink alcohol?

Most of the alcohol you drink is rapidly absorbed into the bloodstream. It is then quickly distributed throughout the body so it appears in almost every organ and tissue. Alcohol is mainly broken down and detoxified by the liver. The rest is disposed of in either sweat or urine. The concentration of alcohol in the body depends on:
• How much you drink
• Whether you have recently eaten
• Your height and weight
• Your sex
If you are smaller or lighter than average, of if you are a woman, you will be more easily affected by alcohol.

Below: Wines vary in their alcoholic strength, so check what proof they are.

Above: Home measures are generally larger than bar measures, so watch how much you are pouring.

Health benefits
• Evidence suggests that drinking alcohol in moderation (as little as one unit a day), can offer protection against a number of diseases including heart disease and stroke, particularly for post-menopausal women and men over 40 years of age.
• A glass of wine provides a small amount of iron and beer provides some B vitamins. Other than that, alcohol has no useful nutrient value and is primarily a source of 'empty calories'.
• Wine consumed with food increases the body's absorption of iron and helps aid digestion.

Health risks
• Drinking large quantities of alcohol on a regular basis puts excess strain on your liver and is bad for your health. It can cause high blood pressure, an increased risk of liver disease, certain cancers and depression. It can also lead to obesity with its attendant health problems.

• Drinking more than one alcoholic drink a day may increase the risk of breast cancer in young women.
• If you are pregnant or planning to fall pregnant, you should not drink more than one or two units of alcohol, once or twice a week, and preferably not drink at all. Alcohol passes from your bloodstream across the placenta and is fed to your baby. This can cause low birth weight and may have a detrimental effect on the baby's health.
• Heavy drinking can lead to vitamin deficiencies, because alcohol may reduce your appetite, thus replacing more nutritious foods.
• Alcoholic drinks provide a reasonable amount of energy, so it is relatively easy to consume a lot of extra calories and thus put on weight. For example, if you were to drink two average glasses of wine ($\frac{1}{6}$th of a bottle each), five days a week, over a year that adds up to 520 glasses, which equates to about 46,800 kcals. All else being equal and without taking extra exercise, this could lead to an average weight gain of about 6.3kg/14lb in one year.
• Mixing alcohol with certain drugs or medicines can be dangerous.

Healthy Limits

The recommended limit for women is two to three units per day and for men it's three to four units per day. A unit of alcohol is 8g, equivalent to:

• 300ml/½ pint /1¼ cups of ordinary beer, lager or cider
• 1 small glass of 8% strength red or white wine (about 125ml/4 floz/½ cup)
• 1 measure of sherry 50ml/3 tbsp or,
• 1 measure of spirits 25ml/1½ tbsp.

You should also aim to have a couple of alcohol-free days each week and not binge drink.

What causes a hangover?

Dehydration is responsible for most of the unpleasant symptoms of a hangover. Alcohol is a diuretic, which means it speeds the loss of water from the body, causing headaches, dizziness and extreme thirst. Nausea, vomiting and indigestion are caused by the direct action of alcohol irritating the stomach lining.

Alcoholic drinks may also contain substances known as congeners, formed by yeast fermentation during their production, and these too can increase the effects of a hangover. They may also contain additives, notably preservatives, which can adversely affect susceptible individuals and trigger migraine attacks.

Why alcohol affects women more than men

In men, between 55 and 65 per cent of the body weight is made up of water. In women, just 45 to 55 per cent is made up of water. Alcohol is distributed throughout the body fluids, so in men the alcohol is more 'diluted' than it is in women. Women also metabolise alcohol more slowly because they usually have smaller livers than men and more body fat. A woman's liver is more likely to suffer alcohol damage than a man's. Alcohol abuse can lead to hepatitis and cirrhosis of the liver – usually a fatal condition.

Right: For most people, drinking is enjoyable, but don't overdo it.

DID YOU KNOW?

• Alcohol is often thought to be a stimulant but it is in fact a depressant. You might feel more relaxed, confident and cheerful after a couple of drinks, but it depresses certain brain functions and affects your judgement, self-control and skills.
• Glasses of wine are frequently larger than the standard measure, so a large (175ml) glass of wine will in fact contain 1.5–2 units of alcohol.
• Many wines, beers and ciders have a stronger alcoholic content, so the units of alcohol provided will be higher. For example, wine varies from 9–14.5% alcohol by volume so a single measure (125ml) could provide up to 2 units of alcohol, for higher alcohol strength wines, as are many from the New World. Similarly, strong beer, lager or cider may be up to 8% alcohol by volume and provide 2 units of alcohol in 300ml/½ pint.
• Alcohol is absorbed into the bloodstream more quickly if drunk on an empty stomach. It's therefore best to drink with a meal or after eating.
• All alcohol is absorbed more quickly if taken with a fizzy drink, so spritzers, spirits with mixers such as tonic water or soda, and alcopops take effect quicker.
• Alcohol dehydrates the body, so try to drink water or non-fizzy, soft drinks in between alcoholic drinks, and drink plenty of water before going to bed.
• Alcohol may make you fall asleep quickly, but it is likely to disturb your sleep pattern so you wake up in the night and can't go back to sleep again.
• On average it take one hour for the body to get rid of the alcohol in one standard drink.
• Do not make the mistake of thinking that a cup of coffee will sober you up if you have had too much to drink. Coffee is also a diuretic and will exacerbate the problem.
• Sulphur-based preservatives used in many alcoholic drinks and histamine (mainly found in red wine), can trigger asthma attacks and other allergic reactions.
• Never drink and drive or drink before operating machinery.
• After heavy drinking, the levels of alcohol in the blood can still be over the limit in the morning.

Health problems and how to help to prevent them with diet

Causes of health problems and disease are numerous. Diet and lifestyle are both known to influence your health. There may be hereditary and environmental factors, and sometimes causes are not known. However, there are many preventative measures you can take to help reduce the risk of common diseases and to manage health conditions. Always seek medical attention for any health problems.

Irritable bowel syndrome (IBS)

This is the most common bowel disorder in the Western world and affects women more often than men. Symptoms are constipation and/or diarrhoea, combined with a stomach-ache, bloating and wind. IBS may be triggered by stress, hormone imbalances or an intolerance to different foods, such as wheat, corn, milk, cheese or oats.

Prevention tips

• High-fibre or low-fibre diet, depending on the cause of the problem. Seek the advice of a dietician.
• Excluding offending foods.
• Stress relief.

High blood pressure

This means that the pressure of blood in your arteries (blood vessels) is too high. High blood pressure usually causes no symptoms, but if left untreated may damage some arteries and put a strain on the heart. High blood pressure increases the risk of developing heart disease, stroke, dementia and kidney damage.

Prevention tips

• Lose weight if you are overweight.
• Eat healthily.
• Eat less salt and cut down on processed foods.
• Exercise for at least 30 minutes, on five or more days a week.
• Cut down on alcohol.
• If you are a smoker, make every effort to give up.

Above: Sugary cakes and biscuits raise blood sugar levels too quickly, causing a temporary high before they plummet.

Diabetes

This is a lifelong condition in which there is too much glucose in the blood. Diabetes develops because the body does not produce enough insulin, a hormone, which allows the body to use glucose (mainly from starches and sugars) for fuel.

• Type 1 diabetes is when little or no insulin is produced.
• Type 2 diabetes is when the body produces some insulin, but not enough for its needs, or when the insulin is not properly used by the body. Type 2 is the most common form of diabetes and usually affects people over 40 years of age. Typical symptoms include increased thirst, passing large amounts of urine, extreme tiredness, weight loss and blurred vision.

Cause and control

The exact cause of diabetes is not known, but good control of the condition requires a healthy, varied diet (that helps to keep blood sugar levels steady), regular exercise and maintaining an ideal weight.

Above: Skimmed and semi-skimmed milk have a slightly higher amount of calcium than full-fat milk.

Osteoporosis

A condition where bone material is lost so the bones become gradually more fragile and likely to break. Bones are at their strongest in the late 20s, then gradually begin to lost their density with increasing age. This process speeds up in women in the ten years after the menopause because the ovaries stop producing the female sex hormone oestrogen, one of the substances that can help to keep the bones strong.

Prevention tips

• Eat a healthy diet, particularly including foods that are high in calcium, such as dairy foods.
• Keep physically active, especially walking or jogging regularly.
• Avoid drinking too much alcohol. High alcohol intake reduces the body's ability to make bone.
• Avoid smoking. Tobacco lowers the oestrogen level in women and may cause early menopause – another risk factor.
• Hormone Replacement Therapy (HRT) can offer benefits.

Arthritis

This causes inflammation and swelling in the joints. The most common type is osteoarthritis, which mainly affects weight-bearing joints such as the hips, knees and spine. It is a degenerative disease caused by the breaking down of cartilage, so the bones rub together causing inflammation. Rheumatoid arthritis is an inflammatory disorder involving the immune system, which for unknown reasons, starts to attack the joints. It can strike at any age, although remissions can occur. Both these forms of arthritis are more common in women.

Prevention tips

• Avoid becoming overweight as obesity increases the risk of developing osteoarthritis by putting undue stress on the joints. Weight control is also vital to minimize stress, reduce pain and optimize mobility, when osteoarthritis has already developed.

• Take regular exercise as this strengthens the muscles responsible for protecting the joints and helps to prevent stiffness.

• A food allergy or intolerance may be linked with rheumatoid arthritis. Seek specialist advice for following an exclusion diet to help identify a possible problem food.

• Fish oils can be helpful for their anti-inflammatory effect on arthritic joints.

Below: Eat more oily fish, such as mackerel, salmon and sardines.

Above: Fruit and vegetables are significant in reducing the risk of certain types of cancer.

Cancer

The sequence of events that leads to a cancer is complex and varied. Most cancers begin when the body is exposed to a carcinogen, a cancer-causing substance present in the environment. Carcinogens can be found in tobacco, food, industrial compounds, or may be a virus. Even the rays of the sun can be carcinogenic. Usually the body's natural defence system is able to destroy these harmful substances before they cause permanent damage to cells, but sometimes the carcinogen escapes and succeeds in changing a cell's structure and thus creating a potentially cancerous cell, which may in time grow into a tumour.

There are many different types of cancer, and all have many different causes, but it is thought that a considerable percentage of all cancers can be prevented by making relatively simple diet and lifestyle changes.

Prevention tips

• Avoid being overweight.

• Eat plenty of fruit and vegetables, as they contain antioxidants and phytochemicals that help to counteract the damaging effects of free radicals.

• Be sure to include plenty of high-fibre foods in your diet, such as whole grains, beans, peas and lentils, to ensure healthy digestion, prevent constipation and allow the speedy removal of toxic waste products.

• Cut down on fatty foods, especially saturated fats.

• Eat less red and processed meats.

• Restrict smoked and cured foods and avoid charred food.

• Restrict high-salt foods.

• Go easy on alcohol.

• Be physically active.

• Avoid smoking.

Carrot and celery juice

This juice is so packed with goodness, you can almost feel it cleansing and detoxing your body. As well as valuable vitamins, the carrots and grapes provide plenty of natural sweetness, which blends perfectly with the mild pepperiness of the celery and fresh scent of parsley. Drink this juice on a regular basis to give your system a thorough clean-out.

Serves 1–2

1 celery stick
300g/11oz carrots
150g/5oz green grapes
several large sprigs of parsley
celery or carrot sticks, to serve

1 Using a sharp knife, roughly chop the celery and carrots. Push half of the celery, carrots and grapes through a juicer, then add the parsley sprigs. Add the remaining celery, carrots and grapes in the same way and juice until thoroughly combined.

2 Pour into one or two glasses and serve with celery or carrot stick stirrers.

Health benefits
When juicing herbs, do not remove their individual stalks because it is the stalks that contain much of the goodness and flavour – and they go through the juicing machine very easily. Parsley contains useful amounts of vitamin C and iron and also works as a natural cleanser and breath freshener.

Energy 77Kcal/322kJ; Protein 1.2g; Carbohydrate 17.9g, of which sugars 17.1g; Fat 0.6g, of which saturates 0.2g; Cholesterol 0mg; Calcium 53mg; Fibre 3.8g; Sodium 50mg.

Cinnamon and squash smoothie

Lightly cooked butternut squash makes a delicious, vitamin-packed smoothie. It has a wonderfully rich, rounded flavour that is lifted perfectly by the addition of tart citrus juice and warm, spicy cinnamon. Imagine pumpkin pie as a gorgeous smooth drink and you're halfway to experiencing the flavours of this lusciously sweet and tantalizing treat.

1 Halve the squash, scoop out and discard the seeds and cut the flesh into chunks. Cut away the skin and discard. Steam or boil the squash for 10–15 minutes until just tender. Drain well and leave to stand until cool.

2 Put the cooled squash in a blender or food processor and add the ground cinnamon. Squeeze the lemons and grapefruit and pour the juice over the squash. Add the honey, if using.

3 Process the ingredients until they are very smooth. If necessary, pause to scrape down the side of the food processor or blender.

4 Put a few ice cubes in two or three short glasses and pour over the smoothie. Serve immediately.

Serves 2–3

1 small butternut squash,
   about 600g/1lb 6oz
2.5ml/½ tsp ground cinnamon
3 large lemons
1 grapefruit
clear honey, to taste
ice cubes

Cook's tip
Squash are not only delicious, but they also contain high levels of magnesium and potassium and are low in calories. If you can only buy a large squash, cook it all and add the leftovers to a stew or soup.

Energy 43Kcal/180kJ; Protein 1.6g; Carbohydrate 8.5g, of which sugars 7.5g; Fat 0.4g, of which saturates 0.2g; Cholesterol 0mg; Calcium 65mg; Fibre 2g; Sodium 4mg.

Lime and watermelon tonic

This refreshing juice will help to cool the body, calm the digestion and cleanse the system – and may even have aphrodisiac qualities. What more could you ask from a juice? It even looks enticing. The real magic of this drink, however, lies in its flavour. The light, watermelon taste is fresh on the palate, while the honey warms the throat – but it is the tart lime that gives it the edge.

Serves 4

1 watermelon
1 litre/1¾ pints/4 cups chilled water
juice of 2 limes
clear honey, to taste
ice cubes, to serve

1 Using a sharp knife, chop the watermelon into chunks, cutting off the skin and discarding the black seeds.

2 Place the watermelon chunks in a large bowl, pour the chilled water over and leave to stand for 10 minutes.

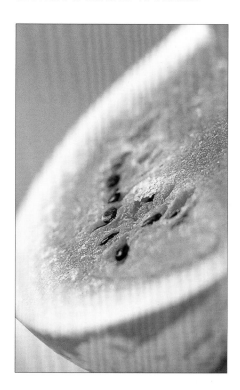

3 Strain the watermelon chunks, then push them through a juicer.

4 Stir in the lime juice and sweeten to taste with honey. Pour into a jug (pitcher), add ice cubes and stir. Serve in wide, chunky glasses.

Cook's tip
If the weather is really hot, why not enjoy this as a frozen slush? Freeze, stirring often, and when crystals begin to form, serve immediately.

Energy 114Kcal/486kJ; Protein 1.3g; Carbohydrate 27.3g, of which sugars 27.3g; Fat 0.8g, of which saturates 0.3g; Cholesterol 0mg; Calcium 18mg; Fibre 0.3g; Sodium 7mg.

Blueberry tonic

Blueberries are not only an excellent source of antioxidant vitamins, they are also rich in antibacterial compounds that can help to prevent gastric and urinary infections. Mixed with dark red fruits, such as blackberries and grapes, they make a highly nutritious and extremely delicious blend that can be enjoyed throughout the day.

Serves 1

90g/3½oz/scant 1 cup blackcurrants
  or blackberries
150g/5oz red grapes
130g/4½oz/generous 1 cup blueberries
ice cubes

1 Remove the blackcurrants, if using, and grapes from their stalks.

2 Push all the fruits through a juicer, saving a few for decoration.

3 Place the ice cubes in a medium glass and pour over the juice. Decorate with the remaining fruit and serve the juice immediately.

Cook's tip
This is a very tangy wake-up drink that can be diluted with chilled mineral water, if you like. Sweeten with a little honey if you find the taste a bit too sharp.

Energy 149Kcal/639kJ; Protein 1.6g; Carbohydrate 37.7g, of which sugars 37.7g; Fat 0.2g, of which saturates 0g; Cholesterol 0mg; Calcium 90mg; Fibre 4.2g; Sodium 12mg.

Orange and raspberry smoothie

This exquisite blend combines the sharp-sweet taste of raspberries and the refreshing fruitiness of oranges with smooth yogurt. It tastes like creamy fruit heaven in a glass. Even better, it takes just minutes to prepare, making it perfect as a quick breakfast juice for boosting the immune system. It may also be enjoyed as a refreshing drink at any other time of day.

Serves 2

250g/9oz/1⅓ cups raspberries, washed
    and chilled
200ml/7fl oz/scant 1 cup low-fat probiotic
    yogurt, chilled
300ml/½ pint/1¼ cups freshly squeezed
    orange juice, chilled

1 Place the raspberries and yogurt in a blender or food processor and process for about 1 minute until the mixture is smooth and creamy.

2 Add the orange juice to the raspberry and yogurt mixture and process for another 30 seconds. Pour into tall glasses and serve immediately.

Cook's tip
For a super-chilled version, use frozen raspberries instead of fresh. You may need to blend the raspberries and yogurt for a little longer to get a smooth result.

Energy 142Kcal/602kJ; Protein 7.6g; Carbohydrate 26.5g, of which sugars 26.5g; Fat 1.5g, of which saturates 0.7g; Cholesterol 1mg; Calcium 237mg; Fibre 3.3g; Sodium 102mg.

Raspberry and oatmeal blend

A spoonful of oatmeal gives substance to this tangy, invigorating drink. If you can, prepare it ahead of time because soaking the raw oats before you blend them helps to break down the starch into natural sugars that are easy to digest.Yogurt provides a useful source of calcium when detoxing, as other dairy foods are temporarily avoided.

Serves 1

25ml/1½ tbsp medium oatmeal
150g/5oz/scant 1 cup raspberries
5–10ml/1–2 tsp clear honey
45ml/3 tbsp low-fat probiotic yogurt

Health benefits
Probiotic yogurt is especially beneficial to the digestive system. However, all live yogurt helps to restore the balance of healthy bacteria in the gut and to reduce most gastro-intestinal problems.

1 Spoon the oatmeal into a large heatproof bowl, then pour in about 120ml/4fl oz/½ cup boiling water. Leave the mixture to stand for about 10 minutes or until the water has been completely absorbed.

2 Put the soaked oats in a blender or food processor and add all but two or three of the raspberries, the honey and about 30ml/2 tbsp of the yogurt. Process until smooth, scraping the mixture down from the side of the bowl if necessary.

3 Pour the raspberry and oatmeal smoothie into a large glass, swirl in the remaining yogurt and top with raspberries. Chill the smoothie in the refrigerator until you are ready to drink it – it will thicken up so you might need to add a little juice or mineral water before serving.

Cook's tips
• If you don't like raspberry pips (seeds) in your smoothies, simply press the fruit through a sieve with the back of a wooden spoon to make a smooth purée, then process with the oatmeal and yogurt as before. Alternatively, you could try using redcurrants instead of the raspberries.
• Although a steaming bowl of porridge cannot be beaten as a warming winter breakfast, this smooth, oaty drink makes a great, light alternative, particularly in warmer months. It is a good way to make sure you get your fill of wholesome oats for breakfast.

Energy 177Kcal/756kJ; Protein 7.5g; Carbohydrate 32.3g, of which sugars 14.1g; Fat 3.1g, of which saturates 0.4g; Cholesterol 1mg; Calcium 137mg; Fibre 5.5g; Sodium 51mg.

Strawberry and tofu smoothie

This energizing blend is simply bursting with goodness. Not only is tofu a great source of protein, it is also rich in minerals, particularly calcium, and contains nutrients that help to protect against diseases. Tofu is naturally bland in flavour and therefore makes an ideal, versatile ingredient for including in smoothies, as it will blend with many different fruits.

Serves 2

250g/9oz silken tofu
200g/7oz/1¾ cups strawberries
45ml/3 tbsp pumpkin or sunflower seeds,
  plus extra for sprinkling
15–30ml/1–2 tbsp clear honey
juice of 2 large oranges
juice of 1 lemon

1 Roughly chop the tofu, then hull the strawberries and chop them. Reserve a few strawberry chunks to garnish.

2 Put all of the ingredients into a blender or food processor and blend until completely smooth and creamy, scraping the mixture down from the side of the bowl, if necessary.

Cook's tips
• Almost any other fruit can be used instead of the strawberries. Those that blend well, such as mangoes, bananas, peaches, plums and raspberries, are especially good substitutes. Frozen mixed berry fruits would also work well and are handy for keeping in the freezer.
• Tofu can be bought fresh or in a long-life pack. Try to find silken tofu, as it has a satiny texture that blends particularly well in a blender or food processor.

3 Pour into tumblers and sprinkle with extra seeds and strawberry chunks.

Energy 289Kcal/1204kJ; Protein 15.7g; Carbohydrate 21.2g, of which sugars 16.9g; Fat 16.1g, of which saturates 1.7g; Cholesterol 0mg; Calcium 684mg; Fibre 2.5g; Sodium 18mg.

Summer fruit smoothie

Long after summer is over you can still summon up the glorious flavours of the season by making this fruity and refreshing drink from frozen summer fruits. This low-fat fruity delight will pep up even the darkest mornings. Revitalize yourself with this blend before you leave for work in the morning to give your body a well-deserved boost.

1 Take the frozen fruits straight from the freezer and tip them into a blender or food processor.

2 Blend until the fruits are finely crushed, scraping down the side of the bowl, if necessary.

3 Add the yogurt to the crushed fruit, then blend again until the mixture is smooth and thick.

4 Taste and add a little honey to sweeten, if necessary.

5 Serve the smoothie immediately, decorated with fruit.

Cook's tip
You can use any mixture of soft berries and currants for this smoothie, either home-grown or bought frozen in bags.

Serves 2

250g/9oz/2 cups frozen summer fruits, plus extra to decorate
200g/7oz/scant 1 cup low-fat probiotic yogurt
clear honey, to taste

Energy 90Kcal/378kJ; Protein 6.1g; Carbohydrate 15g, of which sugars 15g; Fat 1.2g, of which saturates 0.5g; Cholesterol 1mg; Calcium 210mg; Fibre 1.4g; Sodium 91mg.

Apricot and ginger smoothie

Enjoy the perfect option for a healthy and nourishing breakfast in bed without the crumbs. This smoothie is packed with valuable vitamins and minerals and the dried apricots provide natural sweetness – so no added sugar is necessary. Choose whichever non-dairy milk you prefer, such as a rice, almond or soya alternative.

Serves 2

1 piece preserved stem ginger,
   plus 15ml/1 tbsp syrup from
   the ginger jar
50g/2oz/¼ cup ready-to-eat dried
   apricots, halved or quartered
40g/1½ oz/scant ½ cup unsweetened muesli
about 200ml/7fl oz/scant 1 cup
   non-dairy milk, chilled

1 Chop the preserved ginger and put it in a blender or food processor with the syrup, apricots, muesli and milk.

2 Process the mixture until smooth, adding more milk if necessary. Serve immediately in wide glasses.

Energy 167Kcal/706kJ; Protein 6g; Carbohydrate 29.3g, of which sugars 19g; Fat 3.3g, of which saturates 0.6g; Cholesterol 0mg; Calcium 42mg; Fibre 3.1g; Sodium 65mg.

Mango and lime lassi

A tangy, fruity blend of ripe mango, cooling probiotic yogurt, and sharp fresh lime and lemon juice makes a wonderfully satisfying, flavoursome drink that's refreshing and packed with energy. Mango makes a thick purée when it is blended, so chilled mineral water is added to dilute the mixture to a consistency that is suitable for drinking.

Health benefits

Mango is a rich souce of both betacarotene (which the body can convert into vitamin A) and vitamin C. Both these vitamins act as antioxidants, boosting the immune system and helping to prevent cell damage by free radicals.

Serves 2

1 mango
finely grated rind and juice of 1 lime
15ml/1 tbsp lemon juice
clear honey, to taste
100ml/3½fl oz/scant ½ cup low-fat
    probiotic yogurt
mineral water, to dilute
1 extra lime, halved, to serve

1 Peel the mango and cut the flesh from the stone (pit). Put the flesh into a food processor or blender and add the lime rind and juice.

2 Add the lemon juice, honey to taste and probiotic yogurt. Whizz the mixture until completely smooth, scraping down the sides once or twice.

3 Stir a little chilled mineral water into the mixture to thin it down to the required consistency for drinking. Serve immediately, with half a lime on the side of each glass so that more juice can be squeezed in if desired.

Energy 71Kcal/302kJ; Protein 3.1g; Carbohydrate 14.3g, of which sugars 14.1g; Fat 0.7g, of which saturates 0.4g; Cholesterol 1mg; Calcium 104mg; Fibre 2g; Sodium 43mg.

Banana and mango smoothie

Easy to prepare and even easier to drink, this energy-packed smoothie makes a great start to the day. Bananas provide the perfect fuel in the form of slow-release carbohydrate that will keep you going all morning, while vitamin C-rich orange juice and sweet, scented mango will set your tastebuds tingling first thing.

Serves 2

1 mango
1 large banana
1 large orange
15ml/1 tbsp sesame seeds

Health benefits
Sesame seeds not only taste delicious, but they also provide a good source of vitamin E, as well as some calcium. For extra fibre value, add 25ml/1½ tbsp medium oatmeal to the smoothie.

1 Using a small, sharp knife, skin the mango, then slice the flesh off the stone (pit). Peel the banana and break it into short lengths, then place it in a blender or food processor with the mango flesh.

2 Squeeze the juice from the orange and add to the blender or food processor along with the sesame seeds. Whizz until the mixture is smooth and creamy, then pour into glasses and serve.

Energy 148Kcal/625kJ; Protein 3.1g; Carbohydrate 25g, of which sugars 23.9g; Fat 4.7g, of which saturates 0.8g; Cholesterol 0mg; Calcium 90mg; Fibre 4g; Sodium 7mg.

Tropical scented fruit salad

This fresh fruit salad makes a perfect start to the day. For extra flavour and colour, try using two small blood oranges and two ordinary oranges. Other fruit could be added, such as pears, kiwi fruit or bananas. Oranges and strawberries are both great sources of vitamin C, and the passion fruit adds an intense exotic fragrance, as well as further vitamin value and fibre.

Serves 4

400g/14oz/3½ cups strawberries, hulled and halved
4 oranges, peeled and segmented
2 passion fruits
120ml/4fl oz/½ cup fresh, chilled tropical fruit juice

Cook's tip
Passion fruit should feel heavy for their size and have a dimpled skin. If the skin is smooth, the fruit is not quite ripe.

1 Put the hulled and halved strawberries and peeled and segmented oranges into a bowl.

2 Halve the passion fruit and using a teaspoon scoop the flesh into the bowl.

3 Pour the tropical fruit juice over the fruit and toss gently. Cover and chill in the refrigerator or serve immediately.

Energy 87Kcal/371kJ; Protein 2.4g; Carbohydrate 20g, of which sugars 20g; Fat 0.3g, of which saturates 0g; Cholesterol 0mg; Calcium 78mg; Fibre 3.5g; Sodium 14mg.

Fragrant fruit salad

Fruit salads are wonderfully versatile and can include any variety of fresh fruit to suit the season. They can be as simple as you like or fabulously exciting, made with exotic foreign fruits, as typified in this recipe, which includes pineapple, papaya, pomegranate, mango and passion fruit. Fruit salads are best eaten shortly after making, to preserve their full vitamin value.

Serves 4

1 small pineapple
120ml/4 fl oz/½ cup fresh, chilled
   apple juice
juice of 1 lime
1 papaya
1 mango
2 pomegranates
2 passion fruits or kiwi fruit
fine strips of lime peel, to decorate

1 Using a sharp knife, cut the plume and stalk ends from the pineapple.

2 Peel and cut the flesh into bitesize pieces, discarding the core. Put into a serving bowl.

3 Pour over the apple juice and lime juice and stir the mixture together to combine thoroughly.

4 Halve the papaya and scoop out the seeds using a spoon. Cut away the skin with a sharp knife, then cut the flesh into chunks.

5 Cut the mango lengthways into three pieces, along each side of the stone (pit). Peel the skin off the flesh. Cut into chunks and add to the bowl.

6 Halve the pomegranates and scoop out the seeds. Add to the bowl.

7 Halve the passion fruits and scoop out the flesh using a teaspoon or peel and chop the kiwi fruit. Add to the bowl and serve, decorated with lime peel.

Health benefits

Pomegranate is rich in antioxidants and offers good vitamin C and fibre content, plus lots of visual appeal.

Energy 104Kcal/446kJ; Protein 1.3g; Carbohydrate 25.5g, of which sugars 25.4g; Fat 0.4g, of which saturates 0.1g; Cholesterol 0mg; Calcium 46mg; Fibre 4.2g; Sodium 13mg.

Zingy papaya, lime and ginger salad

This refreshing, fruity salad makes a lovely light breakfast, and it is perfect for the summer months. Choose really ripe, fragrant papayas for the best flavour. Papaya is a very nutritious fruit with good antioxidant value provided by vitamins A and C. If they feel hard when you buy them, ripen at room temperature rather than in the refrigerator.

Serves 2–4

2 large ripe papayas
juice of 1 fresh lime
2 pieces preserved stem ginger, finely sliced

Variation

This refreshing fruit salad is delicious made with other tropical fruit. Try using 2 ripe, peeled, stoned (pitted) mangoes in place of the papayas.

1 Cut the papayas in half lengthways and scoop out the seeds, using a teaspoon. Using a sharp knife, thickly slice the flesh and arrange on a platter.

2 Squeeze the lime juice over the slices of papaya and sprinkle them with the finely sliced stem ginger. Serve the fruit salad immediately.

Energy 55Kcal/234kJ; Protein 0.8g; Carbohydrate 13.4g, of which sugars 13.4g; Fat 0.2g, of which saturates 0g; Cholesterol 0mg; Calcium 36mg; Fibre 3.3g; Sodium 8mg.

Figs and pears in honey

A simple breakfast idea that combines lightly cooked fresh figs and pears. Both fruits have good fibre value and therefore help to promote the digestion and to cleanse the system. This makes a tempting combination of fruits for the autumnal months, when pears are at their seasonal best. Alternatively, serve this dish as a dessert.

Serves 4

1 lemon
30ml/2 tbsp clear honey
1 cinnamon stick
1 cardamom pod
2 pears
8 fresh figs, halved

Cook's tip
To vary the flavour, substitute the pears with eating apples or add a kick to the syrup by adding 2.5cm/1in peeled, bruised fresh root ginger in step 2. You could also omit the cardamom or cinnamon stick if you don't like their flavours.

1 Pare the rind from the lemon using a zester or vegetable peeler, avoiding the white pith, then cut into very thin strips.

2 Place the lemon rind, honey, cinnamon stick, cardamom pod and 350ml/12fl oz/1½ cups water in a pan and bring to the boil. Boil for 10 minutes until reduced by about half.

3 Cut the pears into eighths, discarding the cores. Place the pears in the syrup, add the figs and simmer gently for about 5 minutes until the fruit is tender.

4 Remove and discard the cinnamon stick and cardamom pod, then transfer the fruit to a serving bowl. Serve warm or chilled.

Energy 143Kcal/606kJ; Protein 1.7g; Carbohydrate 34.4g, of which sugars 34.4g; Fat 0.7g, of which saturates 0g; Cholesterol 0mg; Calcium 109mg; Fibre 4.7g; Sodium 28mg.

Dried fruit compote

Dried fruit, although slightly higher in sugar – and therefore calories – than fresh, supplies significant amounts of minerals, notably iron and potassium, and fibre as well as useful amounts of energy. This makes a satisfying and sustaining bowlful to start the morning and can be served with low-fat probiotic yogurt if you like.

Serves 4

350g/12oz/2 cups mixed dried fruits,
   such as apples, pears, prunes, peaches
1 cinnamon stick
65g/2½oz/½ cup raisins
30ml/2 tbsp clear honey
juice of ½ lemon
mint leaves, to decorate (optional)

1 Put the mixed dried fruit in a large pan with the cinnamon stick and pour over 300ml/½ pint/1¼ cups water.

2 Heat gently until almost boiling, then cover the pan, lower the heat and cook gently for 12–15 minutes until the fruit is plumped up and softened.

3 Remove the pan from the heat, add the raisins and honey and stir gently.

4 Cover the pan with a lid and leave the compote to cool. Once cooled, remove the cinnamon stick and stir in the lemon juice.

5 Transfer the compote to a serving bowl, cover with clear film (plastic wrap) and keep refrigerated until needed.

6 Before serving, remove the fruit compote from the fridge and allow to return to room temperature.

7 Decorate with a few fresh mint leaves before serving, if you like.

Cook's tip
This compote will keep well, chilled in the refrigerator. If you are following the longer detox plan, for one or two weeks, it is well worth making enough for several servings that you can eat as and when you are ready. Look for unsulphured fruit, which is available from health food stores, especially if you suffer from asthma.

Energy 189Kcal/807kJ; Protein 2.6g; Carbohydrate 46.8g, of which sugars 46.8g; Fat 0.4g, of which saturates 0g; Cholesterol 0mg; Calcium 38mg; Fibre 5.3g; Sodium 20mg.

Apricot and ginger compote

Fresh ginger adds warmth to this stimulating breakfast dish and complements the flavour of the juicy apricots. Dried apricots provide a concentrated source of valuable vitamins and minerals. Unsulphured fruit is free from sulphur dioxide preservative and will not be bright orange in colour. Ready-to-eat dried fruit doesn't require soaking overnight, but does contain preservatives.

Serves 4

350g/12oz/1½ cups dried (preferably
   unsulphured) apricots
4cm/1½in piece fresh root ginger,
   finely chopped
200g/7oz/scant 1 cup low-fat probiotic yogurt

1 Cover the apricots with boiling water, then leave to soak overnight.

Cook's tip
Fresh ginger freezes well. Peel the root and store it in a plastic bag in the freezer.

2 Place the apricots and their soaking water in a pan, add the ginger and bring to the boil.

3 Reduce the heat and simmer for 10 minutes until the fruit is soft and plump and the water becomes syrupy.

4 Strain the apricots over a bowl, reserving the syrup, and discard the ginger. Serve warm with the reserved syrup and a spoonful of yogurt.

Health benefits
• In Chinese medicine, ginger is revered for its health-giving properties. It is antispasmodic, aids digestion and can help treat colds and flu.
• Of all the dried fruits, apricots are the richest source of iron. They also provide calcium, potassium and vitamins A and C.

Energy 166Kcal/708kJ; Protein 6.1g; Carbohydrate 35.7g, of which sugars 35.7g; Fat 1g, of which saturates 0.3g; Cholesterol 1mg; Calcium 159mg; Fibre 5.5g; Sodium 54mg.

Luxury muesli

The benefit of making your own muesli at home is that you can combine a wide variety of seeds, grains, nuts and dried fruits to make a nutrient-packed breakfast, which is also free from added sugar. Use this recipe as a basic guide, but you can alter the balance of ingredients, or substitute others, according to your personal preferences.

Serves 4

50g/2oz/½ cup sunflower seeds
25g/1oz/¼ cup pumpkin seeds
175g/6oz/1½ cups porridge oats
175g/6oz/1½ cups barley flakes
115g/4oz/1 cup raisins
115g/4oz/1 cup chopped
  hazelnuts, roasted
115g/4oz/½ cup dried apricots
  (preferably unsulphured),
  finely chopped
50g/2oz/2 cups dried apple
  slices, halved
25g/1oz/⅓ cup desiccated coconut

1 Put the sunflower and pumpkin seeds in a dry frying pan and cook over a medium heat for 3 minutes until golden, tossing the seeds regularly to prevent them burning.

2 Mix the toasted seeds with the remaining ingredients and leave to cool. Store in an airtight container. Serve with non-dairy milk – this can be a rice, almond or soya substitute.

Granola

Oats, nuts and seeds, combined with sweet dried fruits, make an excellent and nutritious start to the day – without any of the additives often found in pre-packed cereals. Serve the granola with your choice of non-dairy milk or low-fat probiotic yogurt and top with plenty of seasonal fresh fruit. It can also be eaten as a healthy snack at any time of the day.

Serves 4

115g/4oz/1 cup porridge oats
115g/4oz/1 cup jumbo oats
50g/2oz/½ cup sunflower seeds
25g/1oz/2 tbsp sesame seeds
50g/2oz/½ cup hazelnuts, roasted
25g/1oz/¼ cup almonds, roughly chopped
50ml/2fl oz/¼ cup sunflower oil
50ml/2fl oz/¼ cup clear honey
50g/2oz/½ cup raisins
50g/2oz/½ cup dried sweetened cranberries

1 Preheat the oven to 140°C/275°F/ Gas 1. Mix together the oats, seeds and nuts in a bowl.

2 Heat the oil and honey in a pan until combined, then remove from the heat. Add the oat mixture and stir, then spread out on one or two baking sheets.

3 Bake for about 50 minutes until crisp, stirring occasionally to prevent the mixture sticking.

4 Remove from the oven and mix in the raisins and cranberries. Leave to cool, then store in an airtight container.

Health benefits
Oats have been the focus of much publicity in recent years; numerous scientific studies have shown that their soluble fibre content can significantly lower blood cholesterol levels.

Variation
Include any unsalted nuts you like in this granola. Try roughly chopped walnuts, cashews, pecans or Brazil nuts. You can lightly toast the nuts before chopping, if you like.

Top: Energy 813Kcal/3411kJ; Protein 20.8g; Carbohydrate 100.9g, of which sugars 33.4g; Fat 39g, of which saturates 5.5g; Cholesterol 0mg; Calcium 145mg; Fibre 12.4g; Sodium 55mg.
Above: Energy 638Kcal/2674kJ; Protein 14.4g; Carbohydrate 72.3g, of which sugars 27.9g; Fat 34.3g, of which saturates 2.9g; Cholesterol 0mg; Calcium 132mg; Fibre 6.9g; Sodium 39mg.

Traditional Scottish porridge

One of Scotland's oldest foods, oatmeal porridge gets your day off to a super-healthy start. This recipe uses traditional pinhead oatmeal, but you can use rolled oats if you prefer. Oats contain gluten and are therefore unsuitable for people with coeliac disease. If this is the case, millet flakes can be used instead to make a good alternative porridge.

Serves 4

1 litre/1¾ pints/4 cups water
115g/4oz/1 cup pinhead oatmeal
pinch of salt
clear honey, to taste
non-dairy milk, to serve

Variation

Rolled oats can be used, if preferred. This cooks more quickly than pinhead oatmeal. Simmer, stirring to prevent sticking, for about 5 minutes.

1 Put the water, pinhead oatmeal and salt into a heavy pan and bring to the boil over a medium heat, stirring with a wooden spatula. When the porridge is smooth and beginning to thicken, reduce the heat to a simmer.

2 Cook gently for about 25 minutes, stirring occasionally, until the oatmeal is cooked and the consistency smooth. Sweeten to taste with honey, and serve hot with non-dairy milk. Top with fresh fruit, such as banana (optional).

Energy 115Kcal/488kJ; Protein 3.6g; Carbohydrate 20.9g, of which sugars 0g; Fat 2.5g, of which saturates 0g; Cholesterol 0mg; Calcium 16mg; Fibre 2g; Sodium 10mg.

Porridge with dates and pistachio nuts

Full of valuable fibre and nutrients, puréed fresh dates give a natural sweet flavour to this warming winter breakfast dish, so there is no need for any added sugar. The addition of this fruit and nut topping makes your porridge all the more nourishing and exciting. You could use prunes or dried apricots in place of the dates, and any unsalted nuts in place of the pistachios, if you prefer.

Serves 4

250g/9oz/scant 2 cups fresh dates
225g/8oz/2 cups rolled oats
475ml/16fl oz/2 cups non-dairy milk
pinch of salt
50g/2oz/½ cup shelled, unsalted pistachio
nuts, roughly chopped

Health benefits
Oats have a reputation for being warming foods due to their fat and protein content, which is greater than that of most other grains. As well as providing energy and endurance, particularly in the colder months, oats are one of the most nutritious cereals.

1 First make the date purée. Halve the dates and remove the stones (pits) and stems. Cover with boiling water and soak for 30 minutes, until softened. Strain, reserving 90ml/6 tbsp of the soaking water.

2 Remove the skin from the dates and purée them in a food processor with the reserved soaking water.

3 Place the oats in a pan with the milk, 300ml/½ pint/1¼ cups water and salt. Bring to the boil, then reduce the heat and simmer for 4–5 minutes until cooked, stirring frequently.

4 Serve the porridge in warm serving bowls, topped with a spoonful of the date purée and sprinkled with chopped pistachio nuts.

Energy 416Kcal/1754kJ; Protein 13.6g; Carbohydrate 62.5g, of which sugars 21.2g; Fat 13.8g, of which saturates 1.3g; Cholesterol 0mg; Calcium 75mg; Fibre 5.7g; Sodium 127mg.

appetizers and snacks

Whether you want a light lunch or supper dish, a
healthy snack or a tempting appetizer to lead into
a main meal, this section includes delicious ideas
for both everyday and special occasions.
Vegetable dips served with crudités or rice cakes
make a good detox choice, or how about stuffed
vine leaves, sesame falafal or roasted peppers?

Hummus

This creamy purée combines chickpeas, garlic, lemon juice, olive oil and tahini to produce a tasty snack, appetizer or light meal that is rich in vegetable protein. Serve with a selection of raw fruit and vegetable crudités for extra fibre and vitamin value.

1 Put the chickpeas in a bowl, cover with plenty of cold water and leave to soak overnight.

2 Drain, place in a pan and cover with fresh water. Bring to the boil and boil rapidly for 10 minutes. Reduce the heat and simmer gently for about 1 hour until soft. Drain.

3 Process the chickpeas in a food processor or blender until smooth. Add the lemon juice, garlic, olive oil, cayenne pepper and tahini and blend until creamy. Season with pepper and transfer to a serving dish. Sprinkle with oil and cayenne pepper. Garnish with parsley and serve with cherry tomatoes.

4 To make the crudités, trim and peel the carrots and quarter lengthways. Halve the celery sticks lengthways and trim to the same length as the carrots.

5 Core, quarter and thickly slice the apple and pear, then dip into the lemon or lime juice. Arrange with the baby corn in a bowl or on a platter.

Serves 4

150g/5oz/¾ cup dried chickpeas
juice of 2 lemons
2 garlic cloves, sliced
30ml/2 tbsp olive oil
pinch of cayenne pepper
150ml/¼ pint/⅔ cup tahini
freshly ground black pepper
extra olive oil and cayenne pepper,
    for sprinkling
flat leaf parsley, to garnish
cherry tomatoes, to serve

For the crudités
6 baby carrots
2 celery sticks
1 red-skinned eating apple
1 pear
15ml/1 tbsp lemon or lime juice
6 baby corn

Cook's tip
You can use a 400g/14oz can of chickpeas if you prefer.

Energy 453Kcal/1887kJ; Protein 15.7g; Carbohydrate 32.1g, of which sugars 13.8g; Fat 30g, of which saturates 4.2g; Cholesterol 0mg; Calcium 345mg; Fibre 10.5g; Sodium 49mg.

Pea guacamole

This is a variation on the more classic avocado guacamole and provides another delicious idea for including more vegetables in your diet. It's based on frozen peas, which are a good source of vitamin C and fibre, as well as being convenient to use, straight from the freezer.

Serves 4

350g/12oz/3 cups frozen peas, completely defrosted
1 garlic clove, crushed
2 spring onions (scallions), trimmed and chopped
5ml/1 tsp finely grated rind and juice of 1 lime
2.5ml/½ tsp ground cumin
dash of Tabasco sauce
15ml/1 tbsp extra virgin olive oil
30ml/2 tbsp roughly chopped fresh coriander (cilantro)
ground black pepper
pinch of cayenne and lime slices, to garnish
brown rice cakes, to serve

1 Put the peas, garlic, spring onions, lime rind and juice, cumin, Tabasco sauce, olive oil and ground black pepper into a food processor and process for a few minutes until smooth.

2 Add the chopped fresh coriander and process for a few more seconds.

3 Spoon into a serving bowl, cover with clear film (plastic wrap) and chill for about 30 minutes.

4 Sprinkle over the cayenne, garnish with the lime slices and serve with brown rice cakes.

Energy 103Kcal/425kJ; Protein 6.5g; Carbohydrate 10.4g, of which sugars 2.5g; Fat 4.3g, of which saturates 0.7g; Cholesterol 0mg; Calcium 45mg; Fibre 4.8g; Sodium 5mg.

Avocado guacamole

A highly nutritious dip, based on avocados, onion and tomatoes spiked with fresh chilli, garlic, toasted cumin seeds and lime. The avocados are half mashed and half diced for an interesting texture. This makes a great dish to serve with lightly salted corn chips as an appetizer or light meal, or it could be served as a salsa on the side of plain grilled fish or chicken.

Serves 4

2 large ripe avocados
1 small red onion, finely chopped
1 fresh red or green chilli, seeded and
    very finely chopped
1 garlic clove, crushed
finely shredded rind of ½ lime and juice
    of 1–1½ limes
225g/8oz tomatoes, seeded and chopped
30ml/2 tbsp roughly chopped fresh
    coriander (cilantro)
2.5–5ml/½–1 tsp ground toasted
    cumin seeds
15ml/1 tbsp olive oil
ground black pepper
lime wedges and fresh coriander (cilantro)
    sprigs, to garnish
lightly salted corn chips, to serve (optional)

1 Cut one of the avocados in half and lift out and discard the stone (pit). Scrape the flesh from both halves into a bowl and mash it roughly with a fork.

2 Add the onion, chilli, garlic, lime rind, tomatoes and coriander and stir well. Add the ground cumin seeds and pepper to taste, then stir in the olive oil.

3 Halve and stone the remaining avocado. Dice the flesh and stir it into the guacamole.

4 Squeeze in fresh lime juice to taste, mix well, then cover and leave to stand for 15 minutes so that the flavour develops. Serve with lime wedges and garnish with fresh coriander sprigs.

Energy 187Kcal/771kJ; Protein 2.4g; Carbohydrate 4.7g, of which sugars 3.3g; Fat 17.6g, of which saturates 3.5g; Cholesterol 0mg; Calcium 41mg; Fibre 4g; Sodium 14mg.

Artichoke and cumin dip

This dip is easy to make and unbelievably tasty. Globe artichokes contain compounds, including a substance called cynarin, believed to have a range of medicinal properties, including helping to give a boost to a sluggish liver. Serve with raw vegetable crudités for dipping, during your detox, or breadsticks or wholemeal pitta after your detox.

Serves 4

2 x 400g/14oz cans artichoke
  hearts, drained
2 garlic cloves, peeled
2.5ml/½ tsp ground cumin
olive oil
ground black pepper

Cook's tip
For extra flavour, add a handful of fresh basil leaves to the artichokes before blending.

1 Put the artichoke hearts in a food processor with the garlic and ground cumin, and a generous drizzle of olive oil. Process to a smooth purée and season with black pepper to taste.

2 Spoon the purée into a serving bowl and serve with an extra drizzle of olive oil swirled on the top. Serve with a selection of raw vegetable crudités, for dipping.

Energy 76Kcal/315kJ; Protein 2g; Carbohydrate 3.9g, of which sugars 2g; Fat 6g, of which saturates 0.8g; Cholesterol 0mg; Calcium 85mg; Fibre 2.7g; Sodium 121mg.

Stuffed vine leaves

This vegetarian version of the famous Greek dish uses a healthy combination of rice, pine nuts and raisins, flavoured with plenty of fresh herbs, to make a tasty and satisfying stuffing for fresh vine leaves. They are delicious served hot or cold with a salad, and would also be good as light bites for a party or as a healthy snack during the day.

Makes 40

40 fresh vine leaves
60ml/4 tbsp olive oil
a crisp salad and lemon wedges, to serve

For the stuffing
150g/5oz/¾ cup long grain rice, rinsed
2 bunches spring onions (scallions),
   finely chopped
40g/1½oz/¼ cup pine nuts
25g/1oz/scant ¼ cup seedless raisins
30ml/2 tbsp chopped fresh mint leaves
60ml/4 tbsp chopped fresh parsley
2.5ml/½ tsp freshly ground black pepper

1 Cut out the thick, coarse stems from the vine leaves. Blanch the leaves in a large pan of boiling water until they just begin to change colour, then drain. Refresh in cold water and drain again.

2 Mix all the stuffing ingredients together in a bowl.

3 Open out the vine leaves, ribbed side uppermost. Place a heaped teaspoonful of the stuffing on each.

4 Fold over the two outer edges to prevent the stuffing from falling out, then roll up each vine leaf from the stem end to form a neat roll.

5 Arrange the rolls in the base of a steamer and sprinkle over the oil. Steam for 50–60 minutes, or until the rice is cooked. Serve cold or hot, with salad and lemon wedges.

Cook's tip
To boost vitamin, mineral and fibre levels you can substitute wholegrain brown rice for white, cooking the stuffed vine leaves for an extra 15–20 minutes to ensure that the rice is tender.

Energy 38Kcal/156kJ; Protein 0.8g; Carbohydrate 4.4g, of which sugars 1.4g; Fat 1.9g, of which saturates 0.2g; Cholesterol 0mg; Calcium 13mg; Fibre 0.5g; Sodium 2mg.

Sesame falafel with tahini yogurt dip

Sesame seeds are used to give a crunchy coating to these spicy chickpea patties, which are served with a creamy tahini yogurt dip in this recipe. Sesame seeds are a useful source of omega-3 fatty acids, especially for vegetarians. They also provide calcium and vitamin E. You could turn this into a light meal by serving with a large green leafy salad.

Serves 4 (makes 12)

250g/9oz/1⅓ cups dried chickpeas
2 garlic cloves, crushed
1 fresh red chilli, seeded and finely sliced
5ml/1 tsp ground coriander
5ml/1 tsp ground cumin
15ml/1 tbsp chopped fresh mint
15ml/1 tbsp chopped fresh parsley
2 spring onions (scallions), finely chopped
1 large egg, beaten
sesame seeds, for coating
sunflower oil, for shallow frying
ground black pepper

For the tahini yogurt dip
30ml/2 tbsp tahini
200g/7oz/scant 1 cup low-fat probiotic yogurt
5ml/1 tsp cayenne pepper, plus extra
   for sprinkling
15ml/1 tbsp chopped fresh mint
1 spring onion (scallion), finely sliced

1 Place the chickpeas in a bowl, cover with cold water and leave to soak overnight. Drain and rinse the chickpeas, then place in a pan and cover with fresh cold water. Bring to the boil and boil rapidly for 10 minutes, then reduce the heat and simmer gently for about 1 hour until tender.

2 Meanwhile, make the dip. Mix together the tahini, yogurt, cayenne pepper and mint in a bowl. Sprinkle the spring onion and extra cayenne pepper on top and chill.

3 Drain the chickpeas, then combine them with the garlic, chilli, ground spices, herbs, spring onions, egg and seasoning. Process in short bursts in a blender or food processor until the mixture forms a rough paste. If the paste seems too soft, chill it for 30 minutes.

4 Form the chilled chickpea paste into 12 patties with your hands, then roll each one in the sesame seeds to coat.

5 Heat enough oil to cover the base of a large frying pan. Fry the falafel for 6 minutes, turning once. Drain well on kitchen paper.

Energy 372Kcal/1557kJ; Protein 19.3g; Carbohydrate 35.3g, of which sugars 5.8g; Fat 18.1g, of which saturates 2.6g; Cholesterol 48mg; Calcium 280mg; Fibre 8g; Sodium 89mg.

Roasted peppers with sweet cicely

The sweet aniseed flavours of sweet cicely and fennel combine beautifully with the succulent tastes of the peppers and tomatoes and the piquancy of capers. Both sweet cicely and fennel are good herbal aids to digestion. This dish can be served as a light lunch or as an unusual appetizer for a dinner party during the warm summe months.

1 Preheat the oven to 180°C/350°F/ Gas 4. Place the red pepper halves in a large ovenproof dish and set aside.

2 To skin the tomatoes, cut a cross at the base, then put in a bowl and pour over boiling water. Leave them to stand for 1 minute. Cut in half if they are of medium size, or leave whole if small. Place a whole small or half a medium tomato in each half of a pepper cavity.

3 Cover with a scattering of sweet cicely seeds, fennel seeds and capers and about half the sweet cicely flowers. Drizzle the olive oil all over. Bake in for 1 hour. Serve hot, garnished with fresh sweet cicely leaves and flowers.

Serves 4

4 red or yellow (bell) peppers, halved
   and seeded
8 small or 4 medium tomatoes
15ml/1 tbsp semi-ripe sweet cicely seeds
15ml/1 tbsp fennel seeds
15ml/1 tbsp capers, rinsed
4 sweet cicely flowers, newly opened,
   stems removed
60ml/4 tbsp olive oil

For the garnish
a few small sweet cicely leaves
8 more flowers

Variation
If sweet cicely is not available, this dish can be made with a range of different herbs, such as chervil or lovage, although they will all impart a distinctive flavour.

Energy 172Kcal/714kJ; Protein 2.5g; Carbohydrate 14.3g, of which sugars 13.8g; Fat 12g, of which saturates 1.9g; Cholesterol 0mg; Calcium 21mg; Fibre 3.8g; Sodium 16mg.

Griddled polenta with tangy pebre

Polenta is a good wheat-free starchy carbohydrate. Here it is flavoured with chillies and fresh herbs, then left to firm up before being cut into triangles to cook on a griddle. It's served with a tangy salsa from Chile called pebre, which combines onion, chilli, sweet cherry peppers and coriander. It makes an unusual and tasty appetizer.

Serves 6

10ml/2 tsp crushed dried chilli flakes
1.3 litres/2¼ pints/5⅔ cups water
250g/9oz/1¼ cups quick cook polenta
30ml/2 tbsp chopped fresh dill
30ml/2 tbsp chopped fresh
   coriander (cilantro)
45ml/3 tbsp olive oil

For the pebre
½ red onion, finely chopped
4 drained bottled sweet cherry peppers,
   finely chopped
1 fresh medium-hot red chilli, seeded and
   finely chopped
1 small red (bell) pepper, quartered
   and seeded
10ml/2 tsp cider vinegar
30ml/2 tbsp olive oil
4 tomatoes, halved, cored, seeded and
   roughly chopped
45ml/3 tbsp chopped fresh coriander (cilantro)

1 Put the chilli flakes in a pan with the water and bring to the boil. Pour the polenta into the water in a continuous stream, whisking all the time. Reduce the heat and continue to whisk for a few minutes.

2 When the polenta is thick and bubbling, whisk in half the olive oil and herbs. Pour into a greased 33 x 23cm/ 13 x 9in baking tray and leave to cool. Leave uncovered so that the surface firms up and chill overnight.

3 To make the pebre, place the onion, sweet cherry peppers and chilli in a mortar. Dice the red pepper finely and add it to the mortar with the cider vinegar and olive oil.

4 Pound the mixture with a pestle for about 1 minute, then tip into a serving dish. Stir in the tomatoes and coriander. Cover with clear film (plastic wrap) and leave in a cool place.

5 Remove the polenta from the refrigerator and leave it at room temperature for about 30 minutes.

6 Cut into 12 even triangles and brush the top with the remaining olive oil.

7 Heat a griddle until a few drops of water sprinkled on the surface evaporate instantly. Lower the heat to medium and grill the polenta triangles in batches oiled-side down for about 2 minutes, then turn through 180 degrees and cook for 1 minute more, to get a striking chequered effect. Serve immediately, with the pebre.

Variation
Any mixture of fresh herbs can be used in the polenta triangles, such as basil and chives, for a really distinctive flavour without adding any salt.

Energy 254Kcal/1060kJ; Protein 4.8g; Carbohydrate 33.7g, of which sugars 3g; Fat 10.9g, of which saturates 1.4g; Cholesterol 0mg; Calcium 25mg; Fibre 2.2g; Sodium 9mg.

simply sensational soups

Soups are full of vegetable goodness and provide tempting and satisfying lunch or supper dishes all year round, whatever the weather. Tuck into classic favourites such as Fresh Cabbage Soup, or Chilled Tomato and Fresh Basil Soup, or treat your tastebuds to Fragrant Thai Fish Soup or American Red Bean Soup with Guacamole Salsa.

Gazpacho with vegetable garnish

This traditional Spanish soup is packed with fresh vegetables, and because all the vegetables are raw, it provides full vitamin value. The recipe does include a small amount of bread to thicken the texture, but this could be gluten-free bread if preferred. Cool and refreshing, it makes an ideal choice for a healthy lunch in the summer months.

Serves 4

2 slices day-old bread
600ml/1 pint/2½ cups chilled water
1kg/2¼lb ripe tomatoes
1 cucumber
2 red (bell) peppers, seeded and chopped
1 fresh green chilli, seeded and chopped
2 garlic cloves, chopped
30ml/2 tbsp extra virgin olive oil
juice of 1 lime and 1 lemon
a few drops Tabasco sauce
ground black pepper
8 ice cubes, to serve
a handful of basil leaves,
    to garnish

For the vegetable salsa
1 small cucumber
1 small onion
1 red (bell) pepper
1 green (bell) pepper

1 Break the bread into pieces and soak in 150ml/¼ pint/⅔ cup of the chilled water for 5 minutes.

Variation

If you're not following a strict detox diet, you could sprinkle some toasted croûtons over the top. These could be made from corn bread rather than wheat bread.

2 Meanwhile, place the tomatoes in a bowl and cover with boiling water. Leave for 30 seconds, then peel, seed and chop the flesh.

3 Thinly peel the cucumber, then cut it in half lengthways. Scoop out the seeds with a teaspoon. Discard the seeds and chop the flesh.

4 Place the bread (with any free liquid) in a food processor or blender. Add the tomatoes, cucumber, red pepper, chilli, garlic, olive oil, citrus juices and Tabasco, then pour in the remaining 450ml/¾ pint/scant 2 cups water.

5 Blend the mixture until it is well combined but still chunky. Season to taste with black pepper.

6 Pour into a large bowl, leave to cool at room temperature, then chill in the refrigerator for 2–3 hours. Put four serving bowls in the refrigerator at the same time.

7 Just before serving, make the salsa. Peel and finely chop the cucumber and onion and put the pieces in a bowl. Cut the peppers in half, remove the seeds and chop finely. Add to the bowl and combine thoroughly.

8 Ladle the soup into chilled bowls, add the ice cubes, and top each portion with a spoonful of the vegetable salsa.

Energy 190Kcal/798kJ; Protein 5.2g; Carbohydrate 27.6g, of which sugars 20.3g; Fat 7.3g, of which saturates 1.2g; Cholesterol 0mg; Calcium 59mg; Fibre 6g; Sodium 102mg.

Chilled tomato and fresh basil soup

A refreshing chilled soup for late summer when fresh tomatoes are at their most flavoursome. Tomatoes provide valuable amounts of antioxidant vitamins as well as lypocene, which is thought to protect against certain types of cancer. Distinctively peppery basil, a classic partner to tomatoes, aids digestion and calms the nervous system.

Serves 4

45ml/3 tbsp olive oil
1 onion, finely chopped
900g/2lb ripe Italian plum tomatoes,
 roughly chopped
1 garlic clove, roughly chopped
about 1.5 litres/2½ pints/6¼ cups
 vegetable stock
30ml/2 tbsp sun-dried tomato paste
30ml/2 tbsp shredded fresh basil, plus a few
 whole leaves, to garnish
ground black pepper

1 Heat the oil in a large pan. Add the onion and cook gently for about 5 minutes, stirring frequently, until softened but not brown.

2 Stir in the chopped tomatoes and garlic, then add the vegetable stock, sun-dried tomato paste and ground black pepper to season.

3 Bring to the boil, then lower the heat, half cover the pan and simmer gently for 20 minutes, stirring occasionally.

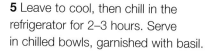

4 Transfer the soup to a blender or food processor, add the shredded fresh basil and process. Press the blended soup through a sieve (strainer) into a clean pan. Gently heat through, stirring. Do not allow the soup to boil. Add more stock if necessary.

5 Leave to cool, then chill in the refrigerator for 2–3 hours. Serve in chilled bowls, garnished with basil.

Energy 107Kcal/448kJ; Protein 2.8g; Carbohydrate 10.3g, of which sugars 9.9g; Fat 6.4g, of which saturates 1g; Cholesterol 0mg; Calcium 49mg; Fibre 3.4g; Sodium 55mg.

Chilled avocado soup with cumin

This delicious cold soup combines mild and creamy avocados with the distinctive flavours of onions, garlic, lemon and cumin. Avocado is one of the few fruits that contains fat, but it is the healthy monounsaturated type that can help to lower blood cholesterol levels. Avocados are also a rich source of vitamin E, which is needed for healthy skin and hair.

Serves 4

3 ripe avocados
1 bunch spring onions (scallions),
   white parts only, trimmed and
   roughly chopped
2 garlic cloves, chopped
juice of 1 lemon
1.5ml/¼ tsp ground cumin
1.5ml/¼ tsp paprika
450ml/¾ pint/scant 2 cups fresh
   vegetable stock
300ml/½ pint/1¼ cups iced water
ground black pepper
roughly chopped fresh flat leaf parsley,
   to garnish

1 Starting half a day ahead, put the flesh of one avocado in a food processor or blender. Add the spring onions, garlic and lemon juice and purée until smooth. Add the second avocado and purée, then add third, along with the spices and seasoning. Purée until smooth.

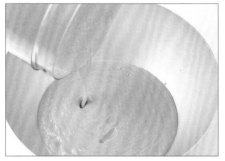

2 Gradually add the vegetable stock. Pour the soup into a metal bowl and chill for 2–3 hours.

3 To serve, stir in the iced water, then season to taste with plenty of black pepper. Garnish with chopped parsley and serve immediately.

Energy 220Kcal/907kJ; Protein 2.7g; Carbohydrate 2.9g, of which sugars 1.3g; Fat 21.8g, of which saturates 4.7g; Cholesterol 0mg; Calcium 22mg; Fibre 4.2g; Sodium 9mg.

Carrot and orange soup

This bright and summery soup with a vibrantly fresh citrus flavour is packed with antioxidant vitamins. Use a good, home-made vegetable stock made with fresh ingredients and no artificial flavourings or excess salt. Here the soup is served warm, but you could chill it in the refrigerator for a few hours and serve it cold on a hot summer's day.

Serves 4

30ml/2 tbsp olive oil
3 leeks, sliced
450g/1lb carrots, sliced
1.2 litres/2 pints/5 cups vegetable stock
rind and juice of 2 oranges
2.5ml/½ tsp freshly grated nutmeg
150ml/¼ pint/⅔ cup low-fat probiotic yogurt
5ml/1 tsp cornflour (cornstarch)
ground black pepper
fresh sprigs of coriander (cilantro),
   to garnish

1 Heat the oil in a large pan. Add the leeks and carrots and stir well, coating the vegetables with the oil. Cover and cook for about 10 minutes, until the vegetables are beginning to soften but not colour.

2 Pour in the stock and the orange rind and juice. Add the nutmeg and season to taste with ground black pepper. Bring to the boil, lower the heat, cover and simmer for about 40 minutes, or until the vegetables are tender.

3 Leave to cool slightly, then purée the soup in a food processor or blender until smooth.

4 Return the soup to the pan. Blend 30ml/2 tbsp of the yogurt with the cornflour, then stir into the soup. Taste and adjust the seasoning, if necessary. Reheat gently.

5 Ladle the soup into warm individual bowls and put a swirl of yogurt in the centre of each. Sprinkle with coriander and serve immediately.

Energy 135Kcal/564kJ; Protein 3.9g; Carbohydrate 16.1g, of which sugars 15g; Fat 6.6g, of which saturates 1.2g; Cholesterol 1mg; Calcium 120mg; Fibre 4.4g; Sodium 63mg.

Pea soup with garlic

This delicious, simple soup has a wonderfully sweet taste and smooth texture, and is really quick and convenient to make. Garlic is beneficial for treating a range of complaints and has numerous therapeutic benefits, such as lowering cholesterol and blood pressure, protecting against infection, and it is believed to help to prevent some types of cancer.

Serves 4

30ml//2 tbsp olive oil
1 garlic clove, crushed
900g/2lb/8 cups frozen peas
1.2 litres/2 pints/5 cups vegetable stock
ground black pepper
fresh mint, to garnish

1 Heat the oil in a large pan and add the garlic. Fry gently for 2 minutes, then add the peas. Cook for 1–2 minutes more, then pour in the stock.

Cook's tip
If you keep a bag of frozen peas in the freezer, you can rustle up this soup at very short notice.

2 Bring the soup to the boil, then reduce the heat to a simmer. Cover and cook for 5–6 minutes, until the peas are tender. Leave to cool slightly, then transfer the mixture to a food processor and process until smooth (you may have to do this in two batches).

3 Return the soup to the pan and heat through gently. Season with pepper to taste. Serve garnished with mint.

Energy 236Kcal/977kJ; Protein 15.7g; Carbohydrate 25.4g, of which sugars 5.2g; Fat 9g, of which saturates 1.5g; Cholesterol 0mg; Calcium 48mg; Fibre 10.6g; Sodium 112mg.

Fresh cabbage soup

This hearty, vegetable soup is good for the digestion. It's based on the popular diet recipe for cabbage soup, but includes a variety of vegetables, namely turnip, carrots, onion and celery as well as apple. You can use any variety of cabbage that's in season or another member of the same family, such as Brussels sprouts or broccoli, shredded or roughly chopped.

Serves 4

45ml/3 tbsp olive oil
1 small turnip, cut into matchstick strips
2 carrots, cut into matchstick strips
1 large onion, sliced
2 celery sticks, sliced
1 white or green cabbage, about
   675g/1½lb, shredded
1.2 litres/2 pints/5 cups vegetable stock
1 sharp eating apple, cored, peeled
   and chopped
2 bay leaves
5ml/1 tsp chopped fresh parsley
10ml/2 tsp lemon juice
ground black pepper
fresh herbs, to garnish
low-fat probiotic yogurt and rye bread,
   to serve

1 Heat the oil in a large pan and gently fry the turnip, carrots, onion and celery for 10 minutes.

Health benefits

Cabbage is an excellent detoxifier and is reputed to aid the digestion, detoxify the stomach and upper bowels, cleanse the liver and reduce the risk of certain cancers. It is also rich in folate, vitamins C and E, potassium, iron, betacarotene and thiamin, and is well known for its potent antiviral and antibacterial qualities.

2 Coarsley shred the cabbage, and add to the pan. Pour in the vegetable stock, add the chopped apple, bay leaves and chopped parsley and bring to the boil. Cover and simmer for 40 minutes or until the vegetables are really tender.

3 Remove and discard the bay leaves, then stir in the lemon juice and season with freshly ground black pepper.

4 Serve hot, garnished with fresh herbs and accompanied by low-fat probiotic yogurt and rye bread.

Variation

Create a red, super-detox version of this cleansing soup by substituting the carrots with beetroot (beets) and the raw white or green cabbage with red cabbage.

Energy 167Kcal/694kJ; Protein 3.6g; Carbohydrate 19g, of which sugars 17.4g; Fat 8.9g, of which saturates 1.2g; Cholesterol 0mg; Calcium 121mg; Fibre 6.3g; Sodium 31mg.

Russian borscht with kvas

Beetroot is the main ingredient of this flavoursome and vibrantly coloured soup. It is a powerful blood cleanser and tonic and can aid the digestive system. It is also a good source of potassium and folate as well as iron. If you are not following a strict detox diet, you could serve this soup with a generous spoonful of creamy yogurt.

3 Add the crushed garlic and chopped tomatoes to the pan and cook, stirring, for 2 more minutes.

4 Place the bay leaf, parsley, cloves and peppercorns in a piece of muslin (cheesecloth) and tie with string.

5 Add the muslin bag to the pan with the stock. Bring to the boil, reduce the heat, cover and simmer for 1¼ hours, until the vegetables are tender. Discard the bag. Stir in the beetroot kvas and season. Ladle into bowls and serve garnished with chives or dill.

Serves 4

900g/2lb raw beetroot (beets), peeled
2 carrots, peeled
2 celery sticks
30ml/2 tbsp olive oil
2 onions, sliced
2 garlic cloves, crushed
4 tomatoes, peeled, seeded and chopped
1 bay leaf
1 large parsley sprig
2 cloves
4 whole peppercorns
1.2 litres/2 pints/5 cups chicken or
  vegetable stock
150ml/¼ pint/⅔ cup beetroot kvas
  (see Cook's Tip)
ground black pepper
chopped fresh chives or sprigs of dill,
  to garnish

1 Cut the beetroot, carrots and celery into thick strips. Heat the oil in a pan and cook the onions over a low heat for 5 minutes, stirring occasionally.

2 Add the beetroot, carrots and celery to the pan and cook for a further 5 minutes, on a low heat, stirring from time to time, until the vegetables are slightly softened.

Cook's tip

Beetroot kvas adds an intense colour and a slight tartness to the soup. Peel and grate 1 beetroot, add 150ml/¼ pint/⅔ cup stock and 10ml/2 tsp lemon juice. Bring to the boil, cover and remove from the heat. Leave for 30 minutes. Strain before using.

Energy 172Kcal/723kJ; Protein 5.1g; Carbohydrate 25.5g, of which sugars 23.5g; Fat 6.2g, of which saturates 0.9g; Cholesterol 0mg; Calcium 75mg; Fibre 6.9g; Sodium 180mg.

Summer vegetable soup

This brightly coloured, fresh-tasting tomato soup makes the most of summer vegetables in season. Diced red and yellow peppers could also be added to make a sweeter version. During a detox, dairy products such as cheese should be avoided, but afterwards a little grated Parmesan cheese may be sprinkled over the the top of this healthy vegetable soup.

Serves 4

450g/1lb ripe plum tomatoes
225g/8oz ripe yellow tomatoes
45ml/3 tbsp olive oil
1 large onion, finely chopped
15ml/1 tbsp sun-dried tomato
   purée (paste)
225g/8oz courgettes (zucchini),
   trimmed and chopped
225g/8oz yellow courgettes,
   trimmed and chopped
3 waxy new potatoes, diced
2 garlic cloves, crushed
about 1.2 litres/2 pints/5 cups chicken or
   vegetable stock or water
60ml/4 tbsp shredded fresh basil
50g/2oz/⅔ cup freshly grated Parmesan
   cheese (optional)
ground black pepper

1 Plunge all the tomatoes in a bowl of boiling water for 30 seconds, refresh in ice cold water, then peel the skin and finely chop the flesh.

2 Heat the oil in a large pan and cook the onion for 5 minutes, until softened. Stir in the tomato purée, tomatoes, courgettes, potatoes and garlic. Mix well and cook gently for 10 minutes.

3 Pour in the stock or water. Bring to the boil, lower the heat, half cover the pan and simmer gently for 15 minutes, or until the vegetables are just tender. Add more stock or water if necessary.

4 Remove the pan from the heat and stir in the basil. Taste for seasoning and serve immediately. Sprinkle with Parmesan cheese, if using.

Energy 221Kcal/925kJ; Protein 6.3g; Carbohydrate 29g, of which sugars 15.5g; Fat 9.7g, of which saturates 1.5g; Cholesterol 0mg; Calcium 74mg; Fibre 5.2g; Sodium 58mg.

Winter farmhouse soup

Colourful fresh root vegetables form the base of this chunky, minestrone-style main meal soup. Always choose organic vegetables if you can and vary them according to what's in season and what is available. During a detox, use non-wheat macaroni or other small non-wheat pasta. The cheese should also be omitted while you are on the diet.

Serves 4

30ml/2 tbsp olive oil
1 onion, roughly chopped
3 carrots, cut into large chunks
175–200g/6–7oz turnips, cut into chunks
175g/6oz swede (rutabaga), cut into chunks
400g/14oz can chopped Italian tomatoes
15ml/1 tbsp tomato purée (paste)
5ml/1 tsp dried mixed herbs
5ml/1 tsp dried oregano
50g/2oz dried (bell) peppers, washed and
    thinly sliced (optional)
1.5 litres/2½ pints/6¼ cups vegetable stock
    or water
50g/2oz/½ cup dried macaroni or
    other pasta
400g/14oz can red kidney beans, rinsed
    and drained
30ml/2 tbsp chopped fresh flat leaf parsley
ground black pepper
freshly grated Parmesan cheese or
    premium Italian-style vegetarian cheese,
    to serve (optional)

1 Heat the olive oil in a large pan, add the onion and cook over a low heat for about 5 minutes until softened.

2 Add the carrot, turnip and swede chunks, canned chopped tomatoes, tomato purée, dried mixed herbs, dried oregano and dried peppers, if using. Stir in plenty of pepper to taste.

3 Pour in the vegetable stock or water and bring to the boil. Stir well, cover the pan, then lower the heat and simmer for 30 minutes, stirring occasionally.

4 Add the pasta to the pan and bring quickly to the boil, stirring. Lower the heat and simmer, uncovered, for about 8 minutes until the pasta is only just tender, or according to the instructions on the packet. Stir frequently.

5 Stir in the kidney beans. Heat through for 2–3 minutes, then remove the pan from the heat and stir in the parsley.

6 Taste the soup for seasoning. Serve hot in warmed soup bowls. Sprinkle with a little grated cheese if liked.

Energy 266Kcal/1118kJ; Protein 10.6g; Carbohydrate 42.3g, of which sugars 18.4g; Fat 7.2g, of which saturates 1.1g; Cholesterol 0mg; Calcium 149mg; Fibre 11.7g; Sodium 432mg.

Spicy pumpkin soup

Pumpkins and the many varieties of winter squash, such as butternut and acorn, are a good source of betacarotene, which the body converts into vitamin A. The delicious flesh is easily digestible and rarely causes problems for those with food sensitivities. Ginger and cumin give the soup its spicy flavour and also help to aid digestion.

Serves 4

900g/2lb pumpkin, peeled and
   seeds removed
30ml/2 tbsp olive oil
2 leeks, trimmed and sliced
1 garlic clove, crushed
5ml/1 tsp ground ginger
5ml/1 tsp ground cumin
900ml/1½ pints/3¾ cups vegetable stock
ground black pepper
fresh coriander (cilantro) leaves, to garnish
60ml/4 tbsp low-fat probiotic yogurt, to serve

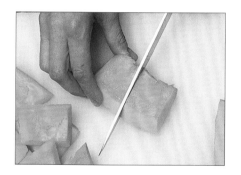

1 Cut the peeled pumpkin into large chunks. Heat the olive oil in a large pan and add the sliced leeks and garlic.

2 Cook gently over a low heat until the vegetables are softened.

3 Stir in the ginger and cumin and cook, stirring, for a further minute.

4 Add the pumpkin and the vegetable stock and season with freshly ground black pepper.

5 Bring the soup to the boil and simmer over a low heat for about 30 minutes, until the pumpkin is tender. Process in batches, if necessary, in a blender or food processor.

6 Warm the soup through again, being careful not to bring it to the boiling point, and serve in warmed individual bowls, with a swirl of yogurt on top. Garnish with fresh coriander leaves.

Cook's tip
Add extra colour and flavour to this soup by stirring in 30ml/2 tbsp chopped fresh coriander (cilantro) leaves before serving.

Energy 101Kcal/420kJ; Protein 3.2g; Carbohydrate 7.9g, of which sugars 6g; Fat 6.5g, of which saturates 1.1g; Cholesterol 0mg; Calcium 89mg; Fibre 4.5g; Sodium 2mg.

Butternut squash soup with tomato salsa

This is a wonderfuly inviting, flavoursome soup, that is perfect for a cold winter's day. Although it appears to use a lot of garlic, the intensity mellows with roasting, so don't be alarmed by the quantity. A spoonful of spicy tomato salsa gives bite to the sweet-tasting soup, and the fresh herbs add fragrance and colour as well as their distinctive flavour.

Serves 4

2 garlic bulbs, outer skin removed
75ml/5 tbsp olive oil
a few fresh thyme sprigs
1 large butternut squash, halved and seeded
2 onions, chopped
5ml/1 tsp ground coriander
1.2 litres/2 pints/5 cups vegetable stock
30–45ml/2–3 tbsp chopped fresh oregano
ground black pepper

For the salsa

4 large ripe tomatoes, halved and seeded
1 red (bell) pepper, halved and seeded
1 large fresh red chilli, halved and seeded
30ml/2 tbsp extra virgin olive oil
15ml/1 tbsp balsamic vinegar
pinch of caster (superfine) sugar

1 Preheat the oven to 220°C/425°F/Gas 7. Place the garlic bulbs on a piece of foil and pour over half the olive oil. Add the thyme, then fold the foil around the garlic bulbs to enclose them. Place the foil parcel on a baking sheet with the butternut squash and brush the squash with 15ml/1 tbsp of the remaining olive oil.

2 Add the tomatoes, red pepper and fresh chilli for the salsa.

3 Roast the vegetables for 25 minutes, then remove the tomatoes, pepper and chilli. Reduce the temperature to 190°C/375°F/Gas 5 and cook the squash and garlic for 20–25 minutes more, or until the squash is tender.

4 Heat the remaining olive oil in a large, heavy pan and cook the onions and ground coriander gently for about 10 minutes, or until softened.

5 Skin the pepper and chilli and process in a food processor or blender with the tomatoes and extra-virgin olive oil. Stir in the vinegar and seasoning to taste, adding a pinch of sugar.

6 Squeeze the roasted garlic out of its papery skin into the onions and scoop the squash out of its skin, adding it to the pan. Add the stock and plenty of black pepper. Bring to the boil and simmer for 10 minutes.

7 Stir in half the oregano and cool the soup slightly, then process in a blender or food processor. Alternatively, press the soup through a sieve (strainer).

8 Reheat the soup without allowing it to boil, then taste for seasoning before ladling it into warmed bowls. Top each with a spoonful of salsa and sprinkle over the remaining chopped oregano. Serve immediately.

Cook's tip
Put the roasted red (bell) pepper and chilli in a plastic bag and allow them to cool. The skins will then slip off easily.

Energy 238Kcal/986kJ; Protein 2.9g; Carbohydrate 11.9g, of which sugars 10.3g; Fat 20.2g, of which saturates 3.1g; Cholesterol 0mg; Calcium 79mg; Fibre 4.1g; Sodium 11mg.

Lentil and garlic soup

This traditional Jewish soup is made with red lentils and vegetables, which are cooked and puréed, then sharpened with lots of lemon juice. Lentils are a good complex carbohydrate, making this a satisfying and sustaining soup. Garlic and lemon juice, added for flavour, both help to aid the digestion as well as offering many health benefits.

Serves 4

45ml/3 tbsp olive oil
1 onion, chopped
2 celery sticks, chopped
1–2 carrots, sliced
8 garlic cloves, chopped
1 potato, peeled and diced
250g/9oz/generous 1 cup red lentils,
   picked over and rinsed
1 litre/1¾ pints/4 cups vegetable stock
2 bay leaves
1–2 lemons, halved
2.5ml/½ tsp ground cumin, or to taste
cayenne pepper or Tabasco sauce,
   to taste
ground black pepper
lemon slices and chopped fresh flat leaf
   parsley, to garnish

1 Heat the oil in a large pan. Add the onion and cook for 5 minutes. Stir in the celery, carrots, half the garlic and all the potato. Cook for a few minutes until beginning to soften.

2 Add the lentils and stock to the pan and bring to the boil. Reduce the heat, cover and simmer for 30 minutes.

3 Add the bay leaves, remaining garlic and half the lemons to the pan and cook the soup for a further 10 minutes, until the lentils and vegetables are tender. Remove the bay leaves. Squeeze the juice from the remaining lemons, then stir into the soup, to taste.

4 Pour the soup into a food processor or blender and process until smooth. (You may need to do this in batches.) Tip the soup back into the pan, stir in the cumin, cayenne pepper or Tabasco sauce, and season to taste.

5 Ladle the soup into bowls and top each portion with lemon slices and a sprinkling of chopped fresh flat leaf parsley.

Energy 349Kcal/1474kJ; Protein 16.7g; Carbohydrate 52.5g, of which sugars 7.2g; Fat 9.5g, of which saturates 1.4g; Cholesterol 0mg; Calcium 59mg; Fibre 5.4g; Sodium 53mg.

Tomato and lentil soup

Lentils are a nourishing staple and make an excellent detox soup to serve as a satisfying lunch or supper dish. Unlike other dried beans and peas, lentils do not need soaking before cooking and therefore make an easy option for a quick meal. You can use brown or green lentils – both retain their shape after cooking, unlike the split variety.

Serves 4

275g/10oz/1¼ cups brown or green lentils,
   thoroughly rinsed
30ml/2 tbsp extra virgin olive oil
1 onion, thinly sliced
2 garlic cloves, sliced into thin matchsticks
1 carrot, thinly sliced
400g/14oz can chopped tomatoes
15ml/1 tbsp tomato purée (paste)
2.5ml/½ tsp dried oregano
1 litre/1¾ pints/4 cups hot water
ground black pepper
30ml/2 tbsp roughly chopped fresh herb
   leaves, to garnish

1 Put the lentils in a pan with cold water to cover. Bring the water to the boil and boil for 3–4 minutes. Strain, discarding the liquid, and set the lentils aside.

2 Wipe the pan clean and add the olive oil. Place it over a medium heat until hot and then add the thinly sliced onion and sauté until translucent.

3 Stir in the sliced garlic, then, as soon as it becomes aromatic, return the lentils to the pan. Add the carrot, tomatoes, tomato purée and oregano. Stir in the hot water and a little ground black pepper to taste.

4 Bring the soup to the boil, then lower the heat, cover the pan and cook gently for 20–30 minutes, or until the lentils are soft. Stir in the chopped herbs just before serving, and taste to check the seasoning.

Energy 298Kcal/1261kJ; Protein 17.6g; Carbohydrate 44.5g, of which sugars 7.3g; Fat 6.8g, of which saturates 1.1g; Cholesterol 0mg; Calcium 50mg; Fibre 5.1g; Sodium 59mg.

Black-eyed bean and tomato broth

This delicious bean soup is delicately flavoured with fragrant spices and tangy lemon, and has a mild chilli kick. It makes a hearty and warming lunch or light supper dish that is perfect for a cold winter day. Like all beans, peas and lentils, these pale, oval beans are an excellent source of fibre and vegetable protein, and they also provide valuable vitamins and minerals.

Serves 4

175g/6oz/1 cup dried black-eyed
   beans (peas)
15ml/1 tbsp olive oil
2 onions, chopped
4 garlic cloves, chopped
1 medium-hot or 2–3 mild fresh
   chillies, chopped
5ml/1 tsp ground cumin
5ml/1 tsp ground turmeric
250g/9oz fresh or canned
   tomatoes, diced
600ml/1 pint/2½ cups vegetable stock
25g/1oz fresh coriander (cilantro) leaves,
   roughly chopped
juice of ½ lemon

1 Put the beans in a pan, cover with cold water, bring to the boil and cook for 5 minutes. Remove from the heat, cover and leave to stand for 2 hours.

2 Drain the beans, return to the pan, cover with fresh cold water, then simmer for 35–40 minutes, or until the beans are tender. Drain and set aside.

Cook's tip
Black-eyed beans have a creamy texture and distinctive flavour. They are characterized by a small black eye, and although they are often called beans, they are also known as black-eyed peas.

3 Heat the oil in a pan, add the onions, garlic and chilli and cook for 5 minutes, or until the onion is soft.

4 Stir in the cumin, turmeric, tomatoes, stock, half the coriander and the beans and simmer for 20–30 minutes.

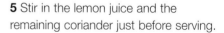

5 Stir in the lemon juice and the remaining coriander just before serving.

Energy 222Kcal/934kJ; Protein 14.3g; Carbohydrate 31.8g, of which sugars 10.9g; Fat 5.1g, of which saturates 0.6g; Cholesterol 0mg; Calcium 273mg; Fibre 13.9g; Sodium 50mg.

North African spiced soup

This mildly spiced soup contains both potatoes and chickpeas, which provide plenty of sustained energy. The addition of lemon juice helps to stimulate the liver to expel toxins.

3 Add 30ml/2 tbsp of the vegetable stock to the spice mixture and mix together to form a paste. Stir the spicy paste into the onion mixture and add the chopped carrots, celery and the remaining vegetable stock.

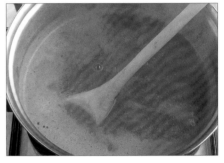

4 Bring the mixture back to the boil, stirring, and reduce the heat. Cover the pan with a lid and gently simmer for a further 5 minutes.

5 Add the tomatoes and potatoes to the soup and simmer gently, covered, for 20 minutes. Add the saffron, chickpeas, coriander and lemon juice, mix well to combine thoroughly, and heat through. Season to taste with pepper and serve with wedges of lemon to squeeze into the soup.

Serves 4

1 large onion, chopped
1.2 litres/2 pints/5 cups vegetable stock
5ml/1 tsp ground cinnamon
5ml/1 tsp ground turmeric
15ml/1 tbsp grated fresh root ginger
pinch of cayenne pepper
2 carrots, diced
2 celery sticks, diced
400g/14oz can chopped tomatoes
450g/1lb floury potatoes, diced
5 strands saffron
400g/14oz can chickpeas, rinsed and drained
30ml/2 tbsp chopped fresh coriander (cilantro)
15ml/1 tbsp lemon juice
ground black pepper
wedges of lemon, to serve

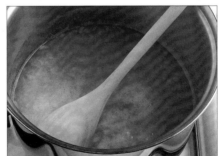

1 Place the chopped onion in a large pan with 300ml/½ pint/1¼ cups of the vegetable stock. Simmer gently for about 10 minutes.

2 Meanwhile, mix together the cinnamon, turmeric, ginger and cayenne pepper.

Cook's tip
The chickpeas in this soup are a good source of fibre, which can relieve constipation. They are also a good source of low-fat protein, vitamins and minerals.

Energy 278Kcal/1173kJ; Protein 11.9g; Carbohydrate 51.6g, of which sugars 16.5g; Fat 4.1g, of which saturates 0.6g; Cholesterol 0mg; Calcium 127mg; Fibre 10.1g; Sodium 276mg.

Cannellini bean soup

A quick, wholesome soup boosted nutritionally with the addition of cavolo nero – a very dark green cabbage. Dark green leafy vegetables are a good source of beneficial phytochemicals.

Serves 4

2 x 400g/14oz cans chopped tomatoes
    with herbs
250g/9oz cavolo nero leaves,
    or Savoy cabbage
400g/14oz can cannellini beans,
    drained and rinsed
60ml/4 tbsp extra virgin olive oil
ground black pepper

1 Pour the tomatoes into a large pan and add a can of cold water. Season with pepper and bring to the boil, then reduce the heat to a simmer.

2 Roughly shred the cabbage leaves and add them to the pan. Partially cover the pan and simmer gently for about 15 minutes, or until the cabbage is just tender.

3 Add the cannellini beans to the pan and warm through for a few minutes. Check the seasoning, then ladle the soup into bowls, drizzle each with a little olive oil and serve immediately.

Energy 416Kcal/1756kJ; Protein 24.4g; Carbohydrate 53.4g, of which sugars 11.8g; Fat 13.1g, of which saturates 2g; Cholesterol 0mg; Calcium 145mg; Fibre 19g; Sodium 41mg.

Borlotti bean and vegetable soup

This is an Italian-style soup, rather like minestrone, but made with beans instead of pasta. It is served ladled over spinach, or other dark green leafy vegetables. You can use any type of canned beans – ideally choose those canned in water. They are wonderfully nutritious and high in dietary fibre, which is essential for healthy digestion.

Serves 4

45ml/3 tbsp olive oil
2 onions, chopped
2 carrots, sliced
4 garlic cloves, crushed
2 celery sticks, thinly sliced
1 fennel bulb, trimmed and chopped
2 large courgettes (zucchini), thinly sliced
400g/14oz can chopped tomatoes
30ml/2 tbsp home-made or bought pesto
900ml/1½ pints/3¾ cups vegetable stock
400g/14oz can borlotti or haricot (navy)
   beans, drained and rinsed
450g/1lb fresh young spinach
ground black pepper

1 Heat 30ml/2 tbsp of oil in a large pan. Add the chopped onions, carrots, crushed garlic, celery and fennel and fry gently for about 10 minutes.

2 Add the courgettes and fry for a further 2 minutes.

Variation
You can use other dark greens, such as chard or cabbage, instead of the spinach; simply shred and cook until tender, then spoon over the soup.

3 Stir in the chopped tomatoes, pesto, stock and beans and bring to the boil. Lower the heat, cover and simmer for 25–30 minutes, until the vegetables are completely tender. Season with black pepper to taste.

4 Heat the remaining oil in a frying pan and quickly stir-fry the spinach for 1 minute, just until wilted. Spoon the spinach into heated soup bowls, then ladle the soup over the spinach. Sprinkle with ground black pepper, and serve immediately.

Energy 359Kcal/1496kJ; Protein 14.3g; Carbohydrate 40.7g, of which sugars 23.4g; Fat 16.5g, of which saturates 2.5g; Cholesterol 0mg; Calcium 353mg; Fibre 15.1g; Sodium 599mg.

Butter bean, tomato and pesto soup

This soup is very quick and easy to make, and uses a combination of store-cupboard ingredients and fresh, preferably home-made, pesto and stock. You could use other types of beans as an alternative to butter beans, if you prefer. Make plenty at once and then freeze in batches so that you have some to hand as a quick meal when you are hungry after a long day.

Serves 4

2 x 400g/14oz cans butter (lima) beans, drained and rinsed
900ml/1½ pints/3¾ cups vegetable stock
60ml/4 tbsp sun-dried tomato purée (paste)
75ml/5 tbsp fresh pesto, (preferably home-made)

Cook's tip

Use a home-made or good-quality bought fresh stock for the best natural flavour. It will also be free from the additives and excess salt found in stock (bouillon) cubes.

1 Put the rinsed and drained beans in a large pan with the stock and bring just to the boil.

2 Reduce the heat and stir in the tomato purée and pesto. Cover, bring back to simmering point and cook gently for 5 minutes.

3 Transfer six ladlefuls of the soup to a blender or food processor, scooping up plenty of the beans. Process until smooth, then return to the pan.

4 Heat gently, stirring frequently, for 5 minutes, then season if necessary. Ladle into four warmed soup bowls.

Energy 255Kcal/1071kJ; Protein 14.9g; Carbohydrate 28.2g, of which sugars 4.4g; Fat 9.9g, of which saturates 2.1g; Cholesterol 5mg; Calcium 96mg; Fibre 9.7g; Sodium 931mg.

American red bean soup with guacamole salsa

This spicy soup is in Tex-Mex style, and it is served with a cooling avocado and lime salsa. It's packed with vitamins, minerals, protective compounds and fibre, all vital in a healthy diet.

2 Cool the soup slightly, then purée it in a food processor or blender until smooth. Return to the pan and season.

3 To make the guacamole salsa, halve, stone (pit) and peel the avocados, then dice them finely. Place in a small bowl and gently, but thoroughly, mix with the finely chopped red onion and chilli, and the coriander and lime juice.

4 Reheat the soup and ladle into bowls. Spoon a little guacamole salsa into the middle of each and serve, offering Tabasco sauce separately, if liked.

Serves 6

30ml/2 tbsp olive oil
2 onions, chopped
2 garlic cloves, chopped
10ml/2 tsp ground cumin
1.5ml/¼ tsp cayenne pepper
15ml/1 tbsp paprika
15ml/1 tbsp tomato purée (paste)
2.5ml/½ tsp dried oregano
400g/14oz can chopped tomatoes
2 x 400g/14oz cans red kidney beans,
    drained and rinsed
900ml/1½ pints/3¾ cups water
ground black pepper
Tabasco sauce, to serve (optional)

For the guacamole salsa
2 avocados
1 small red onion, finely chopped
1 green chilli, seeded and chopped
15ml/1 tbsp chopped fresh coriander (cilantro)
juice of 1 lime

1 Heat the oil in a pan, add the onions and garlic and cook for 4–5 minutes. Add the cumin, cayenne and paprika, and cook for 1 minute. Stir in the tomato purée and cook for a few seconds, then stir in the oregano. Add the chopped tomatoes, kidney beans and water. Bring to the boil and simmer for 15–20 minutes.

Energy 198Kcal/833kJ; Protein 10.4g; Carbohydrate 30.1g, of which sugars 10g; Fat 4.8g, of which saturates 0.7g; Cholesterol 0mg; Calcium 113mg; Fibre 9.7g; Sodium 534mg.

Country mushroom, bean and barley soup

This hearty main meal vegetable soup is perfect on a freezing cold day. Serve in warmed bowls, with plenty of rye or pumpernickel bread on the side.

Serves 6

30ml/2 tbsp haricot (navy) beans, soaked overnight
2 litres/4½ pints/8½ cups water
45ml/3 tbsp green split peas
45ml/3 tbsp yellow split peas
90ml/6 tbsp pearl barley
1 onion, chopped
3 celery sticks, diced or sliced
5 garlic cloves, sliced
2 carrots, sliced
1 large baking potato, peeled and cut into chunks
10g/¼oz mixed dried mushrooms
ground black pepper
chopped fresh parsley, to garnish

1 Put the beans in a large pan, cover with water and bring to the boil. Boil for 10 minutes, then skim any froth from the surface. Add the green and yellow split peas, pearl barley, onion, celery and garlic.

2 Bring the mixture to the boil, then reduce the heat, cover and simmer gently for about 1½ hours, or until the beans are tender.

Cook's tip
Dried beans should be soaked in a bowl of cold water overnight to reduce the cooking time.

3 Add the carrots, potato and dried mushrooms and cook for a further 30 minutes, or until the beans and vegetables are tender.

4 Season to taste, then ladle into bowls, garnish with parsley and serve with rye or pumpernickel bread.

Energy 162Kcal/689kJ; Protein 6.8g; Carbohydrate 34.1g, of which sugars 4.3g; Fat 0.8g, of which saturates 0.1g; Cholesterol 0mg; Calcium 34mg; Fibre 2.9g; Sodium 30mg.

Leek and potato soup

Also called vichyssoise, this less rich version of the popular Scottish soup makes a comforting, warming lunch, which can be taken to work in a flask. The chopped vegetables produce a chunky soup, but if you prefer a smooth texture, press the mixture through a sieve. Onion and related vegetables contain valuable phytochemicals that may help prevent disease.

Serves 4

30ml/2 tbsp vegetable oil
2 leeks, washed and chopped
1 small onion, peeled and finely chopped
350g/12oz potatoes, peeled and chopped
900ml/1½ pints/3¾ cups vegetable stock
ground black pepper
chopped fresh parsley or chives, to garnish

Health benefits
Members of the onion family are good decongestants.

1 Heat the oil in a large pan over a medium heat. Add the leeks and onion and cook gently, stirring occasionally, for about 7 minutes, until they are softened but not browned.

2 Add the potatoes to the pan and cook for about 2–3 minutes, then add the stock and bring to the boil. Cover and simmer for 30–35 minutes.

3 Season to taste with ground black pepper and remove the pan from the heat. Serve sprinkled with the chopped fresh parsley or chives.

Cook's tips
• Don't use a food processor to purée this soup as it can give the potatoes a gluey consistency if you are not careful. The potatoes should be left to crumble and disintegrate naturally as they boil, which means that the the longer you leave them, the thicker the consistency of the soup will be .
• If you have time, you should make your own chicken or vegetable stock by simmering bones and vegetables in water for 2 hours and straining the liquid.

Energy 138Kcal/580kJ; Protein 3.3g; Carbohydrate 18.2g, of which sugars 4.2g; Fat 6.3g, of which saturates 1g; Cholesterol 0mg; Calcium 33mg; Fibre 3.3g; Sodium 12mg.

Fragrant Thai fish soup

This light and aromatic soup is made with chunks of monkfish simmered in a light stock, flavoured with lime, lemon grass, ginger, fresh coriander and chillies. Packed with flavour, it makes a perfect dinner dish. It is an excellent source of low-fat protein and contains many vitamins and minerals that are essential for good health.

Serves 4

1 litre/1¾ pints/4 cups fish stock
4 lemon grass stalks
3 limes
2 small fresh hot red chillies, seeded and
    thinly sliced
2cm/¾in piece fresh root ginger, peeled
    and thinly sliced
6 coriander (cilantro) stalks, with leaves
2 kaffir lime leaves, coarsely
    chopped (optional)
350g/12oz monkfish fillet, skinned and cut
    into 2.5cm/1in pieces
15ml/1 tbsp rice vinegar
30ml/2 tbsp Thai fish sauce
30ml/2 tbsp chopped fresh coriander (cilantro)
    leaves, to garnish

1 Pour the stock into a large pan and bring to the boil. Slice the bulb ends of the lemon grass diagonally into 3mm/⅛in thick pieces. Peel off four wide strips of lime rind with a vegetable peeler, avoiding the white pith. Squeeze the limes and reserve the juice.

2 Add the lemon grass, lime rind, chillies, ginger, and coriander stalks to the stock, with the kaffir lime leaves, if using. Simmer for 1–2 minutes.

3 Add the monkfish, vinegar, Thai fish sauce and half the reserved lime juice. Simmer for 3 minutes, until the fish is just tender. Although cooked, it will still hold its shape.

4 Remove the coriander stalks from the pan and discard. Taste the broth and add more lime juice if necessary. Serve the soup very hot, sprinkled with the chopped coriander leaves.

Variation
Other fish or shellfish such as sole, prawns (shrimp), scallops or squid can be substituted for the monkfish, if you like.

Energy 65Kcal/278kJ; Protein 14.4g; Carbohydrate 1g, of which sugars 0.8g; Fat 0.5g, of which saturates 0.1g; Cholesterol 12mg; Calcium 33mg; Fibre 0.6g; Sodium 554mg.

Chicken, avocado and chickpea soup

Ideally choose organic chicken and use home-made stock to make this soup. It will taste far superior and be free of chemical additives. Turkey breast could be used in place of chicken. Avocado adds a delicious creaminess and chickpeas complete the nutritional balance, making this a tasty, satisfying and nourishing main meal soup.

Serves 4–6

1.5 litres/2½ pints/6¼ cups chicken stock
½ fresh chilli, seeded and thinly sliced
2 skinless, boneless chicken breast fillets
1 avocado
4 spring onions (scallions), finely sliced
400g/14oz can chickpeas, drained
   and rinsed
freshly ground black pepper

1 Pour the chicken stock into a large pan and add the chilli. Bring to the boil, add the whole chicken breast fillets, then lower the heat and simmer gently for about 10 minutes, or until the chicken is cooked.

2 Remove the pan from the heat and lift out the chicken breasts with a slotted spoon. Leave to cool a little.

3 Once it has has cooled, shred the chicken into small pieces using two forks. Set the shredded chicken aside.

Cook's tip
Handle chillies with care as they can irritate the skin and eyes. It is advisable to wear rubber gloves when preparing them.

4 Cut the avocado in half, remove the skin and stone (pit), then slice the flesh into 2cm/¾in pieces.

5 Add the avocado to the stock, with the spring onions and chickpeas.

6 Return the shredded chicken to the pan, and season to taste. Heat gently, then spoon into warmed bowls and serve immediately.

Energy 163Kcal/686kJ; Protein 17.3g; Carbohydrate 11.3g, of which sugars 0.5g; Fat 5.7g, of which saturates 1g; Cholesterol 35mg; Calcium 36mg; Fibre 3.4g; Sodium 178mg.

Chicken and leek soup with prunes

This recipe is based on the traditional Scottish soup cock-a-leekie and makes a warming, tasty and satisfying main meal soup. The unusual sweet and savoury combination of chicken, leeks and prunes is not only delicious, but the prunes add useful fibre. Pearl barley adds further carbohydrate substance and makes a little go a long way.

Serves 6

1 chicken, weighing about 2kg/4½lb
900g/2lb leeks
1 fresh bay leaf
a few each of fresh parsley stalks and
   thyme sprigs
1 large carrot, thickly sliced
2.4 litres/5 pints/10 cups chicken or
   beef stock
115g/4oz/generous ½ cup pearl barley
400g/14oz ready-to-eat prunes
ground black pepper
chopped fresh parsley, to garnish

1 Cut the breasts off the chicken and set aside. Place the remaining chicken carcass in a large pan. Cut half the leeks into 5cm/2in lengths and add them to the pan.

2 Tie the bay leaf, parsley and thyme into a bouquet garni and add to the pan with the carrot and the stock. Bring to the boil, then reduce the heat and cover. Simmer gently for 1 hour. Skim off any scum when the water first boils and occasionally during simmering.

3 Add the chicken breasts and cook for a further 30 minutes. Leave until cool enough to handle, then strain the stock. Reserve the chicken breasts and meat from the chicken carcass. Discard all the skin, bones, cooked vegetables and herbs. Skim as much fat as you can from the stock, then return it to the pan.

4 Meanwhile, rinse the pearl barley thoroughly in a sieve (strainer) under cold running water, then cook it in a large pan of boiling water for about 10 minutes. Drain, rinse well again and drain thoroughly.

5 Add the pearl barley to the stock. Bring to the boil over a medium heat, then lower the heat and cook very gently for 15–20 minutes, until the barley is just cooked and tender.

6 Season to taste with pepper, then add the prunes. Slice the remaining leeks and add them to the pan. Bring to the boil, then simmer for 10 minutes, or until the leeks are just cooked.

7 Slice the chicken breasts and add them to the soup with the chicken meat, sliced or cut into neat pieces.

8 Ladle the soup into deep plates and sprinkle with chopped parsley.

Energy 255Kcal/1083kJ; Protein 17.7g; Carbohydrate 44.4g, of which sugars 27.2g; Fat 2g, of which saturates 0.3g; Cholesterol 35mg; Calcium 69mg; Fibre 7.5g; Sodium 45mg.

main
dish
salads

Tempting, nutritionally balanced salads can be made from an endless variety of ingredients, including vitamin-packed fruit and vegetables, lean poultry, oily fish, seafood, eggs, nuts or seeds for protein, and rice, pasta, potatoes, beans, peas, lentils, or grains. Many are ideal for packed lunches; others make quick weekday suppers.

New spring vegetable salad

This colourful, tempting salad makes a satisfying meal and is ideal for packing into a lunchbox container to take with you to work. It includes a delicious combination of tender new potatoes, young asparagus, baby spinach and cherry tomatoes, all of which are rich sources of vitamin C.

Serves 4

675g/1½lb small new potatoes, scrubbed
400g/14oz can haricot (navy)
  beans, drained
115g/4oz cherry tomatoes, halved
75g/3oz/½ cup walnut halves
30ml/2 tbsp cider vinegar
5ml/1 tsp wholegrain mustard
60ml/4 tbsp olive oil
pinch of sugar
225g/8oz young asparagus spears, trimmed
6 spring onions (scallions), trimmed
ground black pepper
baby spinach leaves, to serve

1 Put the potatoes in a pan, cover with water and bring to the boil. Cook for 15 minutes or until tender. Meanwhile, put the haricot beans in a large bowl, then add the tomatoes and walnuts.

2 Put the cider vinegar, mustard, olive oil and sugar into a jar and season with pepper. Screw the lid on the jar tightly and shake well.

3 Add the asparagus to the potatoes and cook for 3 minutes until just tender.

4 Drain the cooked vegetables well. Cool under cold running water and drain again. Thickly slice the potatoes and cut the spring onions in half.

5 Add the asparagus, potatoes and spring onions to the bowl containing the bean mixture.

6 Pour the dressing over the salad and toss well. Serve on a bed of baby spinach leaves.

Cook's tip
You can use any variety of canned beans for this salad, or you could try fresh, young, cooked broad (fava) beans, if you like.

Energy 469Kcal/1959kJ; Protein 14.7g; Carbohydrate 48.1g, of which sugars 8.7g; Fat 25.5g, of which saturates 3g; Cholesterol 0mg; Calcium 122mg; Fibre 10g; Sodium 414mg.

Summer vegetable salad with hazelnuts

This nutrient-packed salad makes a perfect detox lunch or supper. Nuts supply a good source of vegetable protein, and hazelnuts in particular are rich in the antioxidant vitamin E. The combination of vegetables can be varied according to what is available when you go shopping.

Serves 4

30ml/2 tbsp olive oil
1 shallot, chopped
1 celery stick, sliced
225g/8oz assorted wild and cultivated
   mushrooms such as young ceps, shiitake
   and chanterelles, trimmed and sliced
freshly ground black pepper
175g/6oz small new potatoes, scrubbed
115g/4oz French (green) beans, trimmed
115g/4oz baby carrots, trimmed
   and peeled
50g/2oz baby corn, trimmed
50g/2oz asparagus spears, trimmed
115g/4oz/1 cup broad (fava) beans
30ml/2 tbsp hazelnut oil
15ml/1 tbsp vegetable oil
15ml/1 tbsp lemon juice
5ml/1 tsp chopped fresh thyme
50g/2oz hazelnuts, toasted and chopped

1 Fry the shallot and celery in olive oil until soft but without colouring. Add the mushrooms and cook over a moderate heat until their juices begin to run, then increase the heat to boil off the juices. Season with ground black pepper, then transfer to a bowl.

2 In separate steaming baskets, steam the potatoes for 20 minutes, the French beans, carrots, corn and asparagus for 6 minutes and the broad beans for 3 minutes. Cool under cold running water. Remove the tough outer skins of the broad beans, and cut the potatoes and all the vegetables in half.

3 Combine the steamed vegetables with the mushrooms, then moisten with the hazelnut and vegetable oils. Add the lemon juice and chopped thyme, season with ground black pepper and scatter the toasted hazelnuts over the top.

Health benefits
• Mushrooms are a useful souce of B vitamins as well as providing the minerals potassium and copper. Oriental mushrooms have been at the centre of much attention because of their powerful antiviral properties, which boost the immune system.
• Although hazelnuts, like all nuts, are high in calories, they provide valuable amounts of B group vitamins, vitamin E, calcium and iron, and zinc, as well as essential fatty acids – vital in a balanced diet.

Energy 295Kcal/1224kJ; Protein 7.5g; Carbohydrate 16.3g, of which sugars 5.7g; Fat 22.7g, of which saturates 2.7g; Cholesterol 0mg; Calcium 68mg; Fibre 5.8g; Sodium 166mg.

Red pepper and sprout salad with cashew cream dressing

This satisfying salad has contrasting colours, textures and flavours. The creamy nut dressing, which is full of protein and nutrients, transforms any salad into a wholesome meal.

Serves 1–2

115g/4oz unsalted cashew nuts
1 red (bell) pepper, seeded and diced
90g/3½ oz mung bean, aduki bean or
 chickpea sprouts
½ cucumber
juice of ½ lemon
small bunch fresh parsley, coriander
 (cilantro) or basil, finely chopped
5ml/1 tsp sesame, sunflower or
 pumpkin seeds

1 Put the cashew nuts in a heatproof bowl, pour over 100ml/3½/scant ½ cup boiling water, then leave them to soak for a few hours, preferably overnight, until softened.

2 Process the nuts with their soaking water in a food processor or blender until you have a smooth sauce. Add more water if necessary.

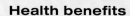

3 Peel away the cucumber skin in strips lengthways to produce a striped effect. Cut the cucumber into dice.

4 Place the pepper, sprouts, cucumber and lemon juice in a bowl and toss together. Serve with the cashew cream dressing and scatter with the herbs and seeds.

Health benefits

The cashew cream makes a smooth dressing that can be used for salads or as a sauce. Cashew nuts are rich in monounsaturated fatty acids, and they are favoured for their heart-protecting and anti-cancer properties.

Sprouting beans and seeds increases their nutritional value without losing any of the plant enzymes that are good for the digestive system. Sprouted beans contain vitamins A and B complex, C and E, and the vitamin content can increase by almost 200 per cent when the sprouts begin to turn green on exposure to light, due to the effect of energy-producing chlorophyll.

Cook's tips

• There are all kinds of sprouts, and beansprouts are one of the most readily available commercially. Rinse in cold water before using in salads and other recipes.
• Choose fresh, crisp sprouts with the seed or bean still attached. Avoid any that are slimy or that smell musty.
• Sprouts are best eaten on the day they are bought, but, if they are fresh, they will keep for 2–3 days tightly wrapped in a plastic bag in the refrigerator.
• You can sprout most whole beans or grains yourself. Favourites include aduki, alfalfa, haricot (navy), lentils, mung, sunflower, cress and wheat sprouts. The smaller beans will sprout more successfully than larger ones. Always use organic, unsprayed beans from a health food store for sprouting. (See instructions for 'How to sprout' on page 44.)

Energy 402Kcal/1668kJ; Protein 14.7g; Carbohydrate 18.9g, of which sugars 10.1g; Fat 30.2g, of which saturates 6g; Cholesterol 0mg; Calcium 86mg; Fibre 5.2g; Sodium 181mg.

Avocado, red onion and spinach salad with polenta croûtons

The simple lemon dressing gives a sharp tang to the creamy avocado, sweet red onions and crisp spinach. Golden polenta croûtons provide a wheat-free alternative to bread croûtons.

Serves 4

1 large red onion, cut into wedges
300g/11oz ready-made polenta, cut into 1cm/½in cubes
olive oil, for brushing
225g/8oz baby spinach leaves
1 avocado, peeled, stoned and sliced
5ml/1 tsp lemon juice

For the dressing
60ml/4 tbsp extra virgin olive oil
juice of ½ lemon
ground black pepper

1 Preheat the oven to 200°C/400°F/ Gas 6.

2 Place the red onion wedges and polenta cubes on a lightly oiled baking sheet and bake in the preheated oven for 25 minutes, or until the onion is tender and the polenta is crisp and golden, turning them regularly to prevent them sticking.

3 Turn the onions and polenta cubes on to kitchen paper and leave to cool.

4 Meanwhile, make the dressing for the salad. Place the olive oil, lemon juice and pepper to taste in a bowl or screw-top jar. Stir or shake thoroughly to combine.

5 Place the baby spinach leaves in a serving bowl. Toss the avocado slices in the lemon juice to prevent them from browning, then add to the spinach with the roasted onions.

6 Pour the dressing over the salad and toss gently to combine. Sprinkle the polenta croûtons on top of the salad or hand them round separately, and serve immediately.

Health benefits
Avocados have been traditionally regarded as a high-fat food that should be avoided. However, although they do contain high amounts of fat, it is beneficial monounsaturated fat, and research has revealed that this type of fat can help to decrease the level of cholesterol in the blood. Avocados also have a valuable vitamin and mineral content, and eating them can help to improve the condition of your skin and hair.

Energy 445Kcal/1849kJ; Protein 8.1g; Carbohydrate 48.3g, of which sugars 1.8g; Fat 23.9g, of which saturates 3.5g; Cholesterol 0mg; Calcium 104mg; Fibre 3.6g; Sodium 81mg.

Mixed bean salad with roasted red pepper dressing

The speckled herb and red pepper dressing adds a vitamin C boost to this salad. Perfect for a healthy detox summer lunch, this salad will provide a steady stream of energy.

Serves 4

1 large red (bell) pepper
60ml/4 tbsp olive oil
1 large garlic clove, crushed
25g/1oz/1 cup fresh flat leaf parsley, basil
    or mint
15ml/1 tbsp lemon juice
400g/14oz can flageolet (pale green) beans,
    drained and rinsed
200g/7oz/1½ cups canned cannellini beans,
    drained and rinsed
ground black pepper

1 Preheat the oven to 200°C/400°F/ Gas 6. Rinse the red pepper under running water, pat dry, then place on a baking sheet, brush with a little of the olive oil and roast for 15–20 minutes, or until wrinkled and soft.

Health benefits

Dried beans, peas and lentils are low in fat and high in fibre and protein and should be a regular part of a healthy balanced diet. They are also a good source of many minerals, including iron, zinc, potassium and magnesium, as well as B complex vitamins.

Canned beans are quick and convenient to use. Choose those canned in water rather than brine, if possible, and rinse thoroughly before using.

2 Remove the pepper from the oven and place in a plastic bag. Seal the bag and leave to cool. (This makes the skin easier to remove.)

3 When the pepper is cool enough to handle, remove it from the bag and carefully peel off the skin. Rinse the peeled pepper under running water.

4 Slice the pepper in half and remove the seeds and stem, gently using a knife to scrape away the membrane that holds the seeds in place. Dice the pepper, retaining any juices. Set aside.

5 Heat the remaining olive oil in a pan and cook the garlic for about 1 minute until softened. Remove from the heat, then add the herbs, the roasted red pepper and any retained juices, and the lemon juice. Stir together gently to combine thoroughly.

6 Put the flageolet and cannellini beans in a large serving bowl and pour over the dressing. Season to taste, then stir gently until well combined. Serve the salad warm or cold.

Energy 265Kcal/1110kJ; Protein 11g; Carbohydrate 29.7g, of which sugars 8.2g; Fat 12.2g, of which saturates 1.8g; Cholesterol 0mg; Calcium 123mg; Fibre 10.3g; Sodium 589mg.

Thai noodle salad

This exciting Asian mixed salad is based on somen noodles, which are Japanese rice noodles. They make a good wheat-free pasta alternative while following a detox diet.

Serves 4

200g/7oz somen noodles
1 large carrot, cut into thin strips
175g/6oz asparagus, trimmed and cut into 4 cm/1½ in lengths
115g/4oz mangetouts (snow peas), halved
115g/4oz baby corn, halved lengthways
1 red (bell) pepper, seeded and thinly sliced
115g/4oz beansprouts
115g/4oz can water chestnuts, drained and finely sliced
50g/2oz/½ cup unsalted peanuts
1 lime, cut into wedges, and fresh coriander (cilantro) leaves, to garnish

For the dressing

30ml/2 tbsp roughly torn fresh basil
45ml/3 tbsp roughly chopped mint
150ml/¼ pint/⅔ cup reduced-fat coconut milk
15ml/1 tbsp dark sesame oil
2 garlic cloves, finely chopped
juice of 1 lime
2 spring onions (scallions), finely chopped
cayenne pepper

Health benefits

Eating plenty of vegetables is essential for good health. Salads are a great way to pack different kinds into one meal.

1 First make the dressing. Combine all the ingredients in a bowl and mix well. Season to taste with salt and cayenne pepper.

2 Cook the noodles in a large pan of boiling water, following the directions on the packet, until just tender. Drain, rinse under cold running water and drain again.

3 Steam the carrots, asparagus, mangetouts and baby corn over a pan of boiling water for about 5 minutes, until they are tender but still crisp.

4 Drain, plunge them immediately into cold water and drain again.

5 Toss the noodles and steamed vegetables together in a large bowl with the red pepper, beansprouts and water chestnuts. Pour over the dressing and toss well to combine.

6 Arrange on individual serving plates, sprinkle over the chopped peanuts and garnish with lime wedges and fresh coriander leaves.

Energy 316Kcal/1318kJ; Protein 11g; Carbohydrate 51.6g, of which sugars 8.3g; Fat 6.8g, of which saturates 1.3g; Cholesterol 0mg; Calcium 60mg; Fibre 4.6g; Sodium 344mg.

Wholewheat pasta salad

This satisfying, high-fibre salad is assembled from any combination of seasonal vegetables. Use a non-wheat pasta for a strict detox or wholewheat pasta for a less restricted regime.

Serves 4

300g/11oz short wholewheat or non-wheat
   pasta, such as fusilli or penne
30ml/2 tbsp olive oil
2 medium carrots
225g/8oz broccoli
175g/6oz/1 cup shelled peas, fresh
   or frozen
1 red or yellow (bell) pepper, seeded
2 sticks celery
4 spring onions (scallions)
2 large tomatoes
75g/3oz/½ cup pitted olives

For the dressing
15ml/1 tbsp cider vinegar
45ml/3 tbsp olive oil
5ml/1 tsp Dijon mustard
15ml/1 tbsp sesame seeds
30ml/2 tbsp chopped mixed fresh herbs
   such as parsley, thyme and basil
ground black pepper
flat leaf parsley, to garnish

1 Cook the pasta in a large pan of rapidly boiling, lightly salted water for 10 minutes until tender, or according to the packet instructions.

2 Drain and rinse under cold water to stop the cooking.

3 Turn the drained pasta into a large bowl. Toss with 30ml/2 tbsp of the olive oil (to prevent the pasta from sticking together) and set aside. Allow it to cool completely before mixing with the other ingredients.

4 Lightly blanch the carrots, broccoli and peas for a few minutes in a large pan of boiling water, or in a steamer placed over a pan of boiling water. Place in a colander and refresh under cold running water. Drain well.

5 Chop the carrots and broccoli into bitesize pieces and add to the pasta with the peas.

6 Thinly slice the pepper, celery and spring onions and chop the tomato. Add to the salad with the olives.

7 Make the dressing in a small bowl by combining the vinegar with the oil and mustard. Stir in the sesame seeds and herbs, and season to taste with pepper.

8 Mix the dressing into the salad and toss well together to combine thoroughly. Garnish with parsley.

Energy 507Kcal/2125kJ; Protein 17.8g; Carbohydrate 64.4g, of which sugars 13g; Fat 21.6g, of which saturates 3.3g; Cholesterol 0mg; Calcium 130mg; Fibre 13.4g; Sodium 554mg.

Bulgur wheat salad with walnuts

Bulgur wheat, often referred to as 'cracked wheat', makes a healthy salad with a nutty flavour. Bulgur contains all the wheat grain except the bran, so it is easy to digest. However, for a wheat-free salad during a strict detox or for a gluten-free alternative grain, substitute long-grain brown rice or quinoa, cooked following the packet instructions.

1 Place the bulgur wheat in a large bowl. Pour the vegetable stock into a pan, add the cinnamon, cumin, cayenne pepper and ground cloves and bring to the boil.

2 Heat the spices in the stock for 1 minute, then pour the flavoured stock over the bulgur wheat and leave to stand for 20–30 minutes.

3 In another bowl, combine the mangetouts, peppers, tomatoes, shallots, olives, herbs and walnuts.

4 Add the lemon juice, olive oil and a little freshly ground black pepper. Stir thoroughly to mix.

5 Strain the bulgur wheat, shaking to remove as much liquid as possible, and discard the cinnamon stick.

6 Place the bulgur wheat in a large serving bowl, stir in the fresh vegetable mixture and serve immediately, garnished with onion rings.

Serves 8

225g/8oz/1 generous cup bulgur wheat
350ml/12fl oz/1½ cups vegetable stock
1 cinnamon stick
generous pinch of ground cumin
pinch of cayenne pepper
pinch of ground cloves
10 mangetouts (snowpeas), topped and tailed
1 red and 1 yellow (bell) pepper, roasted, skinned, seeded and diced
2 plum tomatoes, peeled, seeded and diced
2 shallots, finely sliced
5 black olives, stoned and cut into quarters
30ml/2 tbsp each shredded fresh basil, mint and parsley
30ml/2 tbsp roughly chopped walnuts
30ml/2 tbsp lemon juice
30ml/1fl oz/2 tbsp olive oil
freshly ground black pepper
onion rings, to garnish

Energy 118Kcal/493kJ; Protein 2.7g; Carbohydrate 19g, of which sugars 4.2g; Fat 3.9g, of which saturates 0.5g; Cholesterol 0mg; Calcium 28mg; Fibre 1.5g; Sodium 6mg.

Mushroom rice with cashew nuts

This sustaining warm rice salad combines earthy mushrooms, spicy chillies, fragrant coriander and golden cashew nuts to create a delicious dish that is suitable for lunch or dinner. A wide range of organic mushrooms is readily available. They combine well with rice and garlic chives to make a tasty accompaniment to vegetarian dishes, fish or chicken.

Serves 4

350g/12oz/generous 1¾ cups long
  grain rice
60ml/4 tbsp vegetable oil
1 small onion, finely chopped
2 fresh green chillies, seeded and
  finely chopped
25g/1oz chives, chopped
15g/½oz fresh coriander (cilantro)
600ml/1 pint/2½ cups vegetable stock
250g/9oz mixed mushrooms, thickly sliced
2 garlic cloves, crushed
50g/2oz unsalted cashew nuts
ground black pepper

1 Wash and drain the rice. Heat half the oil in a large pan and cook the onion and chillies over a gentle heat, stirring occasionally, for 10–12 minutes until softened.

2 Set half the chives aside. Cut the stalks off the coriander and set the leaves aside. Blend the remaining chives and the coriander stalks with the stock in a food processor or blender.

3 Add the rice to the onions and stir-fry over a low heat for 4–5 minutes. Pour in the herb stock, then stir in a good grinding of black pepper.

4 Bring to the boil, then stir and reduce the heat to very low. Cover tightly with a lid and cook for 15–20 minutes, or until the rice has absorbed all the liquid.

5 Remove the pan from the heat and lay a clean, folded dish towel over the pan, under the lid, and press on the lid to wedge it firmly in place.

6 Leave the rice to stand for a further 10 minutes, allowing the towel to absorb the steam while the rice becomes completely tender.

7 Meanwhile, heat the remaining oil and cook the mushrooms for 3–4 minutes. Add the remaining chives and cook for another 1–2 minutes.

8 Stir the garlic mushrooms into the rice and add the reserved coriander leaves. Adjust the seasoning to taste, then transfer to a serving dish and serve immediately, sprinkled with the toasted cashew nuts.

Variation
For a higher-fibre alternative use brown rice. Increase the cooking time in Step 3 to 25–30 minutes. Add extra stock as needed.

Energy 507Kcal/2112kJ; Protein 10.7g; Carbohydrate 74g, of which sugars 2g; Fat 18.3g, of which saturates 2.9g; Cholesterol 0mg; Calcium 54mg; Fibre 1.9g; Sodium 44mg.

Citrus fruit salad with avocado

A refreshingly tangy combination – rocket and lamb's lettuce leaves are topped with fresh grapefruit, oranges and avocado in a light, fruity dressing for a vitamin-packed salad. Toasted pine nuts add a crunchy contrast and provide some protein. Almonds, hazelnuts or walnuts could be added as alternatives to the pine nuts, if you like.

Serves 4

1 pink grapefruit
2 large oranges
1 large avocado
50g/2oz/½ cup pine nuts
25ml/1½ tbsp olive oil
10ml/2 tsp cider vinegar
30ml/2 tbsp freshly squeezed orange juice
50g/2oz lamb's lettuce (corn salad)
50g/2oz rocket (arugala)
ground black pepper
15g/½oz fresh chives
fresh herb sprigs, to garnish

1 Halve and segment the grapefruit and oranges and place the segments in a mixing bowl. Prepare over the bowl to catch the juices.

2 Peel, stone (pit) and slice the avocado and add the slices to the bowl. Gently stir in the pine nuts, taking care not to break up the avocado.

3 Whisk together the olive oil, vinegar, orange juice and pepper in a small bowl or jug and stir into the fruit mixture.

4 Arrange the lamb's lettuce and rocket on four serving plates and divide the fruit and dressing evenly over each. Garnish with chives and herb sprigs and serve immediately.

Energy 237Kcal/983kJ; Protein 3.8g; Carbohydrate 10.8g, of which sugars 10.3g; Fat 20.1g, of which saturates 2.7g; Cholesterol 0mg; Calcium 58mg; Fibre 3.6g; Sodium 8mg.

Greek salad

A popular Mediterranean salad, that typifies the healthy diet found in the region. Traditionally it includes feta cheese, which adds protein and calcium to the salad. It may be made from ewe's milk, although usually it is made using cow's milk. For a dairy-free version while following a strict detox, or for those who are lactose intolerant, substitute a soya cheese.

Serves 4

1 small cos or romaine lettuce, sliced
450g/1lb well-flavoured tomatoes, cut
  into eighths
1 cucumber, seeded and chopped
200g/7oz feta cheese, crumbled
4 spring onions (scallions), sliced
50g/2oz/½ cup black olives, pitted and halved

For the dressing
45ml/3 tbsp olive oil
25ml/1½ tbsp lemon juice
ground black pepper

1 Put the lettuce, tomatoes, cucumber, crumbled feta cheese, spring onions and olives in a large salad bowl.

2 For the dressing, whisk together the olive oil and lemon juice, then season. Pour over the salad, toss well and serve immediately.

Energy 248Kcal/1026kJ; Protein 9.8g; Carbohydrate 6.2g, of which sugars 6.1g; Fat 20.6g, of which saturates 8.5g; Cholesterol 35mg; Calcium 242mg; Fibre 2.7g; Sodium 1017mg.

Tofu and wild rice salad

This dish tastes wonderful on its own, or you can add a selection of chargrilled vegetables, such as peppers, tomatoes or courgettes. Tofu is rich in protein and low in fat and makes a nutritious addition to a vegetarian salad. It also provides a wide range of vitamins and minerals and phytoestrogens, which may help to protect against certain diseases and menopausal symptoms.

Serves 4

175g/6oz/scant 1 cup basmati rice
50g/2oz/generous ¼ cup wild rice
250g/9oz firm tofu, drained and cubed
25g/1oz preserved lemon, finely chopped (see Cook's Tip)
20g/¾oz bunch of fresh parsley, chopped

For the dressing
1 garlic clove, crushed
10ml/2 tsp clear honey
10ml/2 tsp of the preserved lemon juice
15ml/1 tbsp cider vinegar
15ml/1 tbsp olive oil
1 small fresh red chilli, seeded and finely chopped
5ml/1 tsp harissa paste (optional)
ground black pepper

1 Cook the basmati rice and the wild rice in separate pans until tender. The basmati will take about 10–15 minutes to cook, while the wild rice will take about 45–50 minutes. (It is possible to buy packets of ready-mixed long grain and wild rice. This takes just 25 minutes to cook because the outer skin of the wild rice has been broken.)

2 Drain, rinse under cold water and drain again, then place in a large bowl.

Cook's tip
Preserved lemons are available from Middle Eastern delicatessens or from some supermarkets.

3 Meanwhile whisk together all the dressing ingredients in a small bowl. Add the tofu, stir to coat and leave to marinate for about 20 minutes while the rice cooks.

4 Gently fold the tofu, marinade, preserved lemon and parsley into the rice, check the seasoning and serve.

Energy 284Kcal/1185kJ; Protein 9.6g; Carbohydrate 47.6g, of which sugars 2.4g; Fat 5.8g, of which saturates 0.7g; Cholesterol 0mg; Calcium 355mg; Fibre 0.6g; Sodium 7mg.

Avocado salad with tofu-dill dressing

In this fresh, crunchy salad the bitterness of the chicory is perfectly complemented by the fresh rocket, crunchy walnuts and smooth avocado. The tofu dressing boosts the nutritional value and makes a lighter, non-dairy alternative to rich mayonnaise. You could substitute any fresh herbs, such as basil or coriander, for the dill, if you like.

Serves 4

3 chicory (Belgian endive) heads, leaves
    separated, washed and dried
50g/2oz rocket (arugula), washed
    and dried
2 large ripe avocados
juice of ½ lemon
90g/3½oz/scant 1 cup walnut halves
sea salt and ground black pepper

For the dressing
15g/½oz/½ cup fresh dill, any tough
    stalks removed
1 garlic clove, crushed
juice of 1 lemon
5ml/1 tsp clear honey
5ml/1 tsp soy sauce
350g/12oz silken tofu
5ml/1 tsp French mustard
50ml/2fl oz/¼ cup olive oil

3 Divide the avocado slices evenly among the serving plates, arranging them attractively among the chicory and rocket leaves.

4 Sprinkle over the walnuts and season lightly with pepper.

5 Make the dressing by blending all the ingredients except the oil in a food processor or blender. With the machine running, gradually add the oil.

6 Season to taste. Drizzle the dressing over the salad and serve immediately.

1 Toss the chicory and rocket leaves together in a large bowl using wooden spoons and then heap on to four individual serving plates.

2 Peel, stone (pit) and slice the avocados, then toss in the lemon juice to prevent the slices from discolouring.

Cook's tip
Keep any remaining dressing in the refrigerator for use on another salad, as it is very versatile.

Energy 319Kcal/1320kJ; Protein 11.8g; Carbohydrate 4.2g, of which sugars 3.7g; Fat 28.5g, of which saturates 3g; Cholesterol 0mg; Calcium 535mg; Fibre 2.4g; Sodium 118mg.

Warm mixed seafood and fresh herb salad

Quick and easy to prepare, this seafood salad makes a great light meal. Shellfish is rich in vitamins and minerals and is a good source of omega-3 fatty acids.

Serves 4

30ml/2 tbsp olive oil
15ml/1 tbsp flavoured oil, such as basil oil or chilli oil
finely grated rind of 1 lemon
15ml/1 tbsp lemon juice
1 garlic clove, crushed
30ml/2 tbsp chopped fresh basil
175g/6oz mixed salad leaves
225g/8oz sugar snap peas, sliced diagonally
400g/14oz packet frozen seafood mix, thawed and drained
ground black pepper

1 Place 15ml/1 tbsp of the olive oil, the flavoured oil, grated lemon rind, lemon juice, garlic and basil in a small bowl or jug (pitcher). Season with pepper and whisk together. Set aside.

2 Place the salad leaves and sugar snap peas in a serving bowl and toss lightly to mix.

3 Heat the remaining olive oil in a large frying pan or wok, add the seafood and stir-fry over a medium heat for about 5 minutes until cooked.

4 Scatter the seafood over the salad leaves, drizzle the dressing over the salad, toss together gently to combine and serve immediately.

Variation
If using cooked seafood, stir-fry for just 2 minutes to warm through, or toss in the dressing and add cold to the salad.

Energy 184Kcal/769kJ; Protein 18.2g; Carbohydrate 4.7g, of which sugars 3g; Fat 10.4g, of which saturates 1.6g; Cholesterol 225mg; Calcium 75mg; Fibre 2.3g; Sodium 117mg.

Buckwheat noodle salad with smoked salmon

Soba is the best known type of Japanese noodle. It is made from buckwheat flour and is satisfying to eat. It makes a nutrient-rich alternative to wheat pasta while following a detox diet.

Serves 4

225g/8oz soba (Japanese
　buckwheat) noodles
15ml/1 tbsp oyster sauce
juice of ½ lemon
30ml/2 tbsp olive oil
115g/4oz smoked salmon, cut into
　fine strips
115g/4oz watercress or rocket (arugula)
2 ripe tomatoes, peeled, seeded and cut
　into strips
15ml/1 tbsp chopped chives
ground black pepper

1 Cook the soba noodles in a large pan of boiling water for about 6 minutes or following the directions on the packet, until tender.

2 Drain, then rinse under cold running water and drain well.

3 Tip the noodles into a large bowl. Mix in the oyster sauce, lemon juice and olive oil, and season with pepper.

4 Add the smoked salmon, watercress or rocket, tomatoes and chives. Toss and serve immediately.

Energy 313Kcal/1307kJ; Protein 11.3g; Carbohydrate 48.9g, of which sugars 3g; Fat 7.2g, of which saturates 1.1g; Cholesterol 10mg; Calcium 65mg; Fibre 1.1g; Sodium 653mg.

Bean salad with tuna and red onion

This salad combines creamy haricot or cannellini beans, crunchy French beans, tuna, fresh tomatoes and a tangy tarragon dressing. It makes a nourishing main meal salad that is easy to pack up and take with you for lunch. Beans are high in fibre, so this salad is good for the digestion as well as filling to eat. It could be accompanied by a mixed green salad if you like.

2 When cooked, drain the beans well and discard the herbs, onion and garlic.

3 Meanwhile, place all the dressing ingredients, apart from the lemon juice and sugar, in a jug (cup) or bowl and whisk until mixed. Season to taste with pepper and add lemon juice and a pinch of sugar, if you like. Leave to stand.

4 Blanch the green beans in plenty of boiling water for 2–3 minutes. Drain, refresh under cold water and drain thoroughly again.

5 Place both types of beans in a large bowl. Add half the dressing and toss to mix. Chop half the remaining parsley and add to the beans with the onion. Flake the tuna into large chunks and add to the salad with the tomatoes.

6 Arrange the salad on four plates. Drizzle the remaining dressing over the salad. Chop the remaining parsley and sprinkle on top. Serve immediately, at room temperature.

Serves 4
250g/9oz/1½ cups dried haricot (navy) or cannellini beans, soaked overnight in cold water
½ onion
1 garlic clove
1 bay leaf
bunch of chopped fresh flat leaf parsley
250g/9oz French (green) beans, trimmed
1 large red onion, very thinly sliced
250g/9oz good-quality canned tuna in olive oil or spring water, drained
200g/7oz cherry tomatoes, halved
ground black pepper

For the dressing
90ml/6 tbsp extra virgin olive oil
15ml/1 tbsp tarragon vinegar
5ml/1 tsp herb mustard
1 garlic clove, finely chopped
5ml/1 tsp grated lemon rind
a little lemon juice (optional)
pinch of caster (superfine) sugar (optional)

1 Drain the haricot or cannellini beans and bring them to the boil in a pan of fresh water. Boil rapidly for about 10 minutes, then reduce the heat and add the ½ onion, garlic, bay leaf and half the parsley. Cook for 1–1½ hours, until tender (the cooking time will depend on the age of the dried beans).

Variation
For an alternative idea, add chickpeas in place of the haricot or cannellini beans. You can use canned instead of dried beans if you don't have time to soak the dried variety overnight.

Energy 336Kcal/1406kJ; Protein 15.2g; Carbohydrate 30.9g, of which sugars 4g; Fat 17.7g, of which saturates 2.6g; Cholesterol 0mg; Calcium 89mg; Fibre 11.5g; Sodium 12mg.

Salad niçoise

This classic French salad combines fresh tuna, hard-boiled eggs, salad leaves, tomato, cucumber, radish and a garlic-flavoured dressing to create a taste sensation. Using fresh tuna makes it all the more appetizing, as well as providing healthy omega-3 fatty acids. The salad ingredients could include sliced red or yellow peppers, and/or thinly sliced fennel.

Serves 2

115g/4oz French (green) beans, trimmed
  and halved
115g/4oz mixed salad leaves
½ small cucumber, sliced
4 ripe tomatoes, quartered
1 tuna steak, weighing about 175g/6oz
olive oil, for brushing
50g/2oz can anchovies, drained, rinsed and
  halved lengthways (optional)
2 eggs, hard-boiled, shelled and quartered
4 small radishes, trimmed
50g/2oz/½ cup black olives, pitted
ground black pepper

For the dressing
45ml/3 tbsp extra virgin olive oil
2 garlic cloves, crushed
15ml/1 tbsp white wine vinegar

3 Preheat the grill (broiler). Brush the tuna lightly with olive oil and season with pepper. Grill (broil) for 3–4 minutes on each side until cooked through. Leave to cool, then flake.

4 Sprinkle the flaked tuna, anchovies, if using, quartered eggs, radishes and olives over the salad. Pour over the dressing and toss lightly to combine, then serve.

1 To make the dressing, whisk all the ingredients together in a bowl and season to taste.

2 Cook the beans in boiling water for 2–3 minutes, until just tender, then drain. In a large shallow bowl, combine the salad leaves, sliced cucumber, tomatoes and beans.

Variation
For a more substantial salad, or to serve more people, add thickly sliced, boiled new potatoes.

Energy 466Kcal/1941kJ; Protein 36.4g; Carbohydrate 8.2g, of which sugars 7.6g; Fat 32.4g, of which saturates 6.1g; Cholesterol 231mg; Calcium 188mg; Fibre 4.3g; Sodium 1674mg.

Warm chicken and tomato salad with hazelnut dressing

This simple, warm salad combines pan-fried chicken, fresh baby spinach leaves and cherry tomatoes with a light hazelnut and fresh herb dressing.

Serves 4

45ml/3 tbsp olive oil
15ml/1 tbsp hazelnut oil
15ml/1 tbsp white wine vinegar or cider vinegar
1 garlic clove, crushed
30ml/2 tbsp chopped fresh mixed herbs
225g/8oz baby spinach leaves
250g/9oz cherry tomatoes, halved
1 bunch of spring onions (scallions), chopped
400g/14oz skinless chicken breast fillets,
   cut into strips
ground black pepper

Variations
Turkey, textured vegetable protein or salmon fillet could all be used as alternatives to chicken.

1 First make the dressing: place 30ml/2 tbsp of the olive oil, the hazelnut oil, vinegar, garlic and chopped herbs in a small bowl or jug (pitcher) and whisk together until mixed. Set aside.

2 Trim any long stalks from the spinach leaves, then place in a large serving bowl with the tomatoes and spring onions, and toss together to mix.

3 Heat the remaining olive oil in a frying pan, and stir-fry the chicken over a high heat for 7–10 minutes, until it is cooked, tender and lightly browned.

4 Arrange the cooked chicken pieces over the salad. Give the dressing a quick whisk to blend, then drizzle it over the salad. Add pepper to taste, toss lightly and serve immediately.

Energy 235Kcal/984kJ; Protein 26.5g; Carbohydrate 3.6g, of which sugars 3.5g; Fat 12.9g, of which saturates 2g; Cholesterol 70mg; Calcium 115mg; Fibre 2.2g; Sodium 146mg.

Warm Oriental chicken and rice stir-fry salad

Succulent chicken pieces are combined with a vibrant selection of vegetables and brown rice in a light chilli dressing, making an exciting salad packed with fibre and nutrients.

Serves 4

50g/2oz mixed salad leaves
50g/2oz baby spinach leaves
50g/2oz watercress or rocket (arugula)
30ml/2 tbsp sweet chilli sauce
30ml/2 tbsp dry sherry
15ml/1 tbsp light soy sauce
15ml/1 tbsp tomato ketchup
10ml/2 tsp olive oil
8 shallots, finely chopped
1 garlic clove, crushed
350g/12oz skinless chicken breast fillets,
  cut into thin strips
1 red (bell) pepper, seeded and sliced
175g/6oz mangetouts (snowpeas), trimmed
400g/14oz can baby corn, drained and
  halved lengthways
275g/10oz brown rice, cooked
ground black pepper
fresh flat leaf parsley, to garnish

1 If any of the mixed salad leaves are large, tear them into smaller pieces and arrange them with the spinach leaves on a serving dish. Add the watercress or rocket, if using and toss together lightly to mix.

2 In a small bowl, mix together the chilli sauce, sherry, soy sauce and tomato ketchup. Set the sauce mixture aside.

3 Heat the olive oil in a large, non-stick frying pan or wok. Add the shallots and garlic and stir-fry over a medium heat for 1 minute.

4 Add the chicken to the pan and stir-fry for a further 3–4 minutes, until cooked through and tender.

5 Add the pepper, mangetouts, baby corn and cooked brown rice, and stir-fry for a further 2–3 minutes, until the vegetables are just tender.

6 Pour in the chilli sauce mixture and stir-fry for 2–3 minutes, until hot and bubbling. Season to taste.

7 Spoon the chicken mixture over the salad leaves, toss together to mix and serve immediately, garnished with a sprig of fresh parsley.

Energy 278Kcal/1173kJ; Protein 29.1g; Carbohydrate 32.8g, of which sugars 9.8g; Fat 4.2g, of which saturates 0.8g; Cholesterol 61mg; Calcium 104mg; Fibre 4.7g; Sodium 1699mg.

vegetable main dishes

Take advantage of the wide variety of cereal grains, dried beans, peas and lentils, and vegetables to make wholesome and satisfying meals, such as Harvest Vegetable and Lentil Casserole, Stir-fried Vegetables and Seeds or Brown Rice Risotto with Mushrooms. These are ideal for a detox diet as they are packed with nutrients, easily digested and filling to eat, and they are suitable for vegetarians. They also lend themselves to flavouring with fresh herbs and spices, which aid the digestion.

Spanish-style vegetables with thyme

This recipe includes courgettes, fennel, onion, peppers, butternut squash and tomatoes, but you can use any combination you like. Cooking the vegetables in this way brings out their flavour magnificently, and the addition of the fresh thyme and a sprinkling of cumin seeds further enhances their flavour and negates the need for added salt.

Serves 4

2–3 courgettes (zucchini)
1 large fennel bulb
1 Spanish (Bermuda) onion
2 large red (bell) peppers
450g/1lb butternut squash
6 whole garlic cloves, unpeeled
60ml/4 tbsp olive oil
juice of ½ lemon
pinch of cumin seeds, crushed
4 sprigs fresh thyme
4 medium tomatoes
ground black pepper

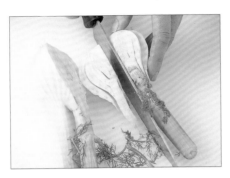

1 Preheat the oven to 220°C/425°F/ Gas 7. Cut all the vegetables into large bitesize pieces. Smash the garlic with the flat of a knife, but leave the skins on.

2 Choose a large roasting pan into which all the vegetables will fit in one layer. Put in all the vegetables except the tomatoes.

3 Mix together the oil and lemon juice. Pour over the vegetables and toss them. Sprinkle with the cumin seeds and pepper and tuck in the thyme sprigs. Roast for 20 minutes.

4 Gently turn the vegetables in the oil and add the tomatoes. Cook for a further 15 minutes, or until tender and slightly charred around the edges.

Variations
• This is a very easy, pretty dish to make and you can vary the choice of vegetables according to what is available and in season. Baby vegetables such as leeks and courgettes (zucchini) are excellent roasted. Judge the roasting time by their size. Wedges of red onion or whole shallots would also be good.
• Aubergines (eggplant) are frequently included in this mixture, and their flavour is delicious, but they turn a slightly unappetizing grey colour when cooked and served plain.
• Fresh rosemary sprigs could be used in place of the fresh thyme, if you like.

Energy 213Kcal/883kJ; Protein 5.7g; Carbohydrate 20.3g, of which sugars 17.5g; Fat 12.6g, of which saturates 2g; Cholesterol 0mg; Calcium 109mg; Fibre 7.3g; Sodium 24mg.

Roasted vegetables with salsa verde

There are endless variations of the Italian salsa verde, which means "green sauce". Usually a blend of fresh chopped herbs, garlic, olive oil, anchovies and capers, this is a simplified version. Here, it is served with a variety of roasted vegetables and rice. The herbs, mint and parsley, both help to aid the digestion and to prevent garlic breath.

Serves 4

3 courgettes (zucchini), sliced lengthways
1 large fennel bulb, cut into wedges
450g/1lb butternut squash, cut into
  2cm/¾in chunks
12 shallots
2 red (bell) peppers, seeded and cut
  lengthways into thick slices
4 plum tomatoes, halved and seeded
45ml/3 tbsp olive oil
2 garlic cloves, crushed
5ml/1 tsp balsamic vinegar
ground black pepper

For the salsa verde
45ml/3 tbsp chopped fresh mint
90ml/6 tbsp chopped fresh flat leaf parsley
15ml/1 tbsp Dijon mustard
juice of ½ lemon
30ml/2 tbsp olive oil

For the rice
15ml/1 tbsp vegetable or olive oil
75g/3oz/¾ cup vermicelli, broken into short
  lengths (optional)
225g/8oz/generous 1 cup long grain rice
900ml/1½ pints/3¾ cups vegetable stock

1 Preheat the oven to 220°C/425°F/ Gas 7. To make the salsa verde, place all the ingredients, with the exception of the olive oil, in a food processor or blender. Blend to a coarse paste, then add the oil, a little at a time, until the mixture forms a smooth purée. Season to taste.

2 To roast the vegetables, toss the courgettes, fennel, squash, shallots, peppers and tomatoes in the olive oil, garlic and balsamic vinegar. Leave to stand for 10 minutes to allow the flavours to mingle.

3 Place all the vegetables – apart from the squash and tomatoes – in a large roasting pan, brush with half the oil and vinegar mixture and season.

4 Roast for 20 minutes, then remove from the oven. Turn the vegetables over and brush with the rest of the oil and vinegar mixture. Add the squash and tomatoes and cook for a further 15–20 minutes until all the vegetables are tender and lightly blackened around the edges.

5 Meanwhile, prepare the rice. Heat the oil in a heavy pan. Add the vermicelli, if using, and fry for about 3 minutes, or until golden and crisp.

6 Rinse the rice under cold running water, then drain well and stir it into the vermicelli. Add the vegetable stock, then cover and cook for 12 minutes until the water is absorbed. Stir the rice, then cover and leave to stand for 10 minutes. Serve with the roasted vegetables and salsa verde.

Cook's tip
The salsa verde will keep for up to 1 week if it is stored in an airtight container in the refrigerator.

Energy 556Kcal/2314kJ; Protein 13.3g; Carbohydrate 83.5g, of which sugars 20.5g; Fat 18.9g, of which saturates 2.8g; Cholesterol 0mg; Calcium 173mg; Fibre 9.3g; Sodium 34mg.

Harvest vegetable and lentil casserole

Take advantage of a wide range of fresh root vegetables when they are in season in order to produce a delicious hearty dish that's full of natural goodness. Lentils are a nutritional superfood – high in protein, starchy carbohydrate and fibre, but very low in sodium and fat. Serve with brown rice, if liked, for a more substantial meal.

3 Cover the casserole and bake in the oven for about 50 minutes, until the vegetables and the lentils are cooked and tender. During the cooking time, remove the casserole from the oven and stir the vegetable mixture once or twice so that it is evenly cooked.

4 Remove the casserole from the oven. Blend the cornflour with 45ml/3 tbsp cold water in a bowl. Stir into the casserole and heat on the stove, stirring continuously, until the mixture comes to the boil and thickens. Simmer gently for 2 minutes.

5 Spoon the vegetable mixture into warm bowls and serve immediately, garnished with thyme sprigs.

Serves 6

15ml/1 tbsp vegetable oil
2 leeks, diagonally sliced
1 garlic clove, crushed
4 celery sticks, diagonally sliced
2 carrots, diagonally sliced
2 parsnips, diced
1 sweet potato, diced
225g/8oz swede (rutabaga), diced
175g/6oz whole brown or green lentils
450g/1lb tomatoes, skinned, seeded
   and chopped
15ml/1 tbsp chopped fresh thyme
15ml/1 tbsp chopped fresh marjoram
900ml/1½ pints/3¾ cups vegetable stock
15ml/1 tbsp cornflour (cornstarch)
ground black pepper
sprigs of fresh thyme, to garnish

1 Preheat the oven to 180°C/350°F/ Gas 4. Heat the oil in a flameproof casserole over a moderate heat. Add the leeks, garlic and celery and cook gently for 3 minutes.

2 Add the carrots, parsnips, sweet potato, swede, lentils, tomatoes, herbs, stock and pepper to taste. Stir well. Bring to the boil, stirring occasionally.

Cook's tip
Although lentils keep well, they toughen with time. Buy from shops with a fast turnover of stock and store them in airtight containers.

Energy 202Kcal/857kJ; Protein 9.4g; Carbohydrate 36.2g, of which sugars 10.3g; Fat 3.2g, of which saturates 0.5g; Cholesterol 0mg; Calcium 70mg; Fibre 6.3g; Sodium 60mg.

Turkish-style new potato casserole

This delicious casserole combines aubergines, courgettes, peppers, onion, peas, beans, tomatoes and potatoes for a really colourful and nutritious hot pot. Together, the many vegetables provide fantastic nutrient value, with plenty of fibre, vitamins, minerals and long-term energy. It is great served on its own or could be an accompaniment to grilled fish or chicken.

Serves 4

60ml/4 tbsp olive oil
1 large onion, chopped
2 small to medium aubergines (eggplants),
    cut into small cubes
4 courgettes (zucchini), cut into small chunks
1 green (bell) pepper, and 1 red or yellow
    (bell) pepper, seeded and chopped
115g/4oz/1 cup fresh or frozen peas
115g/4oz French (green) beans
450g/1lb new potatoes, cubed
2.5ml/½ tsp ground cinnamon
2.5ml/½ tsp paprika
4–5 tomatoes, skinned
400g/14oz can chopped tomatoes
15g/½oz/2 tbsp chopped fresh parsley
3–4 garlic cloves, crushed
350ml/12fl oz/1½ cups vegetable stock
ground black pepper
pitted black olives and fresh parsley,
    to garnish

3 Halve the fresh tomatoes and remove their seeds, using a teaspoon. Chop the flesh and place in a bowl.

4 Mix in the canned tomatoes with their juice, the parsley, crushed garlic and the remaining olive oil.

5 Pour the stock over the aubergine mixture, then spoon the prepared tomato mixture over the top. Cover with foil and bake in the oven for 30–45 minutes until the vegetables are tender. Serve garnished with olives and parsley.

1 Heat the oven to 190°C/375°F/ Gas 5. Heat 45ml/3 tbsp of the oil in a heavy pan, then add the onion and fry until golden. Add the cubed aubergines to the pan, sauté for 3 minutes, then add the courgettes, peppers, peas, beans and potatoes, together with the spices and freshly ground black pepper.

2 Continue to cook the vegetables over a high heat for about 3 minutes, stirring continuously. Transfer them to a large, shallow ovenproof dish.

Energy 307Kcal/1282kJ; Protein 9.4g; Carbohydrate 39.9g, of which sugars 17.8g; Fat 13.3g, of which saturates 2.1g; Cholesterol 0mg; Calcium 92mg; Fibre 8.7g; Sodium 30mg.

Tagliatelle with vegetable ribbons

Narrow strips of lightly cooked courgette and carrot mingle well with tagliatelle to resemble coloured pasta. You can use a non-wheat, gluten-free spaghetti or other pasta, or buckwheat noodles, during a strict detox. Garlic-flavoured olive oil is used in this dish – flavoured oils such as rosemary, chilli or basil are a quick way of adding flavour to pasta.

Serves 4

2 large courgettes (zucchini)
2 large carrots
250g/9oz fresh egg tagliatelle or
   non-wheat pasta
60ml/4 tbsp garlic-flavoured olive oil
ground black pepper

Cook's tip
If you can't find or don't have a garlic- or herb-flavoured oil, you can use plain olive oil and simply add crushed garlic, chopped fresh herbs or chilli to it.

1 Using a vegetable peeler, peel the courgettes and carrots into long thin ribbons. Bring a large pan of water to the boil, then add the courgette and carrot ribbons. Bring the water back to the boil and cook the ribbons for 30 seconds, then drain and set aside.

2 Cook the tagliatelle according to the instructions on the packet. Drain and return it to the pan. Add the vegetable ribbons, garlic flavoured oil and pepper and toss over a medium to high heat until the pasta and vegetables are flavoured through. Serve immediately.

Energy 348Kcal/1464kJ; Protein 9.6g; Carbohydrate 52.1g, of which sugars 7.5g; Fat 12.7g, of which saturates 1.9g; Cholesterol 0mg; Calcium 53mg; Fibre 3.9g; Sodium 16mg.

Penne with green vegetable sauce

Lightly cooked fresh green vegetables are tossed with pasta quills to create this low-fat Italian-style dish, ideal for a light lunch or supper. A wide range of non-wheat, gluten-free pastas, made from buckwheat, corn or rice, are readily available in many health food stores and large supermarkets as alternatives to wheat pasta. Choose any shape or variety you like.

Serves 4

2 carrots
1 courgette (zucchini)
75g/3oz French (green) beans
1 leek, washed
2 ripe Italian plum tomatoes
handful of fresh flat leaf parsley
15ml/1 tbsp extra virgin olive oil
2.5ml/½ tsp sugar
115g/4oz/1 cup frozen peas
350g/12oz/3 cups dried penne
ground black pepper

1 Dice the carrots and the courgette finely. Top and tail the French beans, then cut them into 2cm/¾in lengths. Slice the leek thinly. Skin and dice the tomatoes. Finely chop the parsley.

2 Heat the oil in a medium frying pan. Add the carrots and leek. Sprinkle the sugar over and cook, stirring frequently, for about 5 minutes.

3 Stir in the courgette, French beans and peas and season with black pepper.

4 Cover the frying pan and gently cook the vegetables over a low to medium heat for 5–8 minutes, stirring from time to time, until the vegetables are just tender.

5 Meanwhile, cook the pasta in a large pan of rapidly boiling water for 10–12 minutes or according to the packet instructions, until it is tender but not soggy.

6 Drain the pasta well, return to the pan and cover to keep warm.

7 Stir in the chopped parsley and the diced chopped plum tomatoes and adjust the seasoning to taste. Toss with the pasta and serve immediately.

Energy 401Kcal/1698kJ; Protein 15.5g; Carbohydrate 76.7g, of which sugars 11.3g; Fat 5.7g, of which saturates 0.9g; Cholesterol 0mg; Calcium 99mg; Fibre 8.1g; Sodium 26mg.

Rice noodles with vegetable chilli sauce

Rice noodles are very fine, string-like noodles, sometimes called rice vermicelli. They are made from rice flour, so they are wheat- and gluten-free. They are also very quick to prepare and just require a short soaking in boiling water. Here they are served with a colourful vegetable sauce, flavoured with fresh chilli and coriander to give the dish an aromatic, hot and spicy flavour kick.

3 Meanwhile, place the noodles in a bowl and cover with boiling water. Stir with a fork and leave to stand for 3–4 minutes or according to the packet instructions. Rinse and drain.

4 Stir the chopped fresh coriander into the sauce. Spoon the noodles in to warmed serving bowls, top with the sauce, then garnish with coriander sprigs and serve immediately.

Serves 4

15ml/1 tbsp vegetable oil
1 onion, chopped
2 garlic cloves, crushed
1 fresh red chilli, seeded and finely chopped
1 red (bell) pepper, seeded and diced
2 carrots, finely chopped
175g/6oz baby corn, halved
225g/8oz can sliced bamboo shoots, rinsed and drained
400g/14oz can red kidney beans, rinsed and drained
300ml/½ pint/1¼ cups passata (bottled strained tomatoes)
15ml/1 tbsp soy sauce
5ml/1 tsp ground coriander
250g/9oz rice noodles
30ml/2 tbsp chopped fresh coriander (cilantro)
ground black pepper
fresh coriander, to garnish

1 Heat the oil in a deep frying pan, add the onion, garlic, chilli and red pepper and cook gently for 5 minutes, stirring. Add the carrots, baby corn, bamboo shoots, kidney beans, passata, soy sauce and ground coriander and stir everything together to combine.

2 Bring to the boil, then reduce the heat, cover and simmer for 30 minutes, stirring occasionally, until the vegetables are tender. Season with pepper.

Energy 221Kcal/932kJ; Protein 11.7g; Carbohydrate 35.9g, of which sugars 14.6g; Fat 4.2g, of which saturates 0.6g; Cholesterol 0mg; Calcium 113mg; Fibre 10.1g; Sodium 1345mg.

Stir-fried vegetables and seeds

The contrast between the crunchy seeds and vegetables and the rich, savoury sauce is what makes this dish so delicious. Seeds are nutritional powerhouses, packed with vitamins and minerals, as well as beneficial oils and protein. Oyster mushrooms are included for their delicate texture and in keeping with the Oriental style of this dish. Serve it solo, or with rice or noodles.

Serves 4

30ml/2 tbsp vegetable oil
30ml/2 tbsp sesame seeds
30ml/2 tbsp sunflower seeds
30ml/2 tbsp pumpkin seeds
2 garlic cloves, finely chopped
2.5cm/1in piece fresh root ginger, peeled
   and finely chopped
2 large carrots, cut into matchsticks
2 large courgettes (zucchini), cut
   into matchsticks
90g/3½oz/1½ cups oyster mushrooms,
   torn into pieces
150g/5oz watercress or baby spinach leaves,
   coarsely chopped
small bunch fresh mint or coriander (cilantro),
   leaves and stems chopped
60ml/4 tbsp black bean sauce
30ml/2 tbsp light soy sauce
15ml/1 tbsp light muscovado (brown) sugar
30ml/2 tbsp rice vinegar

1 Heat the oil in a wok or large frying pan. Add the seeds. Toss over a medium heat for 1 minute, then add the garlic and ginger and continue to stir-fry for a further minute. Do not let the garlic burn or it will taste bitter.

2 Add the carrot and courgette matchsticks and the sliced mushrooms to the wok and stir-fry for a further 5 minutes, or until all the vegetables are crisp-tender and golden at the edges.

3 Add the watercress or spinach with the fresh herbs. Toss over the heat for 1 minute, then stir in the black bean sauce, soy sauce, sugar and vinegar. Stir-fry for 1–2 minutes, until combined and hot. Serve immediately.

Cook's tip
Oyster mushrooms are delicate so should be torn rather than cut.

Energy 245Kcal/1015kJ; Protein 7.7g; Carbohydrate 14.2g, of which sugars 11g; Fat 17.7g, of which saturates 2.1g; Cholesterol 0mg; Calcium 163mg; Fibre 4.2g; Sodium 1671mg.

Stir-fried vegetables with cashew nuts

Stir-frying is the perfect way to make a speedy meal that retains the nutrient value of the vegetables. This is also a very flexible dish as you can use any combination of vegetables, according to what's available and your own personal preference. Simply add the firmer vegetables that require longer cooking to the pan first, then finish with leafy or tender varieties.

Serves 4

900g/2lb mixed vegetables (see Cook's Tip)
30ml/2 tbsp vegetable oil
2 garlic cloves, crushed
15ml/1 tbsp grated fresh root ginger
50g/2oz/½ cup unsalted cashew nuts
soy sauce, to taste
ground black pepper

Variation
Substitute a squeeze of lemon juice for the soy sauce, if you prefer.

1 Prepare the vegetables according to which type you are using. Carrots, celery and cucumber should be cut into very fine matchsticks to ensure that they cook quickly.

2 Heat a wok or frying pan, then trickle the oil around the rim so that it runs down to coat the surface. When the oil is hot, add the garlic and ginger and cook for 1–2 minutes, stirring. Add the harder vegetables and toss over the heat for 5 minutes, until they soften.

3 Add the softer vegetables and stir-fry over a high heat for 3–4 minutes.

4 Stir in the cashew nuts and stir-fry for 1–2 minutes until golden. Sprinkle with soy sauce and black pepper to taste. Serve immediately.

Cook's tip
Use a pack of stir-fry vegetables or make up your own mixture. Choose from carrots, baby corn, mangetouts (snowpeas), peppers, beansprouts, mushrooms, and spring onions (scallions). Drained, canned bamboo shoots and water chestnuts are delicious additions.

Energy 205Kcal/849kJ; Protein 3.9g; Carbohydrate 20.1g, of which sugars 17.4g; Fat 12.5g, of which saturates 2.1g; Cholesterol 0mg; Calcium 61mg; Fibre 5.8g; Sodium 93mg.

Spring vegetable stir-fry

Fast, fresh and packed with healthy vegetables, this stir-fry makes an ideal supper dish. Serve it with rice during a wheat-free detox or noodles during a less strict regime. Stir-fries are best flavoured with garlic and ginger, both of which have a distinctive flavour and are great detox spices, helping to stimulate and aid the digestive system.

Serves 4

15ml/1 tbsp vegetable oil
5ml/1 tsp toasted sesame oil
1 garlic clove, chopped
2.5cm/1in piece fresh root ginger,
    finely chopped
225g/8oz baby carrots
350g/12oz broccoli florets
175g/6oz asparagus tips
2 spring onions (scallions), diagonally sliced
175g/6oz/1½ cups spring greens, (collards)
    finely shredded
30ml/2 tbsp soy sauce
15ml/1 tbsp fresh apple juice
15ml/1 tbsp sesame seeds, toasted
rice or noodles, to serve

1 Heat a large frying pan or wok over a high heat. Add the vegetable oil and the sesame oil, and reduce the heat. Add the garlic and sauté gently for 2 minutes.

2 Add the ginger, baby carrots, broccoli and asparagus tips to the pan and stir-fry for about 4 minutes. Add the spring onions and spring greens to the pan and stir-fry for a further 2 minutes.

3 Add the soy sauce and apple juice and cook for 1–2 minutes until the vegetables are tender, adding a little water if they appear dry.

4 Spoon the vegetables into four warmed bowls and sprinkle with toasted sesame seeds. Serve immediately with rice or noodles.

Cook's tip
Look out for reduced-salt soy sauce. Soy sauce is quite high in sodium, so there is no need to add extra salt for seasoning.

Energy 134Kcal/554kJ; Protein 7.8g; Carbohydrate 9.4g, of which sugars 8.6g; Fat 7.4g, of which saturates 1.1g; Cholesterol 0mg; Calcium 195mg; Fibre 6.2g; Sodium 566mg.

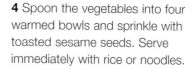

Stir-fried rice and vegetables

The ginger and garlic combine with the array of fresh vegetables to give this flavoursome stir-fry a wonderful aroma, with the added benefit that they boost the dish's therapeutic properties. It's less usual to use brown rice for an Oriental-style dish, but this variety increases the fibre content of the meal significantly and so is worth including.

3 Slice the mushrooms, discarding the stems. Heat the vegetable oil in a wok and stir-fry the carrots for 4–5 minutes until they just start to become tender.

4 Add the mushrooms and baby courgettes and stir-fry for about 3 minutes. Add the broccoli and spring onions and stir-fry for a further 3 minutes, by which time all the vegetables should be tender but still retain a slight "bite".

5 Add the cooked rice to the wok, and toss briefly with the vegetables over the heat to combine well and heat through thoroughly.

6 Sprinkle over the soy sauce and the toasted sesame oil and toss again lightly. Spoon into individual bowls and serve immediately.

Health benefits

• Ginger has long been recognized as an excellent detoxifier. It can provide relief for gastro-intestinal disorders, aid indigestion and help to boost the immune system.
• The starch in brown rice is absorbed slowly by the body, helping to keep blood sugar levels on an even keel, which is very important during a detox. Brown rice is also good for treating digestive disorders, soothing and cleansing the intestinal tract, calming the nervous system and preventing kidney stones.
• All vegetables are highly nutritious and a healthy diet should include at least five portions a day. Broccoli, in particular, is a very good source of vitamins C and E, and betacarotene, and provides folate.

Serves 2

115g/4oz/generous ½ cup brown basmati rice, rinsed and drained
350ml/12fl oz/1½ cups vegetable stock
2.5cm/1in piece of fresh root ginger, finely sliced
1 garlic clove, halved
5cm/2in piece of pared lemon rind
115g/4oz/1½ cups shiitake mushrooms
30ml/2 tbsp vegetable oil
175g/6oz baby carrots, trimmed
225g/8oz baby courgettes (zucchini), halved
175–225g/6–8oz broccoli, broken into florets
6 spring onions (scallions), diagonally sliced
15ml/1 tbsp soy sauce
10ml/2 tsp toasted sesame oil

1 Put the brown rice in a pan and pour in the vegetable stock. Add the root ginger, garlic and lemon rind. Slowly bring to the boil, then cover the pan with a lid and cook very gently for 20–25 minutes until the rice is tender.

2 Drain and remove the ginger, garlic and lemon rind from the rice. Return the rice to the pan and cover with a lid to keep warm. Set aside.

Energy 430Kcal/1788kJ; Protein 12.5g; Carbohydrate 58.2g, of which sugars 11.2g; Fat 16.2g, of which saturates 2.2g; Cholesterol 0mg; Calcium 127mg; Fibre 6.5g; Sodium 569mg.

Thai vegetable curry

Fragrant jasmine rice, subtly flavoured with lemon grass and cardamom, is the perfect accompaniment to this spiced vegetable curry, which combines new potatoes, baby corn, broccoli, red pepper and spinach in a scented coconut milk broth. Don't be put off by the long list of ingredients – this curry is very simple to make.

Serves 4

10ml/2 tsp vegetable oil
400ml/14fl oz/1⅔ cups reduced-fat
    coconut milk
300ml/½ pint/1¼ cups vegetable stock
225g/8oz new potatoes, halved or quartered,
    if large
130g/4½oz baby corn
5ml/1 tsp caster (superfine) sugar
200g/7oz broccoli florets
1 red (bell) pepper, seeded and
    sliced lengthways
115g/4oz spinach, tough stalks removed
    and shredded
30ml/2 tbsp chopped fresh coriander (cilantro)
ground black pepper

For the spice paste
1 fresh red chilli, seeded and chopped
3 fresh green chillies, seeded and chopped
1 lemon grass stalk, outer leaves removed
    and lower 5cm/2in finely chopped
2 shallots, chopped
finely grated rind of 1 lime
2 garlic cloves, chopped
5ml/1 tsp ground coriander
2.5ml/½ tsp ground cumin
1cm/½in fresh galangal or root ginger,
    finely chopped
30ml/2 tbsp chopped fresh coriander (cilantro)

For the rice
225g/8oz/generous 1 cup jasmine rice, rinsed
1 lemon grass stalk, outer leaves removed
    and cut into 3 pieces
6 cardamom pods, bruised

1 Make the spice paste. Place all the ingredients in a food processor or blender and blend to a coarse paste.

2 Heat the oil in a large, heavy pan and fry the spice paste for 1–2 minutes, stirring constantly. Add the coconut milk and stock to the pan, and bring to the boil.

3 Reduce the heat, add the potatoes and simmer for 15 minutes. Add the baby corn, then cook for 2 minutes. Stir in the sugar, broccoli and red pepper, and cook for 2 minutes more until the vegetables are tender. Stir in the shredded spinach and half the fresh coriander. Cook for 2 minutes.

4 Meanwhile, prepare the rice. Put the rinsed rice into a large pan and add the prepared lemon grass and cardamom pods. Pour over 475ml/ 16fl oz/2 cups cold water.

5 Bring to the boil, then reduce the heat, cover, and cook for 10–15 minutes until the water is absorbed and the rice is tender and slightly sticky. Season to taste with pepper, leave to stand for 10 minutes, then fluff up the rice with a fork.

6 Remove the lemon grass and cardomom pods and serve the rice with the curry, sprinkled with the remaining chopped fresh coriander.

Energy 327Kcal/1374kJ; Protein 9.9g; Carbohydrate 64.8g, of which sugars 11.1g; Fat 3.3g, of which saturates 0.6g; Cholesterol 0mg; Calcium 134mg; Fibre 3.9g; Sodium 534mg.

Indian rice with tomatoes and spinach

This tasty rice dish is good solo or can be served as part of an Indian meal with other curries and side dishes. It's based on brown basmati rice, flavoured with onion, garlic and spices, cooked with tomatoes and carrots. Baby spinach is added at the end of the cooking time, then it is attractively served with toasted cashew nuts sprinkled over the top.

Serves 4

30ml/2 tbsp vegetable oil
1 onion, chopped
2 garlic cloves, crushed
3 tomatoes, peeled, seeded and chopped
225g/8oz/generous 1 cup brown basmati rice, rinsed and drained
5ml/1 tsp ground coriander
5ml/1 tsp ground cumin
2 carrots, coarsely grated
900ml/1½ pints/3¾ cups vegetable stock
275g/10oz baby spinach leaves, washed
50g/2oz/½ cup unsalted cashew nuts, toasted
ground black pepper

1 Heat the vegetable oil in a large flameproof casserole and gently fry the chopped onion and garlic for 4–5 minutes until softened. Add the chopped tomatoes and cook for a further 3–4 minutes, stirring until slightly thickened.

2 Add the drained rice to the casserole and cook gently for 1–2 minutes, stirring, until the rice is coated with the tomato and onion mixture.

3 Stir in the coriander and cumin, then add the grated carrots and season with pepper. Pour in the stock and stir well to mix.

4 Bring to the boil, then cover tightly and simmer over a very gentle heat for 20–25 minutes until the rice is tender.

5 Lay the spinach on the surface of the rice, cover again and cook for 2–3 minutes until the spinach has wilted. Fold the spinach into the rest of the rice and check the seasoning. Sprinkle with cashew nuts and serve.

Cook's tip
If you are using large fresh spinach leaves, remove any tough stalks and chop the leaves roughly.

Energy 381Kcal/1586kJ; Protein 9.7g; Carbohydrate 55.8g, of which sugars 8.6g; Fat 13.1g, of which saturates 2.1g; Cholesterol 0mg; Calcium 154mg; Fibre 4g; Sodium 152mg.

Brown rice risotto with mushrooms

This twist on the classic risotto includes health-giving herbs and brown long grain rice. Both fresh and dried porcini mushrooms are included for a really powerful mushroom flavour. This risotto makes a satisfying and hearty main dish that could be accompanied with a leafy green side salad for extra vitamin nourishment, if you like.

Serves 4

15g/½oz/2 tbsp dried porcini mushrooms
15ml/1 tbsp olive oil
4 shallots, finely chopped
2 garlic cloves, crushed
250g/9oz/1⅓ cups brown long grain rice
900ml/1½ pints/3¾ cups vegetable stock
450g/1lb/6 cups mixed mushrooms, wiped
   clean and quartered
45ml/3 tbsp chopped fresh flat
   leaf parsley
ground black pepper

1 Place the dried porcini mushrooms in a bowl and cover with 150ml/¼ pint/⅔ cup hot water. Leave to soak for at least 20 minutes, until the mushrooms are rehydrated.

2 Heat the olive oil in a large pan, add the shallots and garlic and cook gently for 5 minutes, stirring. Drain the porcini, reserving their soaking liquid, and chop roughly. Add the brown rice to the shallot mixture and stir to coat the grains in the oil.

3 Stir the vegetable stock and the porcini soaking liquid into the rice mixture in the pan. Bring to the boil, lower the heat and simmer, uncovered, for about 20 minutes or until most of the liquid has been absorbed, stirring frequently to prevent it from sticking.

Health benefits

Brown rice is a good source of most B vitamins, essential for the release of energy from food. It also contains a good range of minerals and provides fibre, which helps to speed the passage of waste through the body and helps to protect against bowel cancer.

4 Add all the mushrooms, stir well to combine, and cook the risotto for a further 10–15 minutes more until the liquid has been absorbed.

5 Season to taste with freshly ground black pepper. Stir in the chopped fresh parsley, toss through to combine and serve immediately.

Energy 269Kcal/1125kJ; Protein 6.8g; Carbohydrate 51.5g, of which sugars 1.1g; Fat 3.7g, of which saturates 0.5g; Cholesterol 0mg; Calcium 23mg; Fibre 1.5g; Sodium 6mg.

Barley risotto with roasted squash and leeks

This is more like a pilaff made with slightly chewy, nutty-flavoured pearl barley than a classic risotto. Sweet leeks and roasted butternut squash are superb with this earthy grain.

Serves 4

200g/7oz/1 cup pearl barley
1 butternut squash, peeled, seeded and
    cut into chunks
10ml/2 tsp chopped fresh thyme
60ml/4 tbsp olive oil
4 leeks, cut into fairly thick
    diagonal slices
2 garlic cloves, finely chopped
175g/6oz/2½ cups brown cap (cremini)
    mushrooms, sliced
2 carrots, coarsely grated
about 120ml/4fl oz/½ cup vegetable stock
30ml/2 tbsp chopped fresh flat
    leaf parsley
45ml/3 tbsp pumpkin seeds, toasted,
    or chopped walnuts
ground black pepper

1 Rinse the barley, then cook it in simmering water, keeping the pan part-covered, for 35–45 minutes, or until tender. Drain. Preheat the oven to 200°C/400°F/Gas 6.

2 Put the squash in a roasting pan with half the thyme. Season with pepper and toss with half the oil. Roast for 30 minutes, stirring once, until the squash is tender.

3 Heat the remaining olive oil in a large frying pan. Cook the leeks and garlic gently for 5 minutes. Add the mushrooms and remaining thyme, then cook until the liquid from the mushrooms evaporates and they begin to fry.

4 Stir in the carrots and cook for about 2 minutes, then add the barley and most of the vegetable stock. Season well and part-cover the pan. Cook for a further 5 minutes. Pour in the remaining stock if the mixture seems dry.

5 Stir in the roasted squash and the parsley. Add seasoning to taste and serve immediately, sprinkled with the toasted pumpkin seeds or walnuts.

Variations
• Make the risotto with brown rice instead of the pearl barley, if you prefer. Cook the rice according to the packet instructions and continue from Step 2.
• Any type of mushrooms can be used in this recipe – try sliced field (portabello) mushrooms for a hearty, earthy flavour.
• For those not following a strict detox and avoiding dairy products, a little grated parmesan cheese can be stirred through the risotto or sprinkled over before serving.

Energy 398Kcal/1670kJ; Protein 9.1g; Carbohydrate 52.8g, of which sugars 7.7g; Fat 18.1g, of which saturates 2.4g; Cholesterol 0mg; Calcium 121mg; Fibre 5g; Sodium 21mg.

Vegetable couscous with olives and almonds

Couscous is a light, fluffy grain that's low in fat and high in good starchy carbohydrate. It doesn't require cooking, just soaking – making this an easy lunch or supper dish.

Serves 4

275g/10oz/1⅔ cups couscous
525ml/18fl oz/2¼ cups boiling
   vegetable stock
16–20 black olives
2 small courgettes (zucchini)
25g/1oz/¼ cup flaked (sliced)
   almonds, toasted
60ml/4 tbsp olive oil
15ml/1 tbsp lemon juice
15ml/1 tbsp chopped fresh coriander (cilantro)
15ml/1 tbsp chopped fresh parsley
good pinch of ground cumin
good pinch of paprika

3 Add the courgette strips, black olives and toasted almonds to the bowl of couscous and gently mix together to combine thoroughly.

4 Blend together the olive oil, lemon juice, herbs and spices. Pour the dressing over the couscous. Gently stir to combine, and serve.

1 Place the couscous in a heatproof bowl and pour over the boiling vegetable stock. Stir with a fork to combine, then set aside for 10 minutes. When the stock has been absorbed, fluff the grains with a fork.

2 Meanwhile, halve the olives and discard the stones (pits). Top and tail the courgettes and cut into matchsticks.

Variations
• Add extra flavour to this salad by stirring in 10ml/2 tsp grated fresh root ginger.
• Couscous is made from semolina and is therefore a wheat product. For a wheat-free alternative, substitute brown rice or quinoa.

Energy 319Kcal/1326kJ; Protein 6.6g; Carbohydrate 36.9g, of which sugars 1.4g; Fat 16.9g, of which saturates 2.1g; Cholesterol 0mg; Calcium 73mg; Fibre 1.9g; Sodium 287mg.

Tagine of yam, carrots and prunes

This comforting stew has a Moroccan influence. The yam (or sweet potatoes), carrots and prunes give it a delicious sweet flavour, enhanced with honey and warm cinnamon and ginger spices. Chopped fresh herbs add to the tempting combination. Serve it with rice or couscous and a mixed, leafy green salad that includes some bitter leaves.

Serves 4

45ml/3 tbsp olive oil
25–30 baby (pearl) onions, blanched
    and peeled
900g/2lb yam or sweet potatoes, peeled
    and cut into bitesize chunks
2–3 carrots, cut into bitesize chunks
150g/5oz/generous ½ cup ready-to-eat
    pitted prunes
5ml/1 tsp ground cinnamon
2.5ml/½ tsp ground ginger
10ml/2 tsp clear honey
450ml/¾ pint/scant 2 cups vegetable stock
small bunch of fresh coriander (cilantro),
    finely chopped
small bunch of fresh mint,
    finely chopped
ground black pepper

1 Preheat the oven to 200°C/400°F/ Gas 6. Heat the olive oil in a flameproof casserole and stir in the onions. Cook for about 5 minutes until the onions are tender, then remove half of the onions from the pan and set aside.

2 Add the yam or sweet potatoes and carrots to the pan and cook until lightly browned. Stir in the prunes with the cinnamon, ginger and honey, then pour in the stock. Season well, cover the casserole and transfer to the oven for about 45 minutes.

3 Stir in the reserved onions and bake for a further 10 minutes. Gently stir in the chopped coriander and mint, and serve the tagine immediately.

Energy 431Kcal/1825kJ; Protein 5.6g; Carbohydrate 86.4g, of which sugars 23g; Fat 9.5g, of which saturates 1.5g; Cholesterol 0mg; Calcium 97mg; Fibre 7.6g; Sodium 27mg.

Butter bean, tomato and olive stew

This hearty vegetarian stew is based on creamy butter beans. They offer plenty of dietary fibre, essential for a healthy digestive system. Little cherry tomatoes provide plenty of vitamin C and lycopene, both valuable antioxidants, and onions, garlic and ginger all contribute beneficial compounds. Serve on its own or with rice and a side salad.

Serves 4

115g/4oz/⅔ cup butter (lima) beans,
   soaked overnight
30–45ml/2–3 tbsp olive oil
1 onion, chopped
2–3 garlic cloves, crushed
25g/1oz fresh root ginger, peeled and
   finely chopped
pinch of saffron threads
16 cherry tomatoes
pinch of sugar
handful of fleshy black olives, pitted
5ml/1 tsp ground cinnamon
5ml/1 tsp paprika
small bunch of fresh flat leaf parsley
ground black pepper

1 Rinse the beans and place them in a large pan with plenty of water. Bring to the boil and boil for about 10 minutes, and then reduce the heat and simmer gently for 1–1½ hours until tender. Drain the beans and refresh under cold running water, then drain again.

2 Heat the olive oil in a heavy pan. Add the onion, garlic and ginger, and cook for about 10 minutes until softened but not browned. Stir in the saffron threads, followed by the cherry tomatoes and a sprinkling of sugar.

3 As the tomatoes begin to soften, stir in the butter beans. When the tomatoes have heated through, stir in the olives, ground cinnamon and paprika. Season to taste and sprinkle over the chopped parsley. Serve immediately.

Cook's tip

If you are in a hurry, you could use two 400g/14oz cans of butter (lima) beans for this tagine. Make sure you rinse them well before adding, as canned beans are salty if packed in brine.

Energy 138Kcal/578kJ; Protein 5.5g; Carbohydrate 12.8g, of which sugars 3.5g; Fat 7.6g, of which saturates 1.1g; Cholesterol 0mg; Calcium 51mg; Fibre 5.2g; Sodium 605mg.

Mixed bean and aubergine tagine with mint yogurt

In this satisfying Moroccan dish, a mixture of red kidney and black-eyed beans with aubergine provide both texture and flavour, and are enhanced by the herbs and chillies.

Serves 4

115g/4oz/generous ½ cup dried red kidney
    beans, soaked overnight in cold water
    and drained
115g/4oz/generous ½ cup dried black-eyed
    beans (peas) or cannellini beans, soaked
    overnight in cold water and drained
600ml/1 pint/2½ cups water
2 bay leaves
2 celery sticks, each cut into 4 matchsticks
60ml/4 tbsp olive oil
1 aubergine (eggplant), about 350g/12oz,
    cut into chunks
1 onion, thinly sliced
3 garlic cloves, crushed
1–2 fresh red chillies, seeded and chopped
30ml/2 tbsp tomato purée (paste)
5ml/1 tsp paprika
2 large tomatoes, roughly chopped
300ml/½ pint/1¼ cups vegetable stock
15ml/1 tbsp each chopped fresh mint, parsley
    and coriander (cilantro)
ground black pepper
fresh herb sprigs, to garnish

For the mint yogurt

150ml/¼ pint/⅔ cup low-fat probiotic yogurt
30ml/2 tbsp chopped fresh mint
2 spring onions (scallions), chopped

1 Place the soaked and drained kidney beans in a large pan of unsalted boiling water. Bring back to the boil and cook for 10 minutes, then drain.

2 Place the soaked and drained black-eyed or cannellini beans in a separate large pan of boiling unsalted water and boil rapidly for 10 minutes, then drain.

3 Place the 600ml/1 pint/2½ cups of water in a large tagine or casserole, and add the bay leaves, celery and beans. Cover and place in an unheated oven. Set the oven to 190°C/375°F/Gas 5. Cook for 1–1½ hours or until the beans are tender, then drain.

4 Heat 45ml/3 tbsp of the oil in a large frying pan or cast-iron tagine base. Add the aubergine chunks and cook, stirring for 4–5 minutes until evenly browned. Remove and set aside, on a plate.

5 Add the remaining oil to the tagine base or frying pan, then add the sliced onion and cook, stirring, for about 4–5 minutes, until softened.

6 Add the crushed garlic and seeded, chopped red chillies and cook for a further 5 minutes, stirring frequently, until the onion is lightly golden.

7 Reset the oven temperature to 160°C/325°F/Gas 3. Add the tomato purée and paprika to the onion mixture and cook for 1–2 minutes.

8 Add the chopped tomatoes, the pan-fried chunks of aubergine, all the cooked beans and the vegetable stock to the pan, then season to taste with freshly ground black pepper.

9 Cover the tagine base with the lid or, if using a frying pan, transfer the contents to a clay tagine or casserole. Place in the oven and leave to cook for 1 hour.

10 Meanwhile, mix together the yogurt, mint and spring onions in a small serving bowl. Cover and keep chilled.

11 Just before serving, add the fresh mint, parsley and coriander to the tagine and lightly mix through the vegetables. Garnish with fresh herb sprigs and serve with the mint yogurt.

Energy 209Kcal/890kJ; Protein 16.6g; Carbohydrate 33.9g, of which sugars 9.4g; Fat 1.9g, of which saturates 0.5g; Cholesterol 1mg; Calcium 173mg; Fibre 12.3g; Sodium 62mg.

Aromatic chickpea and spinach curry

High in fibre, this hearty, warming curry tastes great and boosts vitality with essential vitamins. Despite its name, the chickpea is not really a pea, but a seed. It is richer in vitamin E than most dried beans, peas and lentils, and like them it is an important source of vegetable protein. Serve it with rice or couscous, if liked, mango chutney and a cooling mint raita.

2 Add the tomatoes and pepper and stir to coat with the spice mixture. Pour in the stock and stir in the tomato purée. Bring to the boil, lower the heat, cover and simmer for 15 minutes.

3 Remove any coarse stalks from the spinach, then rinse the leaves thoroughly, drain them and tear into large pieces. Add them to the pan, in batches, adding a handful more as each batch cooks down and wilts.

4 Stir in the chickpeas, cover and cook gently for 5 minutes more. Add the fresh chopped coriander, season to taste and stir well. Spoon into a warmed serving bowl and sprinkle with the garam masala, if using. Serve immediately.

Serves 4

15ml/1 tbsp vegetable oil
1 large onion, finely chopped
2 garlic cloves, crushed
2.5cm/1in fresh root ginger, finely chopped
1 green chilli, seeded and finely chopped
30ml/2 tbsp medium curry paste
10ml/2 tsp ground cumin
5ml/1 tsp ground turmeric
225g/8oz can chopped tomatoes
1 green or red (bell) pepper, seeded and chopped
300ml/½ pint/1¼ cups vegetable stock
15ml/1 tbsp tomato purée (paste)
450g/1lb fresh spinach
400g/14oz can chickpeas, drained
45ml/3 tbsp chopped fresh coriander (cilantro)
5ml/1 tsp garam masala (optional)

1 Heat the vegetable oil in a large, heavy pan and cook the chopped onion, crushed garlic, root ginger and chilli over a gentle heat for about 5 minutes, or until the onion has softened, but not browned. Stir in the curry paste, mix thoroughly and cook for 1 minute, then stir in the ground cumin and turmeric. Stir over a low heat for 1 minute more.

Energy 221Kcal/925kJ; Protein 12.3g; Carbohydrate 28.7g, of which sugars 11.1g; Fat 7.1g, of which saturates 0.8g; Cholesterol 0mg; Calcium 262mg; Fibre 8.8g; Sodium 396mg.

Tomato and lentil dhal with almonds

Spices have long been recognized for their medicinal qualities, from relieving flatulence to warding off colds and flu. Dhal, made with lentils, is one of the staples of Indian cooking. It can be served either as an accompaniment or as a filling and tasty main dish. Lentils are bland in flavour and are therefore a good carrier of spicy flavours.

Serves 4

30ml/2 tbsp vegetable oil
1 large onion, finely chopped
3 garlic cloves, chopped
1 carrot, diced
10ml/2 tsp cumin seeds
10ml/2 tsp mustard seeds
2.5cm/1in fresh root ginger, grated
10ml/2 tsp ground turmeric
5ml/1 tsp mild chilli powder
5ml/1 tsp garam masala
225g/8oz/1 cup split red lentils
800ml/1½ pints/3¼ cups vegetable stock
  or water
5 tomatoes, peeled, seeded and chopped
juice of 2 limes
60ml/4 tbsp chopped fresh
  coriander (cilantro)
ground black pepper
25g/1oz/¼ cup flaked (sliced) almonds,
  toasted, to serve

1 Heat the oil in a heavy pan. Sauté the onion for 5 minutes until softened, stirring occasionally. Add the garlic, carrot, cumin and mustard seeds, and ginger. Cook for 5 minutes, stirring, until the seeds pop and the carrot softens slightly.

2 Stir in the ground turmeric, chilli powder and garam masala, and cook the mixture on a low heat for 1 minute or until the flavours begin to mingle, stirring continuously to prevent the spices from burning.

3 Add the lentils, stock or water and chopped tomatoes, and season well with freshly ground black pepper. Bring to the boil, then reduce the heat and simmer, covered, for about 45 minutes, stirring occasionally.

4 Stir in the lime juice and 45ml/3 tbsp of the coriander. Cook for a further 15 minutes until the lentils are tender. Sprinkle with the remaining coriander and the flaked almonds.

Health benefits

• Limes are rich in vitamin C, which can aid the absorption of iron.
• Lentils are a useful source of low-fat protein, providing sustained, long-term energy. They contain significant amounts of B vitamins and are rich in zinc and iron.

Energy 326Kcal/1372kJ; Protein 16.9g; Carbohydrate 43.8g, of which sugars 11.5g; Fat 10.5g, of which saturates 1.2g; Cholesterol 0mg; Calcium 102mg; Fibre 6.6g; Sodium 44mg.

Braised beans and lentils

You can use any combination of beans to make this simple yet nourishing dish. Just remember that if you are using dried beans, they need to be soaked overnight to ensure that they will cook evenly and relatively quickly. The lentils do not need soaking. For a variation, pearl barley or brown rice could be used in place of the lentils.

Serves 4

150g/5oz/¾ cup mixed dried beans
75g/3oz/⅔ cup brown or green lentils
45ml/3 tbsp olive oil
1 large onion, finely chopped
2 garlic cloves, crushed
5 or 6 fresh sage leaves, chopped
juice of 1 lemon
3 spring onions (scallions),
  thinly sliced
60ml/4 tbsp chopped fresh dill
ground black pepper

1 Put the beans in a large bowl and cover with cold water. Leave to soak at room temperature for at least 6 hours, or preferably overnight.

2 Drain and rinse the beans, put in a large pan. Cover with cold water, bring to the boil, and cook for 1 hour. Add the lentils and cook for a further 30 minutes, until the beans and lentils are tender. Drain, reserving the cooking liquid. Return the beans and lentils to the pan.

3 Heat the oil in a frying pan and fry the onion until light golden. Add the garlic and sage, cook for 30 seconds, add the mixture to the beans, then stir in the reserved liquid and simmer for 15 minutes. Stir in the lemon juice and season to taste. Serve topped with a sprinkling of spring onions and dill.

Energy 286Kcal/1204kJ; Protein 14.8g; Carbohydrate 38.2g, of which sugars 6.1g; Fat 9.3g, of which saturates 1.3g; Cholesterol 0mg; Calcium 75mg; Fibre 4.6g; Sodium 27mg.

Giant beans baked with tomatoes

Gigantes are a type of white bean originating in Greece. They resemble butter beans but are larger, rounder and much sweeter in flavour. They make a delicious, filling dish when combined with Mediterranean flavours, such as tomatoes, onion, garlic, parsley, thyme and oregano. Serve with a green vegetable side dish or leafy salad for a warming main meal.

Serves 4

400g/14oz/1¾ cups fasolia gigantes
   or similar large dried white beans
45ml/3 tbsp olive oil
2 or 3 onions, total weight about
   300g/11oz, chopped
1 celery stick, thinly sliced
2 carrots, peeled and cubed
3 garlic cloves, thinly sliced
5ml/1 tsp each dried oregano and thyme
400g/14oz can chopped tomatoes
30ml/2 tbsp tomato purée (paste) diluted
   in 300ml/½ pint/1¼ cups hot water
2.5ml/½ tsp sugar
45ml/3 tbsp finely chopped flat
   leaf parsley
ground black pepper

1 Place the beans in a large bowl, cover with plenty of cold water, then leave to soak overnight. The next day, drain the beans, then rinse them under cold water and drain again.

2 Tip the beans into a large pan, pour in plenty of cold water to cover, then bring to the boil. Cover the pan and cook the beans until they are almost tender. Gigantes are not like other beans – they cook quickly, so keep testing them after they have been cooking for 30–40 minutes. They should not be allowed to disintegrate through overcooking.

Cook's tip
Never add salt to dried beans, peas or lentils before they are cooked, as it will make their skins leathery and tough. Season to taste after cooking and only add salt if it is needed. Always taste beans during cooking to ensure that you don't overcook them.

3 When the beans are cooked, tip them into a colander or sieve (strainer) to drain, discarding the cooking liquid, and set them aside. Preheat the oven to 180°C/350°F/Gas 4.

4 Heat the olive oil in the clean pan, add the chopped onions and sauté until light golden. Add the celery, carrots, garlic and dried herbs and stir with a wooden spatula until the garlic becomes aromatic.

5 Stir in the tomatoes, cover and cook for 10 minutes. Pour in the diluted tomato purée, then return the beans to the pan. Stir in the sugar and half the parsley, and season with pepper.

6 Transfer the bean mixture into a large baking dish and bake for 30 minutes, checking the beans once or twice and adding more hot water if they look dry. They should just be moist. Stir in the remaining parsley and serve.

Energy 437Kcal/1844kJ; Protein 25.3g; Carbohydrate 64.7g, of which sugars 19.4g; Fat 10.4g, of which saturates 1.5g; Cholesterol 0mg; Calcium 163mg; Fibre 20.3g; Sodium 67mg.

tofu, egg, fish, shellfish and chicken dishes

This selection of main course dishes adds variety to your diet, especially if you plan to follow a detox regime for two weeks. There are simple ideas for midweek meals, like Salmon Steaks with Mango Salsa, or Spring Vegetable Omelette, as well as delicious "healthy eating" suggestions for casual entertaining, such as Spicy Paella, or Moroccan Fish Tagine. Some ingredients are optional and you can serve your own choice of accompaniments to suit your diet.

Spiced tofu stir-fry

The colours in this aromatic stir-fry are as pleasing to the eye as the flavours are to the palate. Tofu is made from soya beans, the most nutritious of all beans. It is rich in high-quality protein and contains all of the eight essential amino acids that cannot be synthesized in the body. Serve this delicately spiced stir-fry with noodles or rice, if you like.

Serves 4

10ml/2 tsp ground cumin
15ml/1 tbsp paprika
5ml/1 tsp ground ginger
good pinch of cayenne pepper
15ml/1 tbsp caster sugar
275g/10oz firm tofu, rinsed and drained
60ml/4 tbsp vegetable oil
2 garlic cloves, crushed
1 bunch spring onions (scallions), sliced
1 red (bell) pepper, seeded and sliced
1 yellow (bell) pepper, seeded and sliced
225g/8oz/generous 3 cups brown cap
   (cremini) mushrooms, halved or quartered
   if necessary
1 large courgette (zucchini), sliced
115g/4oz French (green) beans, halved
50g/2oz/scant ½ cup pine nuts
15ml/1 tbsp lime juice
15ml/1 tbsp clear honey
ground black pepper

1 In a large bowl, mix together the cumin, paprika, ginger, cayenne and sugar with pepper to season. Cut the tofu into cubes and coat them in the spice mixture.

2 Heat some of the oil in a wok or large frying pan. Cook the tofu over a high heat for 3–4 minutes, turning occasionally (take care not to break up the tofu too much). Remove with a slotted spoon. Wipe out the pan with kitchen paper.

Cook's tip
Choose firm plain tofu for a stir-fry, rather than silken or any other variety of tofu. Firm tofu is sold in blocks and can be easily cubed or sliced before adding to the pan.

3 Add the remaining oil to the pan and cook the garlic and spring onions for 3 minutes. Add the remaining vegetables and cook over a medium heat for 6 minutes, or until beginning to soften and turn golden. Season well.

4 Return the tofu to the pan with the pine nuts, lime juice and honey. Heat through and serve immediately.

Energy 294Kcal/1218kJ; Protein 10.3g; Carbohydrate 11.4g, of which sugars 10.4g; Fat 23.4g, of which saturates 2.4g; Cholesterol 0mg; Calcium 383mg; Fibre 3.3g; Sodium 11mg.

Sweet and sour vegetables with tofu

Crisp, colourful and nutritious, this is a hearty stir-fry that will satisfy even the hungriest appetite. Stir-fries make an easy and convenient meal, as you can prepare the ingredients ahead of time and then they take such a short time to cook. This makes an ideal dish if you are entertaining friends while you are following a detox diet.

Serves 4

4 shallots
3 garlic cloves
30ml/2 tbsp vegetable oil
250g/9oz Chinese leaves (Chinese
  cabbage), shredded
8 baby corn, sliced on the diagonal
2 red (bell) peppers, seeded and thinly sliced
200g/7oz/1¾ cups mangetouts (snow peas),
  trimmed and sliced
250g/9oz firm tofu, rinsed, drained and
  cut in 1cm/½in cubes
60ml/4 tbsp vegetable stock
30ml/2 tbsp light soy sauce
15ml/1 tbsp granulated sugar
30ml/2 tbsp rice vinegar
2.5ml/½ tsp dried chilli flakes
small bunch coriander (cilantro), chopped

1 Slice the shallots thinly using a sharp knife. Finely chop the garlic.

2 Heat the oil in a wok or large frying pan and cook the shallots and garlic for 2–3 minutes over a medium heat, until golden. Do not let the garlic burn or it will taste bitter.

3 Add the shredded cabbage, toss over the heat for 30 seconds, then add the corn and repeat the process.

4 Add the red peppers, mangetouts and tofu in the same way, each time adding a single ingredient and tossing it over the heat for about 30 seconds before adding the next ingredient.

5 Pour in the stock and soy sauce. Mix together the sugar and vinegar in a small bowl, stirring until the sugar has dissolved, then add to the wok or pan. Sprinkle over the chilli flakes and coriander, toss to mix well and serve.

Energy 157Kcal/655kJ; Protein 8.9g; Carbohydrate 11.9g, of which sugars 10.6g; Fat 8.5g, of which saturates 1g; Cholesterol 0mg; Calcium 381mg; Fibre 3.1g; Sodium 828mg.

Tofu and pepper kebabs

A simple coating of ground peanuts pressed on to cubed tofu provides plenty of protein and additional flavour along with the colourful red and green peppers. Use metal or bamboo skewers for the kebabs – if you use bamboo, then soak them in cold water for 30 minutes before using to prevent them from scorching during cooking. Serve with rice and a side salad.

2 If you are making the kebabs in advance, cover them with clear film (plastic wrap) and store them in the fridge until they are needed.

3 Preheat the grill (broiler) to moderate. Halve and seed the peppers, and cut them into large, even chunks. Thread the chunks of pepper on to four large skewers, alternating with the coated tofu cubes, and place on a foil-lined grill rack.

4 Grill (broil) the kebabs, turning frequently, for 10–12 minutes, or until the peppers and peanuts are beginning to brown. (The kebabs can also be cooked on a barbecue, if you prefer.) Transfer the kebabs to plates and serve with the sweet chilli dipping sauce.

Serves 4

250g/9oz firm tofu, rinsed and drained
50g/2oz/½ cup unsalted peanuts
2 red and 2 green (bell) peppers
60ml/4 tbsp sweet chilli dipping sauce

Variation

For an alternative version if you don't like peanuts, toss the tofu cubes in sesame seeds to coat, before threading them on to the skewers with the large chunks of red and green pepper.

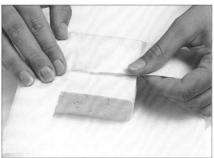

1 Pat the tofu dry on kitchen paper and then cut it into bitesize cubes. Put the peanuts in a blender or food processor and process until coarsely ground, then transfer to a plate. Turn the tofu in the ground nuts to coat.

Energy 187Kcal/778kJ; Protein 10.2g; Carbohydrate 16.8g, of which sugars 15.1g; Fat 9.1g, of which saturates 1.6g; Cholesterol 0mg; Calcium 342mg; Fibre 3.7g; Sodium 214mg.

Provençal stuffed peppers

Peppers make a perfect container for a tasty vegetable filling, including onions, courgettes, mushrooms and tomatoes, flavoured with fresh basil. This dish is bursting with valuable vitamins and the addition of pine nuts supplies useful protein. The vegetable sauce could be used to stuff other vegetables, such as large courgettes or baby aubergines.

Serves 4

15ml/1 tbsp olive oil
1 red onion, sliced
1 courgette (zucchini), diced
115g/4oz mushrooms, sliced
1 garlic clove, crushed
400g/14oz can chopped tomatoes
15ml/1 tbsp tomato purée (paste)
40g/1½oz/scant ⅓ cup pine nuts
30ml/2 tbsp chopped fresh basil
2 red and 2 yellow (bell) peppers
ground black pepper
fresh basil leaves, to garnish

1 Preheat the oven to 180°C/350°F/ Gas 4. Heat the olive oil in a large pan, add the onion, courgette, mushrooms and garlic and cook gently over a medium heat for 3 minutes, stirring from time to time.

2 Stir in the chopped tomatoes and the tomato purée. Bring to the boil, then reduce the heat and simmer, uncovered, for 10–15 minutes, stirring, until thickened slightly.

3 Remove from the heat and stir in the pine nuts, basil and seasoning.

4 Cut the peppers in half lengthways and seed them. Blanch in a pan of boiling water for 3 minutes. Drain.

5 Place the peppers in a shallow, ovenproof dish and fill each one with the vegetable mixture. Cover the dish with foil and bake for 20 minutes.

6 Remove the foil and bake for a further 5–10 minutes until bubbling. Garnish with basil leaves and serve immediately.

Variation

If not following a strict detox, sprinkle the peppers with a little grated hard cheese for the final 5–10 minutes of the cooking time.

Energy 185Kcal/769kJ; Protein 5.5g; Carbohydrate 16.9g, of which sugars 15.9g; Fat 11g, of which saturates 1.2g; Cholesterol 0mg; Calcium 40mg; Fibre 5g; Sodium 19mg.

Spring vegetable omelette

An omelette makes a quick and easy, nourishing meal. Omelettes are very versatile and can be filled with all kinds of ingredients, but this one, packed with seasonal spring vegetables, is particularly healthy. It includes tender asparagus tips, spring greens, onion, baby new potatoes and tomatoes, and is flavoured with fresh mixed herbs.

Serves 4

50g/2oz asparagus tips
50g/2oz spring greens (collards), shredded
15ml/1 tbsp vegetable oil
1 onion, sliced
175g/6oz cooked baby new potatoes,
    halved or diced
2 tomatoes, chopped
6 eggs
30ml/2 tbsp chopped fresh
    mixed herbs
ground black pepper
cherry tomatoes and leafy salad,
    to serve

1 Steam the asparagus tips and spring greens over a pan of boiling water for 5–10 minutes until tender. Drain the vegetables and keep warm.

2 Heat the vegetable oil in a large frying pan, add the onion and cook gently for 5–10 minutes until softened, stirring.

3 Add the cooked baby potatoes and cook for 3 minutes, stirring. Stir in the chopped tomatoes, asparagus and spring greens.

4 Lightly beat the eggs in a small bowl with the herbs, and season with ground black pepper.

5 Pour the beaten eggs over the vegetables, then cook over a gentle heat until the bottom of the omelette is golden brown.

6 Preheat the grill to hot and cook the omelette under the grill for 2–3 minutes until the top is golden brown. Serve with cherry tomatoes and a salad.

Energy 187Kcal/780kJ; Protein 11.4g; Carbohydrate 10.4g, of which sugars 3.5g; Fat 11.6g, of which saturates 2.8g; Cholesterol 285mg; Calcium 82mg; Fibre 1.8g; Sodium 118mg.

Egg and lentil curry

Eggs are an excellent addition to vegetarian curries and, combined with lentils, make a substantial and extremely tasty vegetarian curry. Serve with fluffy basmati rice and mango chutney. Follow this main dish with a vitamin C-rich fruit, such as sliced mango or orange, to ensure maximum absorption of iron from the eggs.

Serves four

75g/3oz/½ cup green lentils
750ml/1¼ pints/3 cups stock
6 eggs
30ml/2 tbsp vegetable oil
3 cloves
1.5ml/¼ tsp black peppercorns
1 onion, finely chopped
2 fresh green chillies, finely chopped
2 garlic cloves, crushed
2.5cm/1in piece of fresh root ginger,
    peeled and chopped
30ml/2 tbsp curry paste
400g/14oz can chopped tomatoes
2.5ml/½ tsp sugar
2.5ml/½ tsp garam masala

1 Wash the lentils thoroughly under cold running water, checking for small stones. Put the lentils in a large, heavy pan with the vegetable stock. Cover and simmer gently for about 15 minutes, or until the lentils are soft. Drain and set aside.

2 Put the eggs in a pan and cover with tepid water. Slowly bring the water to the boil, then reduce the heat and simmer for 7–8 minutes.

3 Remove the eggs from the pan of boiling water with a slotted spoon and place them in a bowl of cold water to cool. When they are cool enough to handle, peel the eggs and cut them in half lengthways.

4 Heat the oil in a large frying pan and fry the cloves and peppercorns for about 2 minutes. Add the onion, chillies, garlic and ginger and fry the mixture for a further 5–6 minutes, stirring frequently.

5 Stir in the curry paste and fry for a further 2 minutes, stirring constantly. Add the chopped tomatoes and sugar and stir in 175ml/6fl oz/¾ cup water. Simmer for about 5 minutes until the sauce thickens, stirring occasionally. Add the boiled eggs, drained lentils and garam masala. Cover and simmer gently for 5 minutes, then serve.

Cook's tip
You can substitute red lentils for the green if liked. Red lentils tend to disintegrate more when cooked.

Energy 238Kcal/997kJ; Protein 14.6g; Carbohydrate 14.2g, of which sugars 4.1g; Fat 14.4g, of which saturates 3.1g; Cholesterol 285mg; Calcium 60mg; Fibre 1.9g; Sodium 121mg.

Roasted cod with fresh tomato sauce

Really fresh cod fillets have a sweet, delicate flavour and pure white flaky flesh. Served with an aromatic fresh tomato sauce on a bed of steamed French beans, they make a delicious and nutritious meal that's quick to prepare. Accompany this simple yet delicious dish with some boiled baby new potatoes for a more substantial meal, if liked.

3 Press the tomato mixture through a fine sieve (strainer), discarding the solids that remain in the sieve. Pour into a small pan and heat gently.

4 Scale the cod fillet and cut on the diagonal into 4 pieces. Season well.

5 Heat the remaining oil in a heavy frying pan and fry the cod, skin side down, until the skin is crisp. Place the fish on a greased baking sheet, skin side up, and roast in the oven for 8–10 minutes, until cooked through. Serve on top of the steamed French beans with the fresh tomato sauce.

Variation
Try haddock, hake, monkfish or any other firm white fish fillet instead of the cod, if you like.

Serves 4

60ml/4 tbsp olive oil
350g/12oz ripe tomatoes
pinch of sugar
2 strips of pared orange rind
1 fresh thyme sprig
6 fresh basil leaves
900g/2lb fresh cod fillet, skin on
ground black pepper
steamed French (green) beans, to serve

1 Preheat the oven to 230°C/450°F/ Gas 8. Using a small, sharp knife, roughly chop the tomatoes, leaving their skins on, and set aside.

2 Heat 15ml/1 tbsp of the olive oil in a heavy pan, add the tomatoes, sugar, orange rind, thyme and basil, and simmer for 5 minutes, until the tomatoes are soft and juicy. Remove the pan from the heat.

Energy 294Kcal/1229kJ; Protein 41.8g; Carbohydrate 2.7g, of which sugars 2.7g; Fat 12.8g, of which saturates 1.9g; Cholesterol 104mg; Calcium 27mg; Fibre 0.9g; Sodium 143mg.

Seared tuna steaks with tomato salsa

Fresh and fruity tomato salsa provides a delicious boost of vitamins to accompany the health-promoting omega-3 fatty acids that can be found in abundance in fresh tuna fish. Take care not to cook the tuna for too long, as the flesh can become dry if it is overcooked. It should remain pinky-red in the centre and be moist and succulent in texture.

Serves 4

4 tuna steaks, each weighing about
   175–200g/6–7oz
30ml/2 tbsp olive oil
5ml/1 tsp cumin seeds, toasted
grated rind and juice of 1 lime
pinch of dried red chilli flakes
1 small red onion, finely chopped
200g/7oz cherry tomatoes, chopped
1 avocado, peeled, stoned (pitted)
   and chopped
2 kiwi fruit, peeled and chopped
1 fresh red chilli, seeded and chopped
15g/½oz fresh coriander (cilantro), chopped
6 fresh mint sprigs, leaves only, chopped
5–10ml/1–2 tsp Thai fish sauce (*nam pla*)
ground black pepper
lime wedges and fresh coriander (cilantro)
   sprigs, to garnish

3 Heat a ridged, cast-iron griddle pan until it is very hot. Carefully lay the tuna steaks in the pan and cook for 2 minutes on each side for rare tuna or a little longer for a medium result.

4 Transfer the tuna steaks to four warmed serving plates and garnish with lime wedges and fresh coriander sprigs. Spoon on the tomato salsa, or transfer it to a serving bowl and offer it separately.

Cook's tip
Do not move the tuna around in the pan while it is cooking. The steak needs to stay in one position to be seared with neat and attractive chargrill lines.

1 Place the tuna steaks on a glass or ceramic plate and drizzle over the olive oil. Sprinkle the steaks with half the toasted cumin seeds, ground black pepper, half the lime rind and the dried chilli flakes. Set aside and leave to stand for about 30 minutes.

2 Meanwhile, make the salsa. Combine the onion, tomatoes, avocado, kiwi fruit, chilli, coriander and mint in a bowl. Add the remaining cumin seeds and lime rind and half the lime juice. Stir in Thai fish sauce to taste. Cover with clear film (plastic wrap) and set aside for about 20 minutes.

Energy 397Kcal/1662kJ; Protein 48.9g; Carbohydrate 5.6g, of which sugars 5.1g; Fat 20g, of which saturates 4.3g; Cholesterol 56mg; Calcium 71mg; Fibre 2.6g; Sodium 105mg.

Barbecued sardines with orange

Sardines are another healthy oil-rich fish and they taste delicious in combination with juicy oranges and fresh parsley. They are ideal for cooking on a barbecue – the meaty flesh holds together, the skin crisps nicely and there are no lingering indoor cooking smells. However, they cook just as well under a grill indoors. Serve them with a selection of salads.

Serves 6

6 whole large sardines, gutted
1 orange, sliced
small bunch of fresh flat leaf
  parsley, chopped
60ml/4 tbsp olive oil
ground black pepper

1 Arrange the sardines and orange slices in a single layer in a large, shallow, non-metallic dish.

2 Sprinkle over half of the chopped fresh parsley and season with ground black pepper.

3 Drizzle the oil over the sardines and orange slices and brush to coat well.

4 Cover the dish with clear film (plastic wrap) and keep chilled in the refrigerator until ready to cook.

5 Meanwhile, prepare the barbecue. Remove the sardines and orange slices from the marinade and cook the fish for 7–8 minutes on each side, until cooked through. Sprinkle with the remaining parsley and serve immediately.

Energy 175Kcal/729kJ; Protein 13.3g; Carbohydrate 1.9g, of which sugars 1.9g; Fat 12.7g, of which saturates 2.6g; Cholesterol 0mg; Calcium 89mg; Fibre 0.8g; Sodium 75mg.

Grilled mackerel with spicy dhal

Mackerel is a well-flavoured, highly nutritious oily fish and it tastes good simply grilled. It is often served with a sharp, fruity sauce, but for a more satisfying dish, these delicious tamarind-flavoured lentils or split peas make an appealing accompaniment. Serve with a tomato and onion salad. If not following a strict detox, flat bread would also be a good accompaniment.

Serves 4

250g/9oz/generous 1 cup red lentils, or yellow split peas rinsed

1 litre/1¾ pints/4 cups water

30ml/2 tbsp vegetable oil

2.5ml/½ tsp each mustard seeds, cumin seeds, fennel seeds and fenugreek or cardamom seeds

5ml/1 tsp ground turmeric

3–4 dried red chillies, crumbled

30ml/2 tbsp tamarind paste

30ml/2 tbsp chopped fresh coriander (cilantro)

4 mackerel

ground black pepper

fresh red chilli slices and finely chopped coriander, to garnish

1 Put the lentils or split peas in a pan. Pour in the water and bring to the boil. Lower the heat, partially cover the pan and simmer the lentils or split peas for 30–40 minutes, stirring occasionally, until they are tender and mushy.

2 Heat the oil in a wok or shallow pan. Add the mustard seeds, then cover and cook for a few seconds until they pop. Remove the lid, add the rest of the seeds, with the turmeric and chillies and fry for a few more seconds.

3 Stir in the lentils or split peas and the tamarind paste and mix well. Bring to the boil, then simmer for 10 minutes until thick. Stir in the coriander.

4 Clean the fish then heat a ridged griddle or the grill (broiler) until very hot. Make six diagonal slashes on either side of each fish and remove the head. Season, then grill for 5–7 minutes on each side. Serve, garnished with sliced red chilli and chopped coriander, accompanied by the dhal.

Energy 578Kcal/2420kJ; Protein 43.5g; Carbohydrate 35.2g, of which sugars 1.5g; Fat 30.2g, of which saturates 5.7g; Cholesterol 80mg; Calcium 49mg; Fibre 3.1g; Sodium 110mg.

Salmon with leeks and peppers

Attractive paper parcels of fish are as healthy as they are tasty. The fillets of fish and the array of fresh vegetables cook in their own juices, so that everything stays moist and succulent, the flavours are locked in and all the valuable nutrients are retained. Serve this delicious dish with plain boiled or steamed rice or floury baked potatoes.

4 Divide the cool vegetable mixture equally among the rounds of parchment or foil and top with a portion of salmon.

5 Drizzle each portion of fish with a little sesame oil and sprinkle with the remaining chives and the chopped fennel fronds. Season with a little more ground black pepper.

6 Fold the baking parchment or foil over to enclose the fish, rolling and twisting the edges together to seal the parcels.

7 Place the parcels on a baking sheet and bake for 15–20 minutes, or until the parcels are puffed up and, if made with parchment, lightly browned. Carefully transfer the parcels to six warmed plates and serve immediately, still wrapped in their baking parchment or foil envelopes.

Serves 6

25ml/1½ tbsp vegetable oil
2 yellow (bell) peppers, seeded and
    thinly sliced
4cm/1½in fresh root ginger, peeled and
    finely shredded
1 large fennel bulb, thinly sliced, fronds
    chopped and reserved
1 fresh green chilli, seeded and
    finely shredded
2 large leeks, cut into 10cm/4in lengths and
    shredded lengthways
30ml/2 tbsp chopped fresh chives
10ml/2 tsp light soy sauce
6 portions salmon fillet, each weighing about
    150–175g/5–6oz, skinned
10ml/2 tsp toasted sesame oil
ground black pepper

1 Heat the vegetable oil in a large non-stick frying pan. Add the yellow peppers, ginger, and fennel bulb and cook, stirring occasionally, for 5–6 minutes, until the vegetables are softened, but not browned.

2 Add the fresh green chilli and leeks to the pan and cook, stirring occasionally, for about 3 minutes. Stir in half the chopped chives and the soy sauce and season to taste with a little salt and freshly ground black pepper. Set the vegetable mixture aside to cool slightly.

3 Meanwhile, preheat the oven to 190°C/375°F/Gas 5. Cut out six 35cm/14in rounds of baking parchment or foil and set aside.

Energy 243Kcal/1014kJ; Protein 22.2g; Carbohydrate 6.5g, of which sugars 5.9g; Fat 14.4g, of which saturates 2.3g; Cholesterol 50mg; Calcium 51mg; Fibre 3.2g; Sodium 410mg.

Salmon steaks with mango salsa

Oil-rich fish contain omega-3 fatty acids that promote good health, and they should be eaten regularly – at least once a week. In this recipe, salmon steaks are chargrilled and served with a fresh fruit salsa, combining diced mango and cucumber with spring onions and coriander. Serve with boiled rice, if liked, for a more substantial meal.

Serves 4

1 ripe mango
115g/4oz cucumber
2 spring onions (scallions)
30ml/2 tbsp chopped fresh coriander
4 salmon steaks, each about 175g/6oz
juice of 1 lemon or lime
ground black pepper
fresh coriander (cilantro) sprigs and lemon
 wedges, to garnish

1 Make the mango salsa. Peel and stone (pit) the mango, chop the flesh and place in a bowl. Peel, seed and finely chop the cucumber; chop the spring onions. Add to the mango with the coriander and pepper to season. Mix, cover and leave for 30 minutes.

2 While the salsa is standing to allow the flavours to mingle, preheat a ridged grill pan or grill (broiler).

3 Place the salmon steaks on the grill pan, drizzle over the lemon or lime juice and cook for about 6 minutes on each side until the steaks are tender and just beginning to flake.

4 Transfer the salmon to serving plates, spoon some mango salsa alongside each steak and serve immediately, garnished with coriander sprigs and lemon wedges.

Energy 341Kcal/1421kJ; Protein 35.9g; Carbohydrate 5.9g, of which sugars 5.7g; Fat 19.4g, of which saturates 3.4g; Cholesterol 88mg; Calcium 49mg; Fibre 1.2g; Sodium 81mg.

Teriyaki salmon

Teriyaki is a popular cooking style in Japan, and is frequently used to flavour fish, poultry and meat. Teriyaki marinade is usually made with soy sauce, rice wine and sugar and although it is easy to make, you can also buy it in bottles from supermarkets and Asian stores. It is a great way of perking up the flavour of salmon fillets for a light and healthy meal.

Serves 4

4 salmon fillets, about 150g/5oz each
75ml/5 tbsp teriyaki marinade
5cm/2in piece of fresh root ginger, peeled and cut into matchsticks
150ml/¼ pint/⅔ cup sunflower oil

1 Put the salmon fillets in a shallow, non-metallic dish and pour over the teriyaki marinade. Turn the fish in the marinade a few times to coat thoroughly. Cover with clear film (plastic wrap), then keep chilled in the refrigerator for 2 hours.

2 Meanwhile, heat the sunflower oil in a small pan and add the ginger. Fry for 1–2 minutes, or until golden and crisp. Remove with a slotted spoon and drain on kitchen paper.

3 Heat a griddle pan until smoking hot. Remove the salmon from the marinade and add, skin side down, to the pan. Cook for 2–3 minutes, then turn over and cook for a further 1–2 minutes, or until cooked through. Remove from the pan and divide among four serving plates. Top the salmon fillets with the crispy fried ginger.

4 Pour the teriyaki marinade into the pan and cook for 1–2 minutes, to heat through and reduce slightly. Pour the marinade over the salmon and serve immediately.

Energy 290Kcal/1208kJ; Protein 30.4g; Carbohydrate 2.2g, of which sugars 2.1g; Fat 17.8g, of which saturates 3g; Cholesterol 75mg; Calcium 33mg; Fibre 0.1g; Sodium 190mg.

Chinese-style steamed trout

Trout is another oily fish that is rich in essential fatty acids, which are vital for good health. Serve this simple Oriental dish with plain boiled rice and a vegetable dish, such as stir-fried spring greens, for a satisfying meal. This would be a great meal for entertaining as it looks impressive, as well as tasting delicious and being super-healthy.

Serves 6

2 trout, each weighing about
    675–800g/1½–1¾lb
25ml/1½ tbsp salted black beans, rinsed
pinch of sugar
30ml/2 tbsp finely shredded fresh
    root ginger
4 garlic cloves, thinly sliced
30ml/2 tbsp Chinese rice wine or dry sherry
30ml/2 tbsp light soy sauce
4–6 spring onions (scallions), finely shredded
    or sliced diagonally
15ml/1 tbsp sesame oil

1 Wash the trout inside and out under cold running water, then pat the fish dry on a sheet of kitchen paper. Using a sharp knife, carefully slash 3–4 deep crosses on each side of each fish.

2 Place half the black beans and the sugar in a small bowl and mash together with the back of a fork. Stir in the remaining whole beans.

3 Place a little ginger and garlic inside the cavity of each fish, then lay them on a plate or dish that will fit inside a large steamer. Rub the bean mixture into the fish, working it into the slashes, then sprinkle the remaining ginger and garlic over the top. Cover with clear film (plastic wrap) and place the fish in the refrigerator for at least 30 minutes.

4 Remove the fish from the refrigerator and place the steamer over a pan of boiling water. Sprinkle the rice wine or sherry and half the soy sauce over the fish and place the plate of fish inside the steamer. Steam for 15–20 minutes, or until the fish is just cooked and the flesh flakes easily when tested with the tip of a knife.

5 Using a fish slice (metal spatula), carefully lift the cooked fish on to a warmed serving dish. Sprinkle the fish with the remaining soy sauce and then sprinkle with the shredded or sliced spring onions.

6 Lightly sprinkle the sesame oil over the cooked fish and spring onions, then serve immediately.

Cook's tip

Black beans and soy sauce are both high in salt, so use reduced-salt soy sauce if available and rinse the black beans under cold running water to remove the excess salt. Salted black beans can often be bought from Chinese restaurants if there is not an Asian grocery store near to where you live.

Energy 235Kcal/990kJ; Protein 36.6g; Carbohydrate 1g, of which sugars 0.9g; Fat 8.9g, of which saturates 1.9g; Cholesterol 149mg; Calcium 61mg; Fibre 0.1g; Sodium 789mg.

Moroccan fish tagine

Firm-fleshed fish, such as monkfish, makes a good low-fat choice for this North African-style dish. It is cooked with onions, aubergines, courgettes and tomatoes with a spicy harissa paste to make a healthy dish that's a bit special. Serve in traditional style with couscous, or for a wheat-free accompaniment, serve with rice, pearl barley or quinoa.

4 Heat the remaining oil in a separate pan. Add the aubergine cubes and fry for 10 minutes. Add the cubed courgettes and fry the vegetables for a further 2 minutes, stirring occasionally.

5 Tip the aubergine mixture into the pan and combine with the onions, then stir in the chopped tomatoes, the passata and fish stock. Bring to the boil, then lower the heat and simmer the mixture for about 20 minutes.

6 Stir the fish cubes and preserved lemon into the pan. Add the olives and stir gently. Cover and simmer over a low heat for about 15–20 minutes until the fish is just cooked through. Season to taste. Stir in the chopped coriander. Garnish with coriander sprigs.

Cook's tip
To boost the fibre value, you could add 225g/8oz/1¼ cups cooked chickpeas to the tagine.

Serves 6–8

1.3kg/3lb firm fish fillets such as
   monkfish or hoki, skinned and cut into
   5cm/2in cubes
60ml/4 tbsp olive oil
4 onions, chopped
1 large aubergine (eggplant), cut into
   1cm/½in cubes
2 courgettes (zucchini), cut into
   1cm/½in cubes
400g/14oz can chopped tomatoes
400ml/14fl oz/1⅔ cups passata (bottled
   strained tomatoes)
200ml/7fl oz/scant 1 cup fish stock
1 preserved lemon, chopped
90g/3½oz/scant 1 cup olives
60ml/4 tbsp chopped fresh coriander (cilantro)
ground black pepper
coriander sprigs, to garnish

For the harissa
3 large fresh red chillies, seeded and chopped
3 garlic cloves, peeled
15ml/1 tbsp ground coriander
30ml/2 tbsp ground cumin
5ml/1 tsp ground cinnamon
grated rind of 1 lemon
30ml/2 tbsp vegetable oil

1 To make the harissa, whizz everything in a food processor to a smooth paste.

2 Put the fish in a wide bowl and add 30ml/2 tbsp of the harissa. Toss to coat, cover and chill for at least 1 hour.

3 Heat half the oil in a shallow pan. Add the onions and cook for 10 minutes. Stir in the remaining harissa; cook for 5 minutes, stirring occasionally.

Energy 230Kcal/968kJ; Protein 28.5g; Carbohydrate 11.7g, of which sugars 9.6g; Fat 8.1g, of which saturates 1.3g; Cholesterol 23mg; Calcium 65mg; Fibre 3.7g; Sodium 406mg.

Spicy paella

Recipes vary from region to region for this famous Spanish rice dish, but this version uses lean chicken breast fillets, white fish and shellfish with plenty of vegetables for a healthy combination. Note that the fish and chicken are marinated, so you need to start preparing this dish a couple of hours before cooking. It's ideal for casual entertaining.

Serves 6

2 large boneless chicken breast fillets
about 150g/5oz prepared squid
8–10 raw king prawns (jumbo shrimp)
325g/11oz cod or haddock fillets
8 scallops, trimmed and halved
350g/12oz raw mussels in shells
30ml/2 tbsp vegetable oil
bunch of spring onions (scallions), cut
    into strips
2 small courgettes (zucchini), cut into strips
1 red (bell) pepper, cut into strips
250g/9oz/1⅓ cups long grain rice, rinsed
400ml/14fl oz/1⅔ cups chicken stock
250ml/8fl oz/1 cup passata
ground black pepper
coriander (cilantro), lemon wedges, to garnish

For the marinade
2 fresh red chillies, seeded
good handful of fresh coriander (cilantro)
10ml/2 tsp ground cumin
15ml/1 tbsp paprika
2 garlic cloves
90ml/6 tbsp olive oil
juice of 1 lemon

1 First blend all the ingredients for the marinade in a food processor.

2 Skin the chicken and cut into bitesize pieces. Place in a glass bowl. Slice the squid into rings and shell the prawns. Skin the fish and cut into bitesize chunks. Place the fish and shellfish (apart from the mussels) in a separate bowl. Divide the marinade between the fish and chicken and mix well. Cover and marinate for 2 hours.

3 Scrub the mussels, discarding any that do not close when tapped sharply. Drain the chicken and fish, and reserve the marinade. Heat the oil in a wok or paella pan and fry the chicken pieces for a few minutes until lightly browned.

4 Add the spring onions to the wok or pan, fry for 1 minute and then add the courgettes and red pepper strips and fry for a further 3–4 minutes until slightly softened. Remove the chicken and then the vegetables with a slotted spoon to separate plates.

5 Scrape the marinade into the pan and cook for 1 minute. Add the rice to the pan and stir-fry for 1 minute. Add the chicken stock, passata and reserved chicken and stir well. Bring to the boil, then reduce the heat, cover and simmer gently for 15–20 minutes until the rice is almost tender.

6 Add the reserved vegetables to the pan and place all the fish and mussels on top. Cover and cook gently for 10–12 minutes until the fish is cooked and the mussels have opened. Discard any mussels that have not opened during cooking. Serve garnished with coriander and lemon wedges.

Energy 352Kcal/1479kJ; Protein 36.4g; Carbohydrate 37.8g, of which sugars 4.1g; Fat 6g, of which saturates 0.9g; Cholesterol 156mg; Calcium 88mg; Fibre 1.3g; Sodium 257mg.

Griddled chicken with tomato salsa

This aromatic dish is a great way to enjoy the flavour, colour and health benefits of good quality fresh ingredients. Plum tomatoes are richly flavoured, less watery and have less seeds than regular tomatoes. If unavailable, use ripe, flavoursome salad tomatoes – sun-ripened would be ideal. For the best result, marinate the chicken overnight.

Serves 4

4 skinless chicken breast fillets, about
  175g/6oz each
30ml/2 tbsp fresh lemon juice
30ml/2 tbsp olive oil
10ml/2 tsp ground cumin
10ml/2 tsp dried oregano
15ml/1 tbsp coarsely ground black pepper

For the salsa

1 fresh green chilli
450g/1lb plum tomatoes, skinned (optional),
  seeded and chopped
3 spring onions (scallions), chopped
15ml/1 tbsp chopped fresh parsley
30ml/2 tbsp chopped fresh coriander (cilantro)
30ml/2 tbsp fresh lemon juice
45ml/3 tbsp olive oil

1 With a meat mallet, pound the chicken between two sheets of clear film (plastic wrap) until thin.

2 In a shallow dish, combine the lemon juice, oil, cumin, oregano and pepper. Add the chicken, cover and leave to marinate for at least 2 hours.

3 To make the salsa, char the chilli over a gas flame or under the grill (broiler). Leave to cool, then carefully rub off the charred skin.

4 Chop the chilli very finely and place in a bowl. Add the seeded and chopped tomatoes, the chopped spring onions, chopped fresh parsley and coriander, lemon juice and olive oil and mix well. Set aside until ready to serve.

5 Remove the chicken from the marinade. Heat a ridged griddle pan. Add the chicken fillets and cook on one side until browned, for about 3 minutes. Turn over and cook for 4 minutes more. Serve with the tomato salsa.

Energy 260Kcal/1096kJ; Protein 43.3g; Carbohydrate 4.1g, of which sugars 4g; Fat 8g, of which saturates 1.4g; Cholesterol 123mg; Calcium 45mg; Fibre 1.9g; Sodium 120mg.

Pan-fried chicken with pesto

Pan-fried chicken, served with warm home-made basil pesto, makes a deliciously quick main course. Make this simple dish in the summer, when basil leaves are plentiful. Omit the Parmesan cheese for a dairy-free pesto. Walnuts make a good alternative to pine nuts. Serve with braised baby carrots and celery, and rice, noodles or potatoes.

Serves 4

15ml/1 tbsp olive oil
4 skinless, chicken breast fillets
fresh basil leaves, to garnish

For the pesto
90ml/6 tbsp olive oil
50g/2oz/½ cup pine nuts
50g/2oz/⅔ cup freshly grated
   Parmesan cheese (optional)
50g/2oz/1 cup fresh basil leaves
15g/½oz/¼ cup fresh parsley
2 garlic cloves, crushed
ground black pepper

1 Heat the 15ml/1 tbsp oil in a frying pan. Add the chicken breasts and cook gently for 15–20 minutes, turning several times until the chicken breasts are tender, lightly browned and thoroughly cooked.

2 Meanwhile, make the pesto. Place the olive oil, pine nuts, Parmesan cheese, if using, basil leaves, parsley, garlic and pepper in a blender or food processor and process until smooth.

3 Remove the chicken from the pan, cover and keep hot. Reduce the heat slightly, then add the pesto to the pan and cook gently, stirring constantly, for a few minutes until the pesto has warmed through.

4 Pour the warm pesto over the chicken, garnish with basil leaves, and serve immediately.

Energy 419Kcal/1745kJ; Protein 37.9g; Carbohydrate 0.6g, of which sugars 0.6g; Fat 29.5g, of which saturates 3.8g; Cholesterol 105mg; Calcium 17mg; Fibre 0.4g; Sodium 91mg.

simple salads
and
side dishes

Eating plenty of vegetables is an essential part of any healthy diet, and having a good proportion of them raw, as salads, ensures that they retain the maximum nutritional value. The recipes in this chapter include a wide selection of hot and cold vegetable, potato, bean and rice ideas to serve as accompaniments. Alternatively, several dishes could be combined to make up a vitamin-packed meal, ideal for a detox regime and providing a healthy option for the entire family.

Spinach and roast garlic salad

Do not worry about the large amount of garlic in this salad. Roasting garlic significantly sweetens and subdues its flavour. It will lose its pungent taste, becoming succulent and subtle and will provide all of the health benefits without the after-effects. Toasted pine nuts are also included in this salad, adding a nutritious crunch and added flavour.

Serves 4

12 garlic cloves, unpeeled
60ml/4 tbsp olive oil
450g/1lb baby spinach leaves
50g/2oz/½ cup pine nuts, lightly toasted
juice of ½ lemon
ground black pepper

Cook's tip

If spinach is to be served raw in a salad, the leaves should be young and tender. Wash well, then drain and pat dry with kitchen paper.

1 Preheat the oven to 190ºC/375ºF/ Gas 5. Place the unpeeled garlic cloves in a small roasting dish, drizzle over 30ml/2 tbsp of the olive oil and toss to coat evenly.

2 Bake for about 15 minutes until the garlic cloves become slightly charred around the edges.

3 While still warm, tip the garlic cloves, still in their skins, into a salad bowl. Add the spinach, pine nuts, lemon juice and remaining olive oil. Toss well and season with pepper to taste.

4 Serve immediately, squeezing the softened garlic out of the skins to eat.

Health benefits

Spinach is a superb source of nutrients, providing a rich supply of antioxidant betacarotene, vitamin C, calcium, folate and iron. Spinach offers the greatest health benefits when eaten raw. Garlic is believed to aid circulation and help fight infections.

Energy 238Kcal/980kJ; Protein 6.9g; Carbohydrate 6.4g, of which sugars 2.6g; Fat 20.6g, of which saturates 2.3g; Cholesterol 0mg; Calcium 198mg; Fibre 3.6g; Sodium 159mg.

Mixed green leaf and herb salad

This cleansing salad makes an ideal light side salad. You can use any combination of soft salad leaves and a variety of delicate herbs, depending on availability and personal preference. The herbs are a good aid to digestion as well as tasting wonderfully aromatic. You could turn it into a more substantial main salad dish by making one of the variations.

Serves 4

15g/½oz/½ cup mixed fresh herbs, such as chervil, dill, basil, marjoram (use sparingly), flat leaf parsley, mint, sorrel, fennel or coriander (cilantro)
350g/12oz mixed salad leaves, such as rocket (arugula), radicchio, chicory (Belgian endive), watercress, baby spinach, oakleaf lettuce and dandelion

For the dressing
50ml/2fl oz/¼ cup extra virgin olive oil
15ml/1 tbsp lemon juice
ground black pepper

1 Wash the herbs and salad leaves under running water and dry them in a salad spinner, or use two clean, dry dish towels to pat them dry.

Variations
If you are making this salad to serve as a light meal, you will need to give it a little more substance. Try adding some of the following combinations of ingredients:
• Tiny new potatoes in their jackets, crumbled hard-boiled egg yolks and beansprouts.
• Cooked baby broad (fava) beans, sliced artichoke hearts and whole cherry tomatoes.
• Cooked chickpeas, asparagus tips and pitted green olives.

2 In a small bowl, blend together the olive oil and lemon juice and season with ground black pepper to taste.

3 Place the mixed salad leaves and herbs in a large serving bowl. Pour over the dressing and mix well, using your hands to toss the leaves.

4 Serve immediately after adding the dressing to prevent the leaves wilting.

Cook's tip
This salad makes the perfect foundation for a detox salad. You can add any number of other ingredients to it, as suggested in the variations, or your own choice of extra ingredients.

Energy 92Kcal/377kJ; Protein 0.7g; Carbohydrate 1.6g, of which sugars 1.6g; Fat 9.2g, of which saturates 1.4g; Cholesterol 0mg; Calcium 26mg; Fibre 0.8g; Sodium 3mg.

Wild rocket and cos lettuce salad with fresh herbs

Rocket makes a delicious addition to a salad. The wild variety has a particularly robust, peppery flavour. Parsley and dill add to the appeal and the digestive qualities of this clean-tasting salad.

Serves 4

a large handful of rocket (arugula) leaves
2 cos or romaine lettuce hearts
3 or 4 fresh flat leaf parsley sprigs,
    roughly chopped
30–45ml/2–3 tbsp finely chopped fresh dill
60ml/4 tbsp extra virgin olive oil
15–30ml/1–2 tbsp lemon juice
ground black pepper

Cook's tip
It is important to balance the bitterness of the rocket (arugula) and the sweetness of the cos or romaine lettuce, and the best way to do so is by taste.

1 If the rocket leaves are young and tender they can be left whole, but older ones should be trimmed of thick stalks and then sliced coarsely. Discard any tough stalks.

2 Slice the cos or romaine lettuce hearts into thin ribbons and place these in a bowl, then add the rocket and the chopped fresh parsley and dill.

3 Make a dressing by whisking the extra virgin olive oil and lemon juice with ground black pepper to taste in a bowl until the mixture emulsifies and thickens. Just before serving, pour the dressing over the salad and toss lightly to coat the leaves in the sharp and fruity dressing.

Energy 111Kcal/458kJ; Protein 0.7g; Carbohydrate 1.5g, of which sugars 1.5g; Fat 11.4g, of which saturates 1.7g; Cholesterol 0mg; Calcium 25mg; Fibre 0.8g; Sodium 3mg.

Cabbage salad with lemon dressing and black olives

An unusual salad with a crisp and refreshing texture. Usually white cabbage is dressed with a rich mayonnaise, so this recipe provides a lighter, healthier alternative idea for a detox regime.

Serves 4

1 white cabbage
12 black olives

For the dressing
75ml/5 tbsp extra virgin olive oil
30ml/2 tbsp lemon juice
1 garlic clove, crushed
30ml/2 tbsp finely chopped fresh flat
   leaf parsley
ground black pepper

1 Cut the cabbage in quarters, discard the outer leaves and trim off any thick, hard stems as well as the hard base. Stone (pit) the olives, if you prefer.

2 Lay each quarter in turn on its side and cut long, very thin slices until you reach the central core, which should be discarded. Shred the cabbage as finely as possible. Place the shredded cabbage in a large bowl and stir in the black olives.

3 Make the dressing by whisking the extra virgin olive oil, lemon juice, garlic, chopped parsley and pepper together in a small bowl until well blended. Pour the dressing over the cabbage and olives, and toss the salad until everything is evenly coated.

Energy 211Kcal/871kJ; Protein 2.9g; Carbohydrate 8.8g, of which sugars 8.6g; Fat 18.4g, of which saturates 2.6g; Cholesterol 0mg; Calcium 115mg; Fibre 4.5g; Sodium 297mg.

Seared mixed onion salad with parsley and balsamic dressing

This is a fine mix of healthy flavours and would make a delicious accompaniment to fish or chicken that has been grilled or cooked on the barbecue. Combine as many different onions as you wish; featuring anything from the fat pink variety sold in West Indian markets to the pink banana shallot, which is shaped like a torpedo. Look out also for the elegant reddish purple-and-white spring onions that Italians call cipolline.

Serves 4–6

6 red spring onions (scallions), trimmed
6 green salad onions, trimmed and
   split lengthways
250g/9oz small or baby (pearl) onions, peeled
   and left whole
2 pink onions, sliced horizontally into
   5mm/¼in rounds
2 red onions, sliced into wedges
2 small yellow onions, sliced into wedges
4 banana shallots, halved lengthways
200g/7oz shallots, preferably Thai
45ml/3 tbsp olive oil, plus extra for drizzling
juice of 1 lemon
45ml/3 tbsp chopped fresh flat leaf parsley
30ml/2 tbsp balsamic vinegar
ground black pepper
kuchai flowers, to garnish (optional)

1 Prepare and light the barbecue or preheat a medium-hot grill (broiler).

2 Spread out the onions and shallots in a large flat dish.

3 Whisk the oil and lemon juice together in a small bowl, then pour the mixture over the onions and shallots. Turn in the dressing to coat evenly. Season to taste with ground black pepper.

4 Once the flames have died down on the barbecue, position a grill rack over the coals to heat. When the coals are medium-hot, or covered in a moderate coating of ash, place a griddle or perforated metal vegetable basket on the grill rack to heat – you do this rather than cooking directly on the rack so that you do not risk losing onions through the gaps.

5 Grill the onions in batches, for 5–7 minutes, turning them occasionally to ensure that they cook evenly. If you are using a grill, spread the onions in batches on a grill pan. As each batch of onions is cooked, lift them on to a platter and keep hot.

6 Just before serving, add the parsley and toss to mix thoroughly, then drizzle over the balsamic vinegar and a little extra olive oil. Garnish with kuchai flowers, if you like.

Health benefits
Members of the onion family not only taste fabulous but they are also medicinal superfoods, containing several beneficial phytochemicals. These compounds are belived to help to reduce blood cholesterol levels, lower blood pressure and help to prevent heart disease and stroke. They also contain flavenoids and sulphurus compounds which are believed to fight cancers; antibiotics which can help to combat colds, flu and bronchitis; and a powerful antioxidant called quercetin.

Cook's tip
When available, scatter the whole salad with a few kuchai flowers. These are the lovely blossoms of the evil-smelling Chinese chive. They are available all year round and are sold in many large Asian food stores.

Energy 120Kcal/497kJ; Protein 3g; Carbohydrate 14.3g, of which sugars 10.6g; Fat 6.1g, of which saturates 0.8g; Cholesterol 0mg; Calcium 68mg; Fibre 3.3g; Sodium 12mg.

Grilled fennel salad with Niçoise olives

Fennel is particularly high in beneficial phytoestrogens, which are believed to help to protect against hormone-related cancers, such as breast or prostate cancer. In this Italian-style recipe, it is cooked on a piping hot griddle with sweet-tasting baby orange peppers, then served with torn savory leaves, juicy olives and sprinkled with a simple vinaigrette.

Serves 6

3 sweet baby orange (bell) peppers
5 fennel bulbs with green tops, total weight
    about 900g/2lb
30ml/2 tbsp olive oil
15ml/1 tbsp cider vinegar or white wine vinegar
45ml/3 tbsp extra virgin olive oil
24 small Niçoise olives
2 sprigs of fresh savory, leaves removed
ground black pepper

1 Heat a griddle pan until a few drops of water sprinkled on to the surface evaporate instantly.

2 Put the baby peppers on the pan and roast, turning them every few minutes, until charred all over.

3 Remove the pan from the heat, place the peppers in a bowl and cover with clear film (plastic wrap).

4 Remove the green fronds from the fennel and reserve. Slice the fennel lengthways into five roughly equal pieces. Place the fennel pieces in a flat dish, coat with the olive oil and season. Rub off the charred skin from the grilled peppers, remove the seeds and cut the flesh into small dice.

5 Reheat the griddle, then lower the heat slightly and grill the fennel slices in batches for about 8–10 minutes, turning frequently, until they are branded with golden grill marks. As each batch cooks, transfer it to a flat serving dish.

6 Whisk the vinegar and olive oil together, then pour over the fennel. Fold in the baby orange peppers and the olives. Tear the savory leaves and fennel fronds and scatter them over the salad. Serve warm or cold.

Cook's tip
If cooking directly on the barbecue, char the peppers when the coals are hot, then cool ready for peeling. Grill the fennel over medium-hot coals and turn frequently once stripes have formed.

Energy 137Kcal/567kJ; Protein 2.2g; Carbohydrate 7.5g, of which sugars 7.1g; Fat 11.1g, of which saturates 1.6g; Cholesterol 0mg; Calcium 50mg; Fibre 5.2g; Sodium 301mg.

Grilled potatoes with chive dressing

There is something very enjoyable about using edible flowering plants and herbs from the garden. This new potato salad includes both the chive stems and the flower heads in the dressing, which is tossed into potates that have been chargrilled on a barbecue. It's served with grilled cherry tomatoes alongside. Both potatoes and tomatoes are a good source of vitamin C.

Serves 4–6

900g/2lb salad potatoes, such as charlottes, Jersey royals or French ratte
15ml/1 tbsp cider vinegar
90ml/6 tbsp olive oil
45ml/3 tbsp chopped chives
about 10 chive flowers
4–6 small bunches yellow cherry tomatoes on the vine
ground black pepper

1 Prepare the barbecue. Boil the potatoes in a large pan of lightly salted water for about 10 minutes, or until just tender. Meanwhile make the dressing by whisking the vinegar with 60ml/4 tbsp of the oil, then stirring in the chives and flowers. Drain the potatoes and cut them in half horizontally. Season to taste.

2 Once the flames have died down, position a grill rack over the coals so that it can heat up.

3 Toss the potatoes in the remaining oil and lay them on the hot grill rack, cut side down. Leave for about 5 minutes, then turn the potatoes over and cook the second side for about 3 minutes.

4 Place the potatoes in a bowl, pour over the dressing and toss to mix.

5 Grill the tomatoes for 3 minutes, or until they are just beginning to blister. Serve with the potatoes, which can be hot, warm or cold.

Energy 215Kcal/902kJ; Protein 3g; Carbohydrate 26.2g, of which sugars 4g; Fat 11.6g, of which saturates 1.8g; Cholesterol 0mg; Calcium 14mg; Fibre 2.2g; Sodium 23mg.

Date, orange and carrot salad

A colourful and unusual salad made with an assortment of exotic ingredients – fresh dates and orange flower water – combined with crisp leaves, carrots, oranges and toasted almonds. This delicious combination of detoxifying fruit and vegetables will not only stimulate the body's cleansing processes but will provide an energy boost as well.

2 Arrange the lettuce leaves in a large salad bowl or on individual serving plates. Place the grated carrot in a mound on top.

3 Peel the oranges and cut them into segments. Arrange them around the mound of grated carrot.

4 Pile the dates on top, then sprinkle with the toasted almonds. Mix together the lemon juice and orange flower water and sprinkle over the salad.

5 Serve the salad chilled with freshly ground black pepper, if you like.

Variation
You can vary the taste of this delicious salad without affecting its cleansing properties by substituting the oranges with another citrus fruit, such as pink grapefruit, clementines or Ugli fruit.

Serves 4

1 Little Gem (Bibb) lettuce
2 carrots, finely grated
2 oranges
150g/5oz fresh dates, stoned (pitted) and cut into eighths, lengthways
25g/1oz/¼ cup toasted whole almonds, chopped
30ml/2 tbsp lemon juice
15ml/1 tbsp orange flower water
ground black pepper (optional)

1 Separate the lettuce leaves, then wash and pat dry with a dish towel.

Energy 137Kcal/578kJ; Protein 3.4g; Carbohydrate 23.4g, of which sugars 22.9g; Fat 4g, of which saturates 0.4g; Cholesterol 0mg; Calcium 86mg; Fibre 4.1g; Sodium 21mg.

Asparagus and orange salad

A slightly unusual combination of ingredients with a simple dressing based on good quality fruity olive oil. Tender spears of asparagus, juicy oranges and ripe tomatoes all provide valuable amounts of vitamin C, and asparagus is also a well-known diuretic and can help to relieve fluid retention. It is also a mild laxative and may help to relieve indigestion.

Serves 4

225g/8oz asparagus, trimmed and cut into
  5cm/2in lengths
2 large oranges
2 flavoursome tomatoes, cut into eighths
50g/2oz cos or romaine lettuce leaves
30ml/2 tbsp extra-virgin olive oil
2.5ml/½ tsp sherry vinegar or balsamic vinegar
ground black pepper

1 Cook the asparagus in boiling, lightly salted water for 3–4 minutes, until just tender. The cooking time may vary according to the size of the asparagus stems. Drain and refresh under cold water, then leave on one side to cool.

4 Mix together the oil and vinegar, and add 15ml/1 tbsp of the reserved orange juice and 5ml/1 tsp of the grated rind. Season with salt and pepper. Just before serving, pour the dressing over the salad and mix gently to coat all the ingredients.

2 Finely grate the rind from half an orange and reserve. Peel both the oranges and cut into segments. Squeeze the juice from the membrane and reserve.

3 Put the asparagus, orange segments, tomatoes and lettuce into a salad bowl.

Cook's tip
The bottom of the asparagus stalk is usually hard and woody, so it will probably need to be cut off with a sharp knife. However, if you are using short, slender stems, sometimes called "spruce", then trimming may not be necessary.

Energy 102Kcal/424kJ; Protein 2.9g; Carbohydrate 9.3g, of which sugars 9.2g; Fat 6.1g, of which saturates 0.9g; Cholesterol 0mg; Calcium 58mg; Fibre 2.9g; Sodium 9mg.

Grated beetroot and celery salad

This simple salad contains beetroot and celery, both of which are effective and well documented detoxifiers. Celery, in particular, is favoured by advocates of detoxing as it contains very few calories and is recognized as being a diuretic and laxative. Be sure to use fresh raw beetroot and not the type that is preserved in vinegar.

Serves 4

450g/1lb raw beetroot (beets), peeled
   and grated
4 celery sticks, finely chopped
30ml/2 tbsp freshly squeezed apple juice
fresh herbs, to garnish

For the dressing
45ml/3 tbsp olive oil
15ml/1 tbsp cider vinegar
4 spring onions (scallions), finely sliced
30ml/2 tbsp chopped fresh parsley
ground black pepper

1 Put the grated beetroot in a large bowl. Add the chopped celery and freshly squeezed apple juice and toss everything together to mix well.

2 Put all the ingredients for the dressing in a small bowl and whisk together with a fork until well blended. Stir half of the dressing into the beetroot and celery mixture.

3 Drizzle the remaining dressing over the top of the salad. Allow to marinate for at least 2 hours before serving, for the fullest flavour.

4 Serve garnished with fresh herbs and season with more pepper, if liked.

Variation
Make a lemony dressing: substitute freshly squeezed lemon juice for the cider vinegar in the dressing. Lemon juice is a powerful astringent and cleanser and will help to stimulate the liver.

Health benefits
Beetroot's naturally rich supply of betacarotene, vitamin C, calcium and iron is at its highest when the vegetable is eaten raw. Malic and tartaric acid, found in apples, boost the digestion and help to remove impurities from the liver. Herbs are particularly beneficial during a detox as they can stimulate and cleanse the system.

Energy 123Kcal/512kJ; Protein 2.3g; Carbohydrate 9.9g, of which sugars 9.2g; Fat 8.5g, of which saturates 1.2g; Cholesterol 0mg; Calcium 42mg; Fibre 2.7g; Sodium 98mg.

Leafy salad with apple and beetroot

Crisp apple, red salad leaves and cooked beetroot combine to make this a super-cleansing salad. Both apples and beetroot are excellent for removing impurities from the liver. Red fruits and vegetables have high levels of vitamins C and E and betacarotene. These antioxidants can help to fight cell damage caused by harmful free radicals.

Serves 4

50g/2oz/⅓ cup whole unblanched almonds
2 red apples, cored and diced
juice of ½ lemon
115g/4oz/4 cups red salad leaves, such
 as lollo rosso, oakleaf and radicchio
200g/7oz cooked beetroot (beets), peeled
 and sliced

For the dressing
30ml/2 tbsp olive oil
15ml/1 tbsp walnut oil
15ml/1 tbsp cider vinegar
ground black pepper

1 Toast the almonds in a dry frying pan for 2–3 minutes until golden brown.

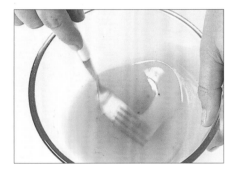

2 Meanwhile, make the dressing. Put the olive and walnut oils, cider vinegar and ground black pepper in a bowl or screw-top jar. Stir or shake thoroughly to combine the ingredients.

3 Toss the diced apples in lemon juice to prevent them browning, then place in a large bowl and add the salad leaves and beetroot.

4 Pour over the dressing and toss gently. Scatter the toasted almonds over the dressed salad and serve.

Cook's tip
If using raw beetroot, it can be cooked by baking in a little water in a covered dish, or it can be simmered for about 1½ hours in boiling water. Trim the stalks, but don't cut away the root or peel it – or the red colour will bleed away.

Energy 191Kcal/793kJ; Protein 4.1g; Carbohydrate 9.5g, of which sugars 8.8g; Fat 15.5g, of which saturates 1.6g; Cholesterol 0mg; Calcium 54mg; Fibre 2.7g; Sodium 58mg.

Mixed salad with capers and olives

Make this refreshing salad in the summer when tomatoes are at their sweetest and full of flavour. Watercress is higly nutritious and supplies a useful amount of iron. If unavailable, baby spinach leaves or rocket could be used as leafy alternatives. Cucumber is an effective diuretic and helps to improve the efficiency of the kidneys.

Serves 4

4 tomatoes
½ cucumber
1 bunch spring onions (scallions), trimmed and chopped
1 bunch watercress or rocket (arugula)
8 stuffed olives
30ml/2 tbsp drained capers, rinsed

For the dressing

30ml/2 tbsp red wine vinegar
5ml/1 tsp paprika
2.5ml/½ tsp ground cumin
1 garlic clove, crushed
75ml/5 tbsp olive oil
ground black pepper

1 Peel the tomatoes and finely dice the flesh. Put them in a salad bowl.

2 Peel the cucumber, dice it finely and add to the tomatoes. Add half the spring onions and mix. Break the watercress into sprigs. Add to the bowl with the olives and capers.

3 To make the dressing, mix the wine vinegar, paprika, cumin and garlic in a bowl. Whisk in the oil and add pepper to taste.

4 Pour over the salad and toss lightly. Serve immediately with the remaining spring onions.

Energy 162Kcal/670kJ; Protein 1.9g; Carbohydrate 4.3g, of which sugars 4.2g; Fat 15.4g, of which saturates 2.3g; Cholesterol 0mg; Calcium 49mg; Fibre 2g; Sodium 243mg.

Warm vegetable salad

This delicious and slightly unusual salad features raw red pepper and sprouted beans, which make a crunchy contrast to the warm steamed broccoli, green beans and carrots. The delicious combination of raw and lightly cooked vegetables offers a powerhouse of cleansing properties along with long-term energy from the new potatoes.

Serves 2

8 new potatoes
225g/8oz broccoli, cut into small florets
200g/7oz/1½ cups French (green)
    beans, trimmed
2 carrots, cut into thin ribbons with a
    vegetable peeler
1 red (bell) pepper, seeded and cut into strips
50g/2oz/½ cup sprouted beans
sprigs of watercress or rocket (arugula),
    to garnish
ground black pepper

For the dressing
45ml/3 tbsp extra virgin olive oil
15ml/1 tbsp toasted sesame oil
juice of ½ lemon

1 Bring a pan of water to the boil, add the potatoes and cook for 15 minutes, until tender. Drain, leave to cool slightly, then halve or thickly slice the potatoes, depending on their size.

2 Meanwhile, place the broccoli and French beans in a steamer placed over a pan of boiling water and steam for 4–5 minutes until just tender, but still crisp to the bite.

3 When the broccoli and beans are nearly cooked, place the prepared carrots in the steamer with the other vegetables and cook lightly for a further 2 minutes, or until all of the vegetables are tender.

4 Meanwhile, make the dressing. In a small bowl, whisk together the olive oil, sesame oil and lemon juice and season with plenty of ground black pepper, to taste.

5 Arrange the cooked vegetables on a serving platter with the red pepper and sprouted beans.

6 Garnish the mixed vegetables with watercress or rocket and pour over the dressing.

Health benefits
Sprouted beans are easily digestible and packed with concentrated goodness. Their nutrients include vitamins B, C and E, protein, potassium and phosphorus. When fresh, their vitamin and enzyme content is at its peak, and they are believed to stimulate the body's ability to cleanse itself.

Energy 435Kcal/1810kJ; Protein 11.6g; Carbohydrate 43.9g, of which sugars 19.3g; Fat 24.7g, of which saturates 3.9g; Cholesterol 0mg; Calcium 146mg; Fibre 10.8g; Sodium 56mg.

Minty broad beans with lemon

Young, tender broad beans have a sweet, mild taste and are delicious served in a simple salad. Take advantage of them when they're in season and make them into this fresh, zesty dish. Green peas – either fresh or frozen – are also delicious served in the same way. All peas and beans are a good souce of fibre, essential for healthy digestion.

Serves 4

450g/1lb broad (fava) beans, thawed if frozen
30ml/2 tbsp garlic-infused olive oil
grated rind and juice of 1 lemon
1 small bunch of fresh mint, roughly chopped
ground black pepper

1 Using your fingers, slip the grey skins off the broad beans and discard – this takes a little time, but the result is well worthwhile for the attractive appearance of the bright green skinned beans.

2 Quickly blanch the skinned beans in a large pan of lightly salted boiling water for 3–4 minutes, or until they are just tender.

3 Drain the beans well and toss with the oil, lemon rind and juice, and mint in a large bowl. Season with pepper, and serve immediately.

Variation
If broad beans are unavailable, you can use drained and rinsed canned flageolet or cannellini beans.

Gingered carrot salad

This fresh and zesty salad is ideal served as an accompaniment to simple grilled chicken or fish. Some food processors have an attachment that can be used to cut the carrots into matchsticks, which makes quick work of the preparation. Root ginger goes perfectly with sweet carrots, and the tiny black poppy seeds not only add taste and texture, but also look stunning.

Serves 4

350g/12oz carrots, peeled and cut into
    fine matchsticks
30ml/2 tbsp garlic-infused olive oil
2.5cm/1in piece of fresh root ginger,
    peeled and grated
15ml/1 tbsp poppy seeds
ground black pepper

1 Put the carrots in a bowl and stir in the oil and grated ginger.

2 Cover with clear film (plastic wrap) and chill for at least 30 minutes, to allow the flavours to develop.

3 Season the salad with pepper to taste. Sprinkle the poppy seeds over the salad just before serving. The black seeds make a stunning contrast against the bright orange of the carrots and also add a pleasing crunch.

Variations
• To make a parsnip and sesame seed salad, replace the carrots with parsnips that have been cut into matchsticks. Blanch the parsnips in lightly salted boiling water for 1 minute before combining with the olive oil and ginger.
• Replace the poppy seeds with the same quantity of lightly toasted sesame seeds. Sesame seeds provide a useful source of calcium and vitamin E and have a distincitve flavour that works well in this salad.

Top: Energy 145Kcal/608kJ; Protein 9.3g; Carbohydrate 13.5g, of which sugars 1.8g; Fat 6.3g, of which saturates 0.9g; Cholesterol 0mg; Calcium 88mg; Fibre 8g; Sodium 13mg.
Above: Energy 103Kcal/424kJ; Protein 1.2g; Carbohydrate 7g, of which sugars 6.5g; Fat 7.9g, of which saturates 1.2g; Cholesterol 0mg; Calcium 47mg; Fibre 2.4g; Sodium 23mg.

Marinated courgette and flageolet bean salad

Serve this healthy salad as a light lunch or as an accompaniment to fish or chicken dishes. It has a wonderful bright green colour and is perfect for a summer lunch.

serves 4

2 courgettes (zucchini), halved lengthways
    and sliced
400g/14oz can flageolet or cannellini beans,
    drained and rinsed
45ml/3 tbsp garlic-infused olive oil
grated rind and juice of 1 lemon
30ml/2 tbsp fresh basil and mint, chopped
ground black pepper

1 Cook the sliced courgettes in a large pan of lightly salted boiling water for 2–3 minutes, or until just tender. Drain well in a colander and refresh under cold running water.

2 Transfer the drained courgettes into a bowl with the beans and stir in the oil, lemon rind and juice and pepper, to season. Cover and chill for 30 minutes. Add the chopped herbs and toss together just before serving.

Energy 183Kcal/766kJ; Protein 7.8g; Carbohydrate 18.7g, of which sugars 4.5g; Fat 9.1g, of which saturates 1.3g; Cholesterol 0mg; Calcium 84mg; Fibre 6.7g; Sodium 391mg.

Butter bean, tomato and red onion salad

Make good use of canned beans in a simple side salad. Serve as an accompaniment to a main dish, or serve several salads together for a healthy main meal.

Serves 4

2 x 400g/14oz cans butter (lima) beans, rinsed and drained
4 plum tomatoes, roughly chopped
1 red onion, thinly sliced
45ml/3 tbsp herb-infused olive oil
ground black pepper

1 Mix together the beans, tomatoes and onion in a large bowl. Season with ground black pepper to taste, and stir in the oil.

2 Cover the bowl with clear film (plastic wrap) and chill in the refrigerator for 20 minutes before serving.

Energy 251Kcal/1055kJ; Protein 12.7g; Carbohydrate 30.3g, of which sugars 6.2g; Fat 9.6g, of which saturates 1.5g; Cholesterol 0mg; Calcium 41mg; Fibre 10.4g; Sodium 850mg.

Potato, caraway seed and parsley salad

Potatoes provide a good steady release of energy. They are high in fibre and especially nutritious when freshly harvested and if eaten in their skins, as here. The caraway seeds and parsley both add a wonderful flavour and help to stimulate the digestion. This recipe would also be delicious made with peeled and chopped, cooked sweet potatoes.

Serves 4–6

675g/1½lb new potatoes, scrubbed
15ml/1 tbsp caraway seeds, lightly crushed
45ml/3 tbsp chopped fresh parsley
45ml/3 tbsp garlic-infused olive oil
 ground black pepper

1 Cook the potatoes in salted, boiling water for about 10 minutes, or until they are just tender.

2 Put the potatoes in a colander and drain, then transfer to a large bowl.

3 Stir the garlic-infused oil, caraway seeds and some pepper into the hot potatoes, set aside to cool, then stir in the parsley and serve.

Energy 131Kcal/549kJ; Protein 2.1g; Carbohydrate 18.3g, of which sugars 1.6g; Fat 5.9g, of which saturates 0.9g; Cholesterol 0mg; Calcium 22mg; Fibre 1.5g; Sodium 15mg.

Herby rice pilaff

A quick and easy recipe to make, this simple pilaff makes a delicious accompaniment or could be served just with a selection of fresh seasonal vegetables, such as broccoli florets, baby corn and carrots, for a light detox meal. Rice provides a good source of starchy carbohydrate, and it is suitable for those with a gluten or wheat sensitivity.

Serves 4

225g/8oz/1 cup mixed brown basmati
    and wild rice
15ml/1 tbsp olive oil
1 onion, chopped
1 garlic clove, crushed
5ml/1 tsp ground cumin
5ml/1 tsp ground turmeric
50g/2oz/½ cup sultanas
750ml/1¼ pints/3 cups vegetable stock
30–45ml/2–3 tbsp chopped fresh herbs
ground black pepper
sprigs of fresh herbs
25g/1oz/¼ cup pistachio nuts, chopped,
    to garnish

1 Wash the rice under cold running water, then drain well.

2 Heat the oil in a large pan, add the onion and garlic and cook gently for 5 minutes, stirring occasionally.

3 Add the spices and rice and cook gently for 1 minute, stirring. Stir in the sultanas and stock, bring to the boil, cover and simmer gently for 20–25 minutes, stirring occasionally.

4 Stir in the chopped mixed fresh herbs and season to taste with pepper.

5 Spoon the pilaff into a warmed serving dish and garnish with fresh herb sprigs and a scattering of chopped pistachio nuts. Serve immediately, or cool, then cover and keep chilled to serve as a cold rice salad.

Energy 304Kcal/1271kJ; Protein 5.8g; Carbohydrate 55.3g, of which sugars 9.9g; Fat 6.6g, of which saturates 0.9g; Cholesterol 0mg; Calcium 29mg; Fibre 0.9g; Sodium 36mg.

Stir-fried broccoli with sesame seeds

Purple sprouting broccoli has been used for this recipe, but when it is not available an ordinary variety of broccoli, such as calabrese, will also work very well. Broccoli should form a regular part of your everyday diet, even when you are not on a detox diet. It is exceptionally rich in antioxidant vitamins and minerals, and it is believed to reduce the risk of certain cancers.

Serves 2

225g/8oz purple sprouting broccoli
15ml/1 tbsp olive oil
15ml/1 tbsp soy sauce
15ml/1 tbsp sesame seeds, toasted
ground black pepper

Cook's tip
To toast sesame seeds, put them on a large baking sheet and brown under a medium-hot grill (broiler).

1 Using a sharp knife, cut off and discard any thick stems from the broccoli, then cut the remainder into long, slender florets.

2 Heat the olive oil in a wok or large frying pan and add the broccoli.

3 Stir-fry for 3–4 minutes, or until tender, adding a splash of water if the pan becomes too dry.

4 Add the soy sauce, then season with ground black pepper to taste.

5 Add the lightly toasted sesame seeds to the pan and toss well to combine thoroughly. Transfer to a large dish and serve immediately.

Energy 135Kcal/558kJ; Protein 6.6g; Carbohydrate 2.7g, of which sugars 2.3g; Fat 10.9g, of which saturates 1.7g; Cholesterol 0mg; Calcium 115mg; Fibre 3.5g; Sodium 545mg.

Roasted plum tomatoes with garlic

These roast tomatoes flavoured with garlic and bay leaves are so simple to prepare, yet taste absolutely wonderful. Cooking the tomatoes in a shallow earthenware dish will allow them to char slightly around the edges, adding colour, texture and flavour. Plum tomatoes are used here, but the dish would be equally good with halved beefsteak tomatoes.

Serves 4

8 plum tomatoes
12 garlic cloves, unpeeled
20ml/4 tsp extra virgin olive oil
3 bay leaves
ground black pepper
45ml/3 tbsp fresh oregano leaves, to garnish

1 Preheat the oven to 230°C/450°F/ Gas 8. Cut the plum tomatoes in half lengthways with a sharp knife, leaving a small part of the green stem intact for the final decoration.

2 Select an ovenproof dish that will hold all the tomatoes snugly together in a single layer. Place them in the dish with the cut side facing upwards, and push each of the whole, unpeeled garlic cloves among them.

3 Lightly brush the tomatoes with the oil, add the bay leaves and sprinkle black pepper over the top.

4 Bake for about 35–45 minutes until the tomatoes have softened and are sizzling in the dish, and slightly charred around the edges. Season with a little black pepper. Garnish with the fresh oregano leaves and serve immediately.

Variation

For a sweet alternative, use halved and seeded red or yellow (bell) peppers instead of the tomatoes.

Energy 114Kcal/474kJ; Protein 2g; Carbohydrate 7.1g, of which sugars 5.6g; Fat 8.8g, of which saturates 1.4g; Cholesterol 0mg; Calcium 14mg; Fibre 2.2g; Sodium 16mg.

Braised red cabbage

Red cabbage is a hardy vegetable that makes a good seasonal choice during the winter months. In this dish it is gently braised with onions, apples and warm spices. Red cabbage provides useful amounts of the B vitamin folate and vitamin C, as well as the mineral potassium. Apples are particularly good for helping to remove impurities from the liver.

3 Layer the shredded cabbage in a large ovenproof dish with the onions, apples, spices, sugar, and ground black pepper to season. Drizzle the vinegar over the mixture.

4 Cover the dish with a lid and cook in the preheated oven for about 1½ hours, stirring a couple of times, until the cabbage is very tender. Serve immediately, garnished with the parsley.

Serves 4–6

1kg/2¼lb red cabbage
2 cooking apples
2 onions, chopped
5ml/1 tsp freshly grated nutmeg
1.5ml/¼ tsp ground cloves
1.5ml/¼ tsp ground cinnamon
15ml/1 tbsp soft dark brown sugar
45ml/3 tbsp cider or red wine vinegar
ground black pepper
chopped flat leaf parsley, to garnish

1 Preheat the oven to 160ºC/325ºF/ Gas 3.

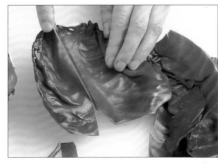

2 Cut away and discard the large white ribs from the outer cabbage leaves using a large, sharp knife, then finely shred the cabbage. Peel, core and coarsely grate the apples.

Energy 90Kcal/381kJ; Protein 3.1g; Carbohydrate 19.4g, of which sugars 18g; Fat 0.5g, of which saturates 0g; Cholesterol 0mg; Calcium 98mg; Fibre 5g; Sodium 14mg.

Young vegetables with tarragon

This delicious side dish contains a variety of tender young vegetables, which are just lightly cooked to bring out their different flavours and to retain as much nutrient value as possible. The tarragon adds a wonderful depth to this bright, fresh dish. It goes well as a light accompaniment to simple fish, seafood and poultry dishes.

Serves 4

5 spring onions (scallions)
30ml/2 tbsp olive oil
1 garlic clove, crushed
115g/4oz asparagus tips
115g/4oz mangetouts (snow peas), trimmed
115g/4oz broad (fava) beans
2 Little Gem (Bibb) lettuces
5ml/1 tsp finely chopped fresh tarragon
ground black pepper

1 Cut the spring onions into quarters lengthways with a sharp knife. Heat the olive oil in a large frying pan, add the spring onions and the crushed garlic and fry gently over a medium-low heat for a few minutes, until softened.

2 Add the asparagus tips, mangetouts and broad beans to the pan and stir around. Mix well, covering all the vegetables with oil.

3 Just cover the base of the pan with water, season, and allow to simmer gently for a few minutes.

4 Cut the Gem lettuce into quarters with a sharp knife and add to the frying pan. Cook for 3 minutes then remove the pan from the heat.

5 Transfer the cooked vegetables to a warmed serving dish, add the chopped tarragon, and serve immediately.

Energy 103Kcal/428kJ; Protein 5g; Carbohydrate 6.8g, of which sugars 3.5g; Fat 6.3g, of which saturates 0.9g; Cholesterol 0mg; Calcium 63mg; Fibre 3.9g; Sodium 6mg.

delicious healthy desserts

A range of desserts can be enjoyed while following a detox diet and provide a great opportunity to include plenty of vitamin-packed fruit in your diet. All fruit is good for you, whether fresh, frozen, dried or canned (ideally in natural juice), so go ahead and tuck into fruit salads, baked stuffed fruits and frozen yogurt, sorbet or granita.

Fresh fruit salad

A healthy diet should include plenty of fresh fruit, and the wide variety available throughout the seasons means that it's always easy to put together a delicious combination of fruit for a healthy dessert or snack. Fruit salads are especially beneficial during a detox regime, as fruit helps to eliminate toxins. This simple version could also be enjoyed for breakfast.

Serves 4

16–20 strawberries
2 peaches
2 oranges
2 eating apples
30ml/2 tbsp lemon juice
15–30ml/1–2 tbsp orange flower
  water (optional)
a few fresh mint leaves, to decorate

Variations
There are no rules with this fruit salad, and you could add any other fruit that you like, such as bananas and grapes.

1 Hull the strawberries and cut them in half. Put the peaches in a bowl, pour boiling water over them and leave them to stand for 1 minute.

2 Remove from the water, using a slotted spoon. Peel, then cut the flesh into thick slices. Discard the stones (pits).

3 Peel the oranges, removing all the pith, and segment, catching any juice in a small bowl. Peel, core and chop the apples. Place all the fruit in a large serving bowl.

4 Combine the lemon juice, orange flower water, if using, and any reserved orange juice. Pour the fruit juice mixture over the salad and serve decorated with a few fresh mint leaves.

Health benefits
Fruit cleanses and rejuvenates the body, as well as providing minerals, vitamins and fibre.

Dried fruit salad

This wonderful combination of fresh and dried fruit makes an excellent detox dessert. Both types are packed with nutrients and will provide plenty of energy. The dried selection includes apricots and peaches, and the fresh selection includes pear, apple, orange, blackberries and raspberries, but you can ring the changes with your own favourite combination.

Serves 4

115g/4oz/½ cup dried apricots
115g/4oz/½ cup dried peaches
1 pear
1 apple
1 orange
50g/2oz/½ cup blackberries
1 cinnamon stick
45ml/3 tbsp clear unblended honey
30ml/2 tbsp lemon juice
50g/2oz/½ cup raspberries

1 Place the apricots and peaches in a bowl and cover with water. Leave to soak for 1–2 hours or overnight in the refrigerator until plump, then drain. Cut the soaked fruit into equal size pieces with a sharp knife.

2 Peel and core the pear and apple and cut into cubes. Peel the orange with a sharp knife, removing all the pith, and cut into wedges. Place all the prepared fruit in a large pan with the blackberries.

3 Add 600ml/1 pint/2½ cups water, the cinnamon and honey to the pan and bring to the boil.

4 Cover and simmer very gently for 10–12 minutes, then remove the pan from the heat. Stir in the lemon juice and raspberries. Allow the mixture to cool, then pour into a bowl. Cover and chill in the refrigerator for about 1 hour before serving.

Cook's tips
• Ideally, choose unsulphured dried fruit. Much dried fruit is treated with sulphur-based preservatives to prevent discoloration and enhance the colour, but it is best avoided, especially by those with asthma.
• Avoid ready-to-eat dried fruit, as it contains lots of preservatives.

Top: Energy 78Kcal/331kJ; Protein 2.1g; Carbohydrate 18g, of which sugars 18g; Fat 0.2g, of which saturates 0g; Cholesterol 0mg; Calcium 50mg; Fibre 3.5g; Sodium 8mg.
Above: Energy 162Kcal/689kJ; Protein 3.1g; Carbohydrate 38.6g, of which sugars 38.6g; Fat 0.5g, of which saturates 0g; Cholesterol 0mg; Calcium 70mg; Fibre 5.9g; Sodium 13mg.

Fresh fruit with mango coulis

A flavourful fruit sauce, or coulis, is easy to prepare and ideal for transforming a simple fruit salad into something special. Making a coulis also provides an opportunity for adding extra fruit to this dessert. Mangoes make a luscious coulis, but other soft fruits, such as raspberries, strawberries or peaches, would make good alternatives.

Serves 4–6

1 large ripe mango, peeled, stoned
   and chopped
rind of 1 orange
juice of 3 oranges
caster (superfine) sugar, to taste
2 peaches
2 nectarines
1 small mango, peeled
2 plums
1 pear or ½ small melon
juice of 1 lemon
50g/2oz/2 heaped tbsp wild
   strawberries (optional)
50g/2oz/2 heaped tbsp raspberries
50g/2oz/2 heaped tbsp blueberries
small fresh mint sprigs, to decorate

1 In a food processor fitted with a metal blade, blend the chopped flesh of the large mango until smooth. Add the orange rind and juice and a little sugar to taste and process again until very smooth. Press through a sieve (strainer) into a bowl and chill.

2 Slice and stone the peaches, nectarines, small mango and plums. Quarter the pear and remove the core or, if using, slice the melon thinly and remove the skin.

3 Place the sliced fruits on a large plate, sprinkle with the lemon juice and chill, covered with clear film (plastic wrap), for up to 3 hours. (Some fruits discolour if cut too far ahead of time.)

4 To serve, arrange the sliced fruits on serving plates, spoon the berries on top, drizzle with a little mango coulis and decorate with mint sprigs. Serve the remaining coulis separately.

Cook's tip
Ideally choose unwaxed or organic citrus fruit, if you are going to be using the rind. If they are not unwaxed, wash the fruit thoroughly before using, because the waxes contain fungicide.

Energy 82Kcal/351kJ; Protein 1.9g; Carbohydrate 19.2g, of which sugars 19.1g; Fat 0.3g, of which saturates 0.1g; Cholesterol 0mg; Calcium 22mg; Fibre 3.3g; Sodium 5mg.

Exotic fruit platter with ginger

Pineapple, papaya, melon and pomegranates offer an impressive range of detoxifying qualities. There is no need to save this refreshing platter for dessert. Fruit prepared in this way is delicious as an energy-boosting snack or breakfast during a detox. Serve on its own or with some low-fat probiotic yogurt. Omit the ground ginger, if you prefer.

Serves 4–6

1 pineapple
2 papayas
1 melon
juice of 2 limes
2 pomegranates
ground ginger, to taste
sprigs of mint, to decorate

1 Peel the pineapple. Remove the core, then cut the flesh lengthways into thin wedges. Peel the papayas, cut them in half, remove the seeds, then slice into thin wedges.

2 Halve the melon and remove the seeds from the middle. Cut into thin wedges and remove the skin.

Health benefits
Fresh mint has traditionally been used as a cure for indigestion and is also effective in stimulating and cleansing the system.

Variation
The selection of fruit can be varied. Apples and bananas make a simple salad, or guavas and mangoes a more exotic combination. Rather than using ginger, simply season with freshly ground black pepper.

3 Arrange the fruit on six individual plates and sprinkle with the lime juice. Cut the pomegranates in half and scoop out the seeds, discarding any pith. Scatter the seeds over the fruit. Serve, sprinkled with a little ginger to taste, and a few sprigs of mint.

Energy 91Kcal/389kJ; Protein 1.2g; Carbohydrate 22.1g, of which sugars 22.1g; Fat 0.4g, of which saturates 0g; Cholesterol 0mg; Calcium 48mg; Fibre 3.4g; Sodium 32mg.

Strawberries with passion fruit sauce

Fragrant strawberries are always a treat, but they are full of nutrients too. They are rich in antioxidants, including betacarotene and vitamin C, which help to neutralize harmful free radicals in the body. Berry fruits taste best when they are served at room temperature, so remove strawberries from the refrigerator at least one hour before serving.

Serves 4

350g/12oz/2 cups raspberries, fresh or frozen
30ml/2 tbsp clear honey
1 passion fruit
700g/1½lb/6 cups small strawberries

1 Place the raspberries and honey in a pan and warm over a very gentle heat to release the juices. When the juices start to run, simmer for 5 minutes, stirring occasionally. Set aside and allow the mixture to cool.

2 Halve the passion fruit and, using a teaspoon, carefully scoop out the seeds and juice into a small bowl.

3 Put the raspberries into a food processor or blender, add the passion fruit and blend until smooth.

4 Place the raspberry and passion fruit sauce in a fine nylon sieve and press the purée through to remove the gritty seeds.

5 Divide the strawberries among serving bowls, spoon over some of the sauce and serve. Offer extra sauce separately, in a small jug (pitcher).

Energy 92Kcal/391kJ; Protein 2.8g; Carbohydrate 20.5g, of which sugars 20.5g; Fat 0.5g, of which saturates 0.1g; Cholesterol 0mg; Calcium 51mg; Fibre 4.2g; Sodium 15mg.

Lemon grass skewers

Grilled fruits make a delicious end to a cleansing meal. The lemon grass skewers give the fruit a subtle lemon tang. The fruits used here make an ideal exotic mix, but almost any soft fruit that will thread easily on to skewers can be substituted as preferred. If lemon grass is unavailable, use bamboo skewers that have been pre-soaked, to prevent them from burning.

Serves 4

4 long fresh lemon grass stalks
1 mango, peeled, stoned (pitted) and cut into chunks
1 papaya, peeled, seeded and cut into chunks
1 star fruit, cut into thick slices and halved
8 fresh bay leaves
a little nutmeg
60ml/4 tbsp clear honey
low-fat probiotic yogurt, to serve

1 Preheat the grill (broiler). Cut the top of each lemon grass stalk into a point. Bruise each with the back of a knife.

2 Thread each lemon grass stalk with the prepared fruit and bay leaves.

3 Cover a large baking sheet in kitchen foil, raising the edges slightly, and lay the skewers on top.

Cook's tip
Only fresh lemon grass will work as skewers for this recipe. It is now possible to buy lemon grass stalks in jars, but they are too soft to use as skewers.

4 Grate nutmeg over each of the fruit skewers and drizzle with honey. Grill for 5 minutes, until they are lightly browned. Serve immediately with probiotic yogurt.

Energy 92Kcal/393kJ; Protein 0.9g; Carbohydrate 23.2g, of which sugars 23.1g; Fat 0.2g, of which saturates 0g; Cholesterol 0mg; Calcium 29mg; Fibre 3.5g; Sodium 7mg.

Minted pomegranate yogurt with grapefruit salad

The vitamin-rich jewel-like seeds of the pomegranate make any dessert look beautiful. Here they are stirred into yogurt to make a stunning sauce for a refreshing grapefruit salad.

Serves 3–4

300ml/½ pint/1¼ cups low-fat probiotic yogurt
2–3 ripe pomegranates
small bunch of fresh mint, finely chopped
clear honey or caster (superfine) sugar, to
    taste (optional)

For the grapefruit salad
2 red grapefruits
2 pink grapefruits
1 white grapefruit
15–30ml/1–2 tbsp orange flower water

To decorate
handful of pomegranate seeds
fresh mint leaves

1 Put the yogurt in a bowl and beat well. Cut open the pomegranates and scoop out the seeds, removing and discarding all the bitter pith. Fold the pomegranate seeds and chopped mint into the yogurt. Sweeten with a little honey or sugar, if using, then chill until ready to serve.

2 To make the salad, peel the red, pink and white grapefruits, cutting off and discarding all the pith.

3 Holding each fruit in the palm of your hand, cut between the membranes to remove the segments. Prepare the fruit over a bowl to catch the juices.

4 Discard the membranes and mix the fruit segments with the reserved fruit juices. Sprinkle the segments with the orange flower water and add a little honey or sugar, if using. Stir gently to mix, then decorate with a few pomegranate seeds.

5 Just before serving, decorate the chilled yogurt with a sprinkling of pomegranate seeds and mint leaves.

6 Serve the minted pomegranate yogurt with the grapefruit salad.

Variation
Alternatively, you can use a mixture of oranges and blood oranges, interspersed with thin segments of lemon. Lime segments work well with the grapefruit and mandarins or tangerines could be used too. As the idea is to create a refreshing, scented salad, juicy melons and kiwi fruit would also make an ideal combination.

Energy 115Kcal/482kJ; Protein 6g; Carbohydrate 21.7g, of which sugars 21.7g; Fat 1.1g, of which saturates 0.4g; Cholesterol 1mg; Calcium 210mg; Fibre 3.4g; Sodium 73mg.

Rose water-scented oranges with pistachio nuts

This delightfully fragrant and refreshing dessert combines three favourite Middle Eastern ingredients. If you don't have pistachio nuts, use hazelnuts instead.

Serves 4

4 large oranges
30ml/2 tbsp rose water
30ml/2 tbsp unsalted shelled pistachio nuts, roughly chopped

Cook's tip

Rose-scented sugar is delicious lightly sprinkled over fresh fruit salads. To make, wash and dry a handful of rose petals and place them in a sealed container filled with caster (superfine) sugar for 2–3 days. Remove the petals before using the sugar.

1 Slice the top and bottom off one of the oranges to expose the flesh. Using a small serrated knife, slice down between the pith and the flesh, working around the orange, to remove all the peel and pith. Slice the orange into six rounds, reserving any juice. Repeat with the remaining oranges.

2 Arrange the orange rounds on a serving dish. Mix the reserved juice with the rose water and drizzle over the oranges. Cover the dish with clear film (plastic wrap) and chill for about 30 minutes. Sprinkle the chopped pistachio nuts over the oranges just before serving.

Energy 91Kcal/384kJ; Protein 2.7g; Carbohydrate 11.3g, of which sugars 11.1g; Fat 4.3g, of which saturates 0.6g; Cholesterol 0mg; Calcium 67mg; Fibre 2.6g; Sodium 46mg.

Papaya and green grapes with mint sauce

Papaya is rich in vitamin C and betacarotene, and provides a useful amount of dietary fibre. It is easy to digest and has a tonic effect on the stomach.

Serves 4

2 large papayas
225g/8oz/2 cups seedless green grapes
juice of 3 limes
2.5cm/1in fresh root ginger, peeled and
    finely grated
15ml/1 tbsp clear honey
5 fresh mint leaves, cut into thin strips,
    plus extra whole leaves, to decorate

1 Peel the papayas and cut into small cubes, discarding the seeds. Cut the grapes in half.

2 In a large mixing bowl, thoroughly combine the lime juice, ginger, honey and shredded mint leaves.

3 Add the papaya and grapes to the bowl and toss together gently. Cover with clear film (plastic wrap) and leave in a cool place to allow the flavours to mingle for 1 hour.

4 Serve in a large glass dish or individual stemmed glasses, decorated with whole fresh mint leaves, if liked.

Orange granita with strawberries

A granita is a refreshing alternative to ice cream, and makes the ideal dessert after a spicy main dish such as a curry. It's made with just frozen freshly-squeezed fruit juice and is therefore dairy-free. The combination of orange juice in the granita and the accompanying portion of fresh, ripe strawberries provides a generous amount of vitamin C.

Serves 4

6 large juicy oranges
350g/12oz ripe strawberries
finely pared strips of orange rind, to decorate

1 Juice the oranges and pour into a shallow freezerproof bowl.

Cook's tips
• Granita will keep for up to 3 weeks in the freezer. If you prefer a more tart ice, use sweet pink grapefruits or blood oranges or, alternatively, add a little fresh lemon or lime juice.
• Look out for Valencia oranges. They are the best variety for juicing.

2 Place the bowl in the freezer. Remove after 30 minutes and beat the semi-frozen juice thoroughly with a wooden spoon. Repeat this process at 30-minute intervals over a 4-hour period. This will break the ice crystals down into small particles and prevent the granita from freezing solid.

3 Halve the strawberries and arrange them on a serving plate. Scoop the granita into serving glasses, decorate with strips of orange rind and serve immediately with the strawberries.

Top: Energy 90Kcal/382kJ; Protein 0.9g; Carbohydrate 22.5g, of which sugars 22.5g; Fat 0.2g, of which saturates 0g; Cholesterol 0mg; Calcium 36mg; Fibre 3.2g; Sodium 8mg.
Above: Energy 79Kcal/336kJ; Protein 2.4g; Carbohydrate 18g, of which sugars 18g; Fat 0.2g, of which saturates 0g; Cholesterol 0mg; Calcium 85mg; Fibre 3.5g; Sodium 13mg.

Summer berry frozen yogurt

Any combination of summer fruits will work for this deliciously creamy yet tangy dish, as long as they are frozen, because this helps to create a chunky texture. If using individual fruits, choose a mixture of red and blue currants and berries. They are all rich in vitamin C, which helps to boost the immune system and is a powerful antioxidant.

Serves 6

350g/12oz/3 cups frozen summer fruits,
    plus whole fresh or frozen berries,
    to decorate
200g/7oz/scant 1 cup low-fat probiotic yogurt
25g/1oz icing (confectioners') sugar

Variation

To make a more creamy ice cream, use Greek (US strained plain) yogurt. This will still be healthy, although slightly higher in fat.

1 Put all the ingredients into a food processor and process until combined but still quite chunky. Spoon the mixture into six 150ml/¼ pint/⅔ cup ramekin dishes.

2 Cover each dish with clear film (plastic wrap) and place in the freezer for about 2 hours, or until firm.

3 To turn out the frozen yogurts, dip the ramekin dishes briefly in hot water, taking care not to allow water to get on to the dessert itself. Invert the ramekins on to small serving plates. Tap the base of the dishes and the yogurts should come out.

4 Serve immediately, decorated with fresh or frozen berries, such as blueberries, blackberries or raspberries.

Energy 51Kcal/215kJ; Protein 2.2g; Carbohydrate 10.4g, of which sugars 10.4g; Fat 0.4g, of which saturates 0.2g; Cholesterol 0mg; Calcium 75mg; Fibre 0.7g; Sodium 32mg.

Strawberry and lavender sorbet

Delicately perfumed with just a hint of lavender, this delightful, pastel pink sorbet is perfect for a special-occasion dinner, if entertaining while following a longer detox programme. It is made with a light sugar syrup, rather than the rich custard used for making ice cream, and captures the flavours and nutrient value of fresh strawberries. It is ideal for a low-fat summer dessert.

Serves 6

150g/5oz/¾ cup caster (superfine) sugar
300ml/½ pint/1¼ cups water
6 fresh lavender heads
500g/1¼lb/5 cups strawberries, hulled
1 egg white
lavender flowers, to decorate

1 Put the sugar and measured water into a pan and bring to the boil, stirring constantly until the sugar has completely dissolved.

2 Take the pan off the heat, add the lavender flower heads and leave to infuse (steep) for 1 hour. If time permits, chill the syrup before using.

3 Purée the strawberries in a food processor or in batches in a blender, then press the purée through a large sieve (strainer) into a bowl.

Cook's tip
The size of the lavender flowers may vary; if they are very small you may need to use 8 instead of 6. The intensity of the flavour may also vary depending on the variety of the lavender. To double check, taste a little of the cooled lavender syrup. If you think the flavour is a little mild, add 2–3 more flowers, reheat and cool again before using.

4 Spoon the purée into a freezerproof container, strain in the lavender syrup and freeze for 4 hours, or until the mixture is mushy. Alternatively, churn the strawberry and lavender mixture for 20 minutes, or until thick.

5 Whisk the egg white until it has just turned frothy.

6 Scoop the sorbet from the tub into a food processor, process it until smooth, then add the egg white. Spoon the sorbet back into the tub and freeze for 4 hours, or until firm. If using an ice cream machine, add the egg white to the bowl and continue to churn until the sorbet is firm enough to scoop. Serve immediately, or transfer to a freezerproof container and freeze until needed.

7 Serve in scoops in individual glasses, decorated with lavender flowers.

Energy 123Kcal/523kJ; Protein 1.3g; Carbohydrate 31.1g, of which sugars 31.1g; Fat 0.1g, of which saturates 0g; Cholesterol 0mg; Calcium 27mg; Fibre 0.9g; Sodium 17mg.

Poached pears in scented honey syrup

Pears are among the least allergenic of foods and they contain vitamin C and provide a useful amount of potassium, essential for helping to regulate blood pressure. Delicate and pretty to look at, these scented pears, poached in a honey and lemon syrup with saffron, cinnamon and lavender, would provide an exquisite finishing touch to a detox meal.

Serves 4

45ml/3 tbsp clear honey
juice of 1 lemon
250ml/8fl oz/1 cup water
pinch of saffron threads
1 cinnamon stick
2–3 dried lavender heads
4 firm pears

Variation

If pears are not available, you can use whole, peeled nectarines or peaches instead.

1 Heat the honey and lemon juice in a heavy pan that will hold the pears snugly. Stir over a gentle heat until the honey has dissolved. Add the water, saffron threads, cinnamon stick and flowers from 1–2 lavender heads. Bring the mixture to the boil, then reduce the heat and simmer for 5 minutes.

2 Peel the pears, leaving the stalks attached. Add the pears to the pan and simmer for 20 minutes, turning and basting at regular intervals, until they are tender. Allow to cool, then serve at room temperature, decorated with a few lavender flowers.

Energy 93Kcal/392kJ; Protein 0.5g; Carbohydrate 23.6g, of which sugars 23.6g; Fat 0.2g, of which saturates 0g; Cholesterol 0mg; Calcium 17mg; Fibre 3.3g; Sodium 6mg.

Nectarines baked with nuts

Fresh nectarines stuffed with a ground almond and chopped pistachio nut filling are baked in orange juice until tender and juicy, then served with a fragrant sauce made by stirring passion fruit seeds into the fruity cooking juices. Peaches could be used instead of nectarines. Both fruits contain plenty of vitamin C and the nuts provide protein and vitamin E.

Serves 4

50g/2oz/½ cup ground almonds
15ml/1 tbsp caster (superfine) sugar
1 egg yolk
50g/2oz/½ cup unsalted shelled pistachio
 nuts, chopped
4 nectarines
250ml/8fl oz/scant 1 cup orange juice
2 ripe passion fruits

1 Preheat the oven to 200°C/400°F/ Gas 6.

2 Mix together the ground almonds, sugar and egg yolk in a bowl to make a paste, then stir in the pistachio nuts.

3 Cut the nectarines in half and carefully remove the stones (pits). Pile the ground almond and pistachio filling into the nectarine halves, packing in plenty of filling, and then place them in a single layer in the base of a shallow ovenproof dish.

4 Pour the orange juice around the nectarines, then cover the dish with a lid or foil and place in the preheated oven. Cook for 15 minutes.

5 Remove the lid and bake for a further 5–10 minutes, or until the nectarines are soft. Transfer the nectarines to individual, warmed serving plates and keep warm.

6 Cut the passion fruits in half, scoop out the seeds and stir them into the cooking juices in the dish. Place the nectarines on serving plates and spoon the sauce over and around them. Serve immediately.

Energy 264Kcal/1106kJ; Protein 8g; Carbohydrate 24.8g, of which sugars 24.2g; Fat 15.5g, of which saturates 1.9g; Cholesterol 50mg; Calcium 68mg; Fibre 3.6g; Sodium 78mg.

Baked peaches

This is an excellent dessert to serve in summer, when peaches are in season and at their juiciest and most fragrant. Baking brings out their wonderful flavour, which is enhanced by the addition of a sweet apple, almond and honey juice, drizzled over the top. Serve warm from the oven or chilled with a spoonful of low-fat probiotic yogurt.

Serves 4

4 ripe peaches
45ml/3 tbsp fresh apple juice
45ml/3 tbsp clear honey
10ml/2 tsp almond extract
low-fat probiotic yogurt, to serve

Cook's tips
• You can cook these peaches over a barbecue. Place them on sheets of foil, drizzle over the fruit juice mixture, then scrunch the foil around them to seal. Cook for 15–20 minutes.
• If you are not on a detox diet, you could use Amaretto di Sarone liqueur in place of the apple juice.

1 Preheat the oven to 190°C/375°F/ Gas 5. Cut each of the peaches in half and twist each of the two halves in opposite directions to separate them. Once you have separated the two halves, prise out the stones (pits) with the point of the knife.

2 Place the peaches cut side up in a roasting pan.

3 In a small bowl, mix the apple juice with the honey and almond extract, and drizzle over the halved peaches, covering them evenly.

4 Bake the peaches for 20–25 minutes, or until tender. Place two peach halves on each serving plate and drizzle with the pan juices. Serve immediately, with low-fat probiotic yogurt.

Energy 70Kcal/299kJ; Protein 1.1g; Carbohydrate 17.3g, of which sugars 17.3g; Fat 0.1g, of which saturates 0g; Cholesterol 0mg; Calcium 8mg; Fibre 1.5g; Sodium 3mg.

Baked apples with figs and walnuts

Apples help to boost the digestion and remove impurities from the liver. Their cleansing properties are further enhanced by their high fibre content, which helps to remove toxins and purify the system. Serve these delicious apples stuffed with a mixture of walnuts and dried figs with a spoonful of low-fat probiotic yogurt or an egg custard sauce made with non-dairy milk.

Serves 6

4 medium cooking apples
50g/2oz/⅓ cup ready-to-eat dried
   figs, chopped
150ml/¼ pint/⅔ cup apple juice

1 Preheat the oven to 180°C/350°F/ Gas 4. Using an apple corer, remove the cores from the apples and discard. Place the apples in a small, shallow roasting pan or ovenproof dish.

2 Mix together the figs and walnuts, then stuff evenly into the cavity in the centre of each apple.

3 Pour over the apple juice. Cover the pan or dish tightly with foil and cook for about 30 minutes.

4 Remove the foil and cook for a further 10 minutes, or until the apples are tender and the juices have reduced slightly. Serve immediately with any remaining juices drizzled over the top.

Energy 56Kcal/241kJ; Protein 0.6g; Carbohydrate 14g, of which sugars 14g; Fat 0.2g, of which saturates 0g; Cholesterol 0mg; Calcium 24mg; Fibre 1.9g; Sodium 7mg.

Index

additives 11, 13, 14, 16, 22, 25, 43, 68
alcohol 14, 19, 22, 32, 34, 40, 47, 55, 61, 73, 74–5
allergies 40, 41, 75
see also food allergies
almonds 31
Tomato and Lentil Dhal with Almonds 185
Vegetable Couscous with Olives and Almonds 179
antioxidants 11, 15, 18, 21, 26, 28, 31, 40, 41, 69
apples 26
Baked Apples with Figs and Walnuts 251
Leafy Salad with Apple and Beetroot 221
apricots: Apricot and Ginger Compote 97
Apricot and Ginger Smoothie 89
aromatherapy 48, 49
artichokes: Artichoke and Cumin Dip 107
artichoke extract 21, 40
globe 28, 40
arugula see rocket
Asparagus and Orange Salad 219
aubergines (eggplants): Aubergine Dip 109
Mixed Bean and Aubergine Tagine with Mint Yogurt 182
avocados: Avocado Guacamole 106
Avocado, Red Onion and Spinach Salad with Polenta Croûtons 146
Avocado Salad with Tofu-dill Dressing 155
Chicken, Avocado and Chickpea Soup 138
Chilled Avocado Soup with Cumin 118
Citrus Fruit Salad with Avocado 152

bacteria, beneficial 18, 20, 23, 32, 41
balsamic vinegar: Seared Mixed Onion Salad with Parsley and Balsamic Dressing 214
Banana and Mango Smoothie 91
barley 16, 17, 24, 29
Barley Risotto with Roasted Squash and Leeks 178
Country Mushroom, Bean and Barley Soup 135
Chilled Tomato and Fresh Basil Soup 117
baths 50, 62, 63
beans 29, 43, 68
American Red Bean Soup with Guacamole Salsa 134
Bean Salad with Tuna and Red Onion 158
Black-eyed Bean and Tomato Broth 129
Borlotti Bean and Vegetable Soup 132
Braised Beans and Lentils 186
Butter Bean, Tomato and Olive Stew 181
Butter Bean, Tomato and Pesto Soup 133
Butter Bean, Tomato and Red Onion Salad 227
Cannellini Bean Soup 131
Country Mushroom, Bean and Barley Soup 135
Giant Beans Baked with Tomatoes 187
Marinated Courgette and Flageolet Bean Salad 226
Minty Broad Beans with Lemon 224
Mixed Bean and Aubergine Tagine with Mint Yogurt 182
Mixed Bean Salad with Roasted Red Pepper Dressing 147
beetroot 27
Grated Beetroot and Celery Salad 220
Leafy Salad with Apple and Beetroot 221
Russian Borscht with Kvas 122
betacarotene 18, 26, 28, 40, 90
blood pressure 14, 15, 16, 22, 24, 28, 40, 41, 50, 51, 74, 76
blood sugar levels 15, 24, 35
Blueberry Tonic 84
bread 24
Lebanese Flatbread 109
breast-feeding 7, 52, 63
breathing 20, 21, 51

broccoli 27
Stir-fried Broccoli with Sesame Seeds 230
bulgur wheat 24
Bulgur Wheat Salad with Walnuts 150
butter 17, 23, 70, 72
butternut squash: Barley Risotto with Roasted Squash and Leeks 178
Butternut Squash Soup with Tomato Salsa 126
Cinnamon and Squash Smoothie 82

cabbages: Braised Red Cabbage 232
Cabbage Salad with Lemon Dressing and Black Olives 213
Fresh Cabbage Soup 121
caffeine 6, 13, 14, 15, 19, 21, 22, 34, 47, 59
cakes 24, 70, 72
calcium 34, 36, 40, 97
calories 19, 24, 31, 72
'empty' 22, 74
capers: Mixed Salad with Capers and Olives 222
caraway seeds 38
Potato, Caraway Seed and Parsley Salad 228
carbohydrates 21, 24, 47, 68
cardamom 38
carrots 27
Carrot and Celery Juice 62, 81
Carrot and Orange Soup 119
Date, Orange and Carrot Salad 218
Gingered Carrot Salad 224
Spiced Carrot Dip 108
Tagine of Yam, Carrots and Prunes 180
cashew nuts: Mushroom Rice with Cashew Nuts 151
Red Pepper and Sprout Salad with Cashew Cream Dressing 144
Stir-fried Vegetables with Cashew Nuts 172
celery 27
Carrot and Celery Juice 62, 81
Grated Beetroot and Celery Salad 220
chamomile 38
Cheddar cheese 71
cheese 14, 17, 23, 70, 72
types of 71
see also individual cheeses

chervil 39
chicken 31
Chicken, Avocado and Chickpea Soup 138
Chicken and Leek Soup with Prunes 139
Griddled Chicken with Tomato Salsa 206
Pan-fried Chicken with Pesto 207
Warm Chicken and Tomato Salad with Hazelnut Dressing 160
Warm Oriental Chicken and Rice Stir-fry Salad 161
chickpeas 35
Aromatic Chickpea and Spinach Curry 184
Chicken, Avocado and Chickpea Soup 138
chillies 38
chives 38
Grilled Potatoes with Chive Dressing 217
chocolate 13, 14, 22, 47, 60, 72
cholesterol 25, 28, 29, 31, 35, 40, 41, 72
cinnamon 38
Cinnamon and Squash Smoothie 82
circulation 21, 28, 40, 46, 48, 49, 50, 55, 62
citrus fruits 14, 26
Cinnamon and Squash Smoothie 82
Citrus Fruit Salad with Avocado 152
co-enzyme Q10 40
cod 31
Roasted Cod with Fresh Tomato Sauce 196
Spicy Paella 205
coffee 22, 55, 59, 60, 73, 75
complementary therapies 6, 18, 19, 48–51, 55, 60
cooking, healthy 44–5
coriander leaf/seed 38
cottage cheese 71
couscous: Vegetable Couscous with Olives and Almonds 179
cream 17, 23, 70
cumin 38
Artichoke and Cumin Dip 107
Chilled Avocado Soup with Cumin 118
cynarin 21, 28, 40

dairy products 13, 23, 35, 70
dandelion 38, 40

dates: Date, Orange and Carrot
Salad 218
Porridge with Dates and
Pistachio Nuts 101
dehydration 14, 22, 75
detox diet 6, 7
benefits 6, 18–19
the body's natural detoxifiers 20
complementary therapies and
relaxation techniques 48–51
detox supplements 40–41
essential vitamins and
minerals 36–7
exercise for body and mind 46–7
following the detox programme
56–9
food allergy and intolerance
16–17
foods to avoid 22–5
foods to include 26–33
health problems and how to
prevent them with diet 76–7
healthy cooking 44–5
healthy shopping 42–3
herbs and spices for health 38–9
how diet affects health 12–15
how to boost your vital
organs 21
long-term healthy eating 68–73
one- and two-week detox meal
planners 64–7
people who shouldn't detox 7
preparing to detox 52–5
safe drinking 74–5
toxins 10–11
vital nutrients 34–5
a weekend detox 60–63
dhal: Grilled Mackerel with Spicy
Dhal 199
Tomato and Lentil Dhal with
Almonds 185
dill 38
Avocado Salad with Tofu-dill
Dressing 155
drinking, safe 74–5

eggs 13, 17, 23, 32, 35, 71
Egg and Lentil Curry 195
Spring Vegetable Omelette 194
eggplants see aubergines
essential fatty acids 21, 22
exercise 6, 7, 15, 18, 19, 21, 46,
47, 55, 60, 62

family meals 57
farm-box schemes 42, 43
farmers' markets 43
fast foods 25
fats 7, 19, 21, 25, 101
hard 72

monounsaturated 72
polyunsaturated 72
saturated 23, *23*, 25, 30, 43,
68, 70, 71, 72
trans 25, 72
unsaturated 72
fennel 38
Grilled Fennel Salad with
Niçoise Olives 216
fenugreek seeds 39
feta cheese 71
Greek Salad 153
fibre 25, 26, 31, 35, 41, 60, 68
figs: Baked Apples with Figs and
Walnuts 251
Figs and Pears in Honey 95
fish 31, 35, 68, 71
Moroccan Fish Tagine 204
see also individual names of fish
flaxseeds 31
folate (folic acid) 14, 35, 37
food: allergies 7, 12, 13, 15, 16,
23, 25, 68
aversion 16
cravings/addictions 13
diary 12
intolerance 12, 14, 15, 16,
20, 68
sensitivities 7, 13, 14
free radicals 10–11, 21, 26, 33
fromage frais 70
fruit 26, 42, 43, 44, 56, 57, 60, 62,
63, 69
boosting intake 70
Citrus Fruit Salad with
Avocado 152
Dried Fruit Compote 96
dried fruits 27, 43
Dried Fruit Salad 236
Exotic Fruit Platter with
Ginger 239
Fragrant Fruit Salad 93
Fresh Fruit Salad 236
Fresh Fruit with Mango
Coulis 238
Summer Berry Frozen
Yogurt 246
Summer Fruit Smoothie 88
super fruits 26
Tropical Scented Fruit Salad 92
Zingy Papaya, Lime and Ginger
Salad 94

garlic 28, 39
Lentil and Garlic Soup 127
Pea Soup with Garlic 120
Roasted Plum Tomatoes with
Garlic 231
Spinach and Roast Garlic
Salad 210

Gazpacho with Vegetable
Garnish 116
ginger 28, 39
Apricot and Ginger Compote 97
Apricot and Ginger Smoothie 89
Exotic Fruit Platter with
Ginger 239
Gingered Carrot Salad 224
Pineapple and Ginger Juice 80
Zingy Papaya, Lime and Ginger
Salad 94
ginkgo biloba 40
gluten 12, 16–17, 29
goat's cheese 71
Granola 98
grapefruit: Minted Pomegranate
Yogurt with Grapefruit
Salad 242
grapes: Papaya and Green
Grapes with Mint Sauce 244
guacamole: American Red Bean
Soup with Guacamole
Salsa 134
Avocado Guacamole 106
Pea Guacamole 105

haddock 31
hazelnuts: Summer Vegetable
Salad with Hazelnuts 143
Warm Chicken and Tomato
Salad with Hazelnut
Dressing 160
health problems, and
prevention 76–7
healthy eating, long-term 68–73
herbs 38–9, 43, 81
Herby Rice Pilaff 229
Mixed Green Leaf and Herb
Salad 211
Warm Mixed Seafood and Fresh
Herb Salad 156
Wild Rocket and Cos Lettuce
Salad with Herbs 212
hoki: Moroccan Fish Tagine 204
honey: Figs and Pears in Honey 95
Poached Pears in Scented
Honey Syrup 248
horseradish 39
Hummus 104

illnesses: anaemia 14, 17, 34
arthritis 26, 40, 77
asthma 10–13, 16, 17, 22, 24,
48, 49, 75, 96
bloating 7, 12, 15, 16, 17, 20,
24, 33, 68
cancer 7, 11, 18, 24, 26, 28, 30,
31, 35, 42, 72, 74, 77
cirrhosis 20, 41, 75
coeliac disease 12, 14, 16–17, 24

constipation 7, 12, 20, 24, 29,
31, 33, 40
depression 7, 15, 20, 48, 74
diabetes 7, 14, 52, 63, 76
digestive problems 10, 12, 17,
40, 49
eczema 7, 12, 13, 16, 17, 28,
40, 50
fluid retention 24, 33, 40
headaches 7, 14, 15, 20, 33,
47, 59, 68, 75
heart disease 7, 11, 15, 18, 25,
29, 31, 41, 50, 72, 73
hepatitis 20, 41, 75
indigestion 16, 17, 75
insomnia 19, 22, 47, 48
irritable bowel syndrome (IBS)
12, 20, 32, 76
kidney problems 14, 22, 24
osteoporosis 22, 24, 30, 34, 76
respiratory problems 10, 13,
20, 28
rheumatism 28, 40
sinus problems 7, 13, 20, 23, 49
stroke 24, 29, 73
immune system 6, 16, 18, 28,
34, 40
iodine 36, 40
iron 36, 37, 40, 74, 81, 97
juices 6, 21, 44, 60, 73
Blueberry Tonic 84
Carrot and Celery Juice 62, 81
Lime and Watermelon Tonic 83
Pineapple and Ginger Juice 80

kelp 28, 40
kitchen essentials 53

lavender 39
Strawberry and Lavender
Sorbet 247
leeks: Barley Risotto with Roasted
Squash and Leeks 178
Chicken and Leek Soup with
Prunes 139
Leek and Potato Soup 136
Salmon with Leeks and
Peppers 200
lemon balm 39

Lemon Grass Skewers 241
lemons: Cinnamon and Squash
Smoothie 82
Minty Broad Beans with
Lemon 224
lentils 29
Braised Beans and Lentils 186
Egg and Lentil Curry 195
Harvest Vegetable and Lentil
Casserole 166
Lentil and Garlic Soup 127
Tomato and Lentil Dhal with
Almonds 185
Tomato and Lentil Soup 128
lettuce: Wild Rocket and Cos
Lettuce Salad with Herbs 212
limes: Lime and Watermelon
Tonic 83
Mango and Lime Lassi 90
Zingy Papaya, Lime and Ginger
Salad 94
linseeds see flaxseeds
liquorice 41
liver 20, 21, 41, 62
disease 74, 75
function 14, 28, 40
lycopene 28
lymphatic drainage massage 48
lymphatic system 20, 21, 46, 48, 50

mackerel 71
Grilled Mackerel with Spicy
Dhal 199
magnesium 29, 36, 82
manganese 36
mangoes: Banana and Mango
Smoothie 91
Fresh Fruit with Mango
Coulis 238
Mango and Lime Lassi 90
Salmon Steaks with Mango
Salsa 201
marjoram 39
massage 19, 21, 47–8
foot 49
lymphatic drainage 48
shoulder 49
meat products 23, 25, 35, 68, 71
medication 7, 52, 63
meditation 18, 47, 51
migraine 7, 14, 16, 22, 28, 49
milk 70
lactose intolerance 17
milk allergy 16, 17
non-dairy milk choices 32
milk thistle 41
millet 27
minerals 18, 23, 26, 28, 29, 31, 36,
44, 60, 68, 69, 70
mint 39, 239

Minted Pomegranate Yogurt
with Grapefruit Salad 242
Minty Broad Beans with
Lemon 224
Mixed Bean and Aubergine
Tagine with Mint Yogurt 182
Papaya and Green Grapes with
Mint Sauce 244
monkfish: Fragrant Thai Fish
Soup 137
Moroccan Fish Tagine 204
mozzarella cheese 71
muesli: Luxury Muesli 98
mushrooms: Brown Rice Risotto
with Mushrooms 177
Mushroom Rice with Cashew
Nuts 151
Country Mushroom, Bean and
Barley Soup 135
mycoprotein (quorn) 30, 71

Nectarines Baked with Nuts 249
noodles: Buckwheat Noodle Salad
with Smoked Salmon 157
Thai Noodle Salad 148
nutmeg 39
nuts 17, 31, 43
Nectarines Baked with Nuts 249
see also individual nut types

oats 16, 17, 24, 29, 98
Porridge with Dates and
Pistachio Nuts 101
Raspberry and Oatmeal Blend 86
Traditional Scottish Porridge 100
oils 33, 49, 72
olives: Butter Bean, Tomato and
Olive Stew 181
Cabbage Salad with Lemon
Dressing and Black Olives 213
Grilled Fennel Salad with
Niçoise Olives 216
Mixed Salad with Capers and
Olives 222
Vegetable Couscous with Olives
and Almonds 179
omega-3 fatty acids 31, 44, 72
omega-6 fatty acids 31, 72
onions 28

Avocado, Red Onion and
Spinach Salad with Polenta
Croûtons 146
Bean Salad with Tuna and Red
Onion 158
Butter Bean, Tomato and Red
Onion Salad 227
Seared Mixed Onion Salad with
Parsley and Balsamic
Dressing 214
oranges: Asparagus and Orange
Salad 219
Barbecued Sardines with
Orange 198
Carrot and Orange Soup 119
Citrus Fruit Salad with
Avocado 152
Date, Orange and Carrot
Salad 218
Orange Granita with
Strawberries 244
Orange and Raspberry
Smoothie 85
Rose Water-scented Oranges
with Pistachio Nuts 243
oregano 39
papaya 26
Papaya and Green Grapes with
Mint Sauce 244
Zingy Papaya, Lime and Ginger
Salad 94
Parmesan cheese 71
parsley 39
Potato, Caraway Seed and
Parsley Salad 228
Seared Mixed Onion Salad with
Parsley and Balsamic
Dressing 214
passion fruits: Fragrant Fruit
Salad 93
Strawberries with Passion Fruit
Sauce 240
pasta 24
Wholewheat Pasta Salad 149
peaches: Baked Peaches 250
pears: Figs and Pears in Honey 95
Poached Pears in Scented
Honey Syrup 248
peas: dried 29
Pea Guacamole 105
Pea Soup with Garlic 120
Penne with Green Vegetable
Sauce 169
peppers: Mixed Bean Salad with
Roasted Red Pepper
Dressing 147
Provençal Stuffed Peppers 193
Red Pepper and Sprout Salad
with Cashew Cream
Dressing 144

Roasted Peppers with Sweet
Cicely 112
Salmon with Leeks and
Peppers 200
Tofu and Pepper Kebabs 192
pineapples 26
Pineapple and Ginger Juice 80
pistachio nuts: Porridge with
Dates and Pistachio Nuts 101
Rose Water-scented Oranges
with Pistachio Nuts 243
plants 54, 55
polenta: Avocado, Red Onion and
Spinach Salad with Polenta
Croûtons 146
Griddled Polenta with Tangy
Pebre 113
pomegranates 26
Minted Pomegranate Yogurt
with Grapefruit Salad 242
porridge: Porridge with Dates and
Pistachio Nuts 101
Traditional Scottish Porridge 100
potassium 22, 36, 40, 41, 82, 97
potatoes: Grilled Potatoes with
Chive Dressing 217
Leek and Potato Soup 136
Turkish-style New Potato
Casserole 167
poultry 6, 31, 35, 71
pregnancy 7, 52, 63, 74
preservatives 11, 42, 75
protein 19, 21, 23, 30, 31, 101
prunes: Chicken and Leek Soup
with Prunes 139
Tagine of Yam, Carrots and
Prunes 180
psyllium husks 41
pumpkin seeds 31
Stir-fried Vegetables and
Seeds 171
pumpkins 28
Spicy Pumpkin Soup 125

quark 70
quinoa 29
quorn 30, 71

raspberries: Orange and
Raspberry Smoothie 85
Raspberry and Oatmeal Blend 86
relaxation 6, 19, 47, 48, 61, 62
rice 17, 29, 43
Barley Risotto with Roasted
Squash and Leeks 178
Brown Rice Risotto with
Mushrooms 177
Herby Rice Pilaff 229
Indian Rice with Tomatoes and
Spinach 176

Mushroom Rice with Cashew Nuts 151
Spicy Paella 205
Stir-fried Rice and Vegetables 174
Tofu and Wild Rice Salad 154
Warm Oriental Chicken and Rice Stir-fry Salad 161
Rice Noodles with Vegetable Chilli Sauce 170
ricotta cheese 71
rocket: Wild Rocket and Cos Lettuce Salad with Herbs 212
Rose Water-scented Oranges with Pistachio Nuts 243
rosehip 41
rosemary 39
rye 16, 17, 24, 29

sage 39
salads: Asparagus and Orange Salad 219
Avocado, Red Onion and Spinach Salad with Polenta Croûtons 146
Bean Salad with Tuna and Red Onion 158
Buckwheat Noodle Salad with Smoked Salmon 157
Bulgur Wheat Salad with Walnuts 150
Cabbage Salad with Lemon Dressing and Black Olives 213
Citrus Fruit Salad with Avocado 152
Date, Orange and Carrot Salad 218
Dried Fruit Salad 236
Exotic Fruit Platter with Ginger 239
Fragrant Fruit Salad 93
Fresh Fruit Salad 236
Fresh Fruit with Mango Coulis 238
Gingered Carrot Salad 224
Grated Beetroot and Celery Salad 220
Greek Salad 153
Grilled Fennel Salad with Niçoise Olives 216
Leafy Salad with Apple and Beetroot 221
Marinated Courgette and Flageolet Bean Salad 226
Minted Pomegranate Yogurt with Grapefruit Salad 242
Mixed Bean Salad with Roasted Red Pepper Dressing 147
Mixed Green Leaf and Herb Salad 211

Mixed Salad with Capers and Olives 222
New Spring Vegetable Salad 142
Potato, Caraway Seed and Parsley Salad 228
Red Pepper and Sprout Salad with Cashew Cream Dressing 144
Salad Niçoise 159
Seared Mixed Onion Salad with Parsley and Balsamic Dressing 214
Spinach and Roast Garlic Salad 210
Summer Vegetable Salad with Hazelnuts 143
Thai Noodle Salad 148
Tofu and Wild Rice Salad 154
Tropical Scented Fruit Salad 92
Warm Chicken and Tomato Salad with Hazelnut Dressing 160
Warm Mixed Seafood and Fresh Herb Salad 156
Warm Oriental Chicken and Rice Stir-fry Salad 161
Warm Vegetable Salad 223
Wholewheat Pasta Salad 149
Wild Rocket and Cos Lettuce Salad with Herbs 212
Zingy Papaya, Lime and Ginger Salad 94
salmon 31, 71
Buckwheat Noodle Salad with Smoked Salmon 157
Salmon with Leeks and Peppers 200
Salmon Steaks with Mango Salsa 201
Teriyaki Salmon 202
salt 15, 21, 24, 25, 34, 43, 68, 73
sardines 31, 71
Barbecued Sardines with Orange 198
seaweeds 28, 40
seeds 31, 43
selenium 15, 21, 31, 36
sesame seeds 31, 91
Sesame Falafel with Tahini Yogurt Dip 111
Stir-fried Broccoli with Sesame Seeds 230
shellfish 31, 71
Warm Mixed Seafood and Fresh Herb Salad 156
shopping, healthy 42–3
side effects, possible 59
skin 20, 21

dry skin brushing 19, 21, 50, 62
improved 6, 18
problems 7, 13, 17, 40, 41, 47
sleep 6, 7, 19, 21, 47, 61
smoking 7, 10, 11, 19, 54, 55, 61
smoothies: Apricot and Ginger Smoothie 89
Banana and Mango Smoothie 91
Cinnamon and Squash Smoothie 82
Orange and Raspberry Smoothie 85
Raspberry and Oatmeal Blend 86
Strawberry and Tofu Smoothie 87
Summer Fruit Smoothie 88
snacks 7, 21, 24, 59, 72, 73
sodium 36, 41
sorbet: Strawberry and Lavender Sorbet 247
soups: American Red Bean Soup with Guacamole Salsa 134
Black-eyed Bean and Tomato Broth 129
Borlotti Bean and Vegetable Soup 132
Butter Bean, Tomato and Pesto Soup 133
Butternut Squash Soup with Tomato Salsa 126
Cannellini Bean Soup 131
Carrot and Orange Soup 119
Chicken, Avocado and Chickpea Soup 138
Chicken and Leek Soup with Prunes 139
Chilled Avocado Soup with Cumin 118
Chilled Tomato and Fresh Basil Soup 117
Fragrant Thai Fish Soup 137
Fresh Cabbage Soup 121
Gazpacho with Vegetable Garnish 116
Leek and Potato Soup 136
Lentil and Garlic Soup 127
North African Spiced Soup 130
Country Mushroom, Bean and Barley Soup 135
Pea Soup with Garlic 120
Russian Borscht with Kvas 122
Spicy Pumpkin Soup 125
Summer Vegetable Soup 123
Tomato and Lentil Soup 128
Winter Farmhouse Soup 124
soya 30, 32
spices 38–9
spinach 28
Aromatic Chickpea and Spinach Curry 184

Avocado, Red Onion and Spinach Salad with Polenta Croûtons 146
Indian Rice with Tomatoes and Spinach 176
Spinach and Roast Garlic Salad 210
sprouts 29
how to sprout 44
Red Pepper and Sprout Salad with Cashew Cream Dressing 144
strawberries: Orange Granita with Strawberries 244
Strawberries with Passion Fruit Sauce 240
Strawberry and Lavender Sorbet 247
Strawberry and Tofu Smoothie 87
stress 47
sugar(s) 19, 24, 68, 72, 73
sulphites 11, 13, 16, 22
sunflower seeds 31
Stir-fried Vegetables and Seeds 171
supplements 40–1
sweet cicely: Roasted Peppers with Sweet Cicely 112

Tagliatelle with Vegetable Ribbons 168
tahini 31
Sesame Falafel with Tahini Yogurt Dip 111
tarragon 39
Young Vegetables with Tarragon 233
tea 7, 18, 21, 22, 55, 73
ginger 28
herbal 19, 22, 33, 47, 55, 59, 60, 62, 73
Teriyaki Salmon 202
thiamin 22, 37
thyme 39
Spanish-style Vegetables with Thyme 164
tofu 30, 71
Avocado Salad with Tofu-dill Dressing 155

Spiced Tofu Stir-fry 190
Strawberry and Tofu Smoothie 87
Sweet and Sour Vegetables
    with Tofu 191
Tofu and Pepper Kebabs 192
Tofu and Wild Rice Salad 154
tomatoes 13, 28
    Black-eyed Bean and Tomato
        Broth 129
    Butter Bean, Tomato and Olive
        Stew 181
    Butter Bean, Tomato and Pesto
        Soup 133
    Butter Bean, Tomato and Red
        Onion Salad 227
    Butternut Squash Soup with
        Tomato Salsa 126
    Chilled Tomato and Fresh Basil
        Soup 117
    Giant Beans Baked with
        Tomatoes 187
    Griddled Chicken with Tomato
        Salsa 206
    Indian Rice with Tomatoes and
        Spinach 176
    Roasted Cod with Fresh
        Tomato Sauce 196
    Roasted Plum Tomatoes with
        Garlic 231
    Seared Tuna Steaks with
        Tomato Salsa 197
    Tomato and Lentil Dhal with
        Almonds 185
    Tomato and Lentil Soup 128
    Warm Chicken and Tomato
        Salad with Hazelnut
        Dressing 160
toxins 7, 10–11
trout 31, 71
    Chinese-style Steamed Trout 203

tuna 31, 71
    Bean Salad with Tuna and Red
        Onion 158
    Seared Tuna Steaks with
        Tomato Salsa 197
turmeric 39
TVP (textured vegetable protein) 71

vegetable stock, homemade 45
vegetables 26, 42, 43, 44, 56,
        57, 60, 69
    boosting intake 70
    Borlotti Bean and Vegetable
        Soup 132
    cooking 45
    Gazpacho with Vegetable
        Garnish 116
    Harvest Vegetable and Lentil
        Casserole 166
    New Spring Vegetable Salad 142
    Penne with Green Vegetable
        Sauce 169
    Rice Noodles with Vegetable
        Chilli Sauce 170
    Roasted Vegetables with Salsa
        Verde 165
    sea 28
    Spanish-style Vegetables with
        Thyme 164
    Spring Vegetable Omelette 194
    Spring Vegetable Stir-fry 173
    Stir-fried Rice and Vegetables 174
    Stir-fried Vegetables and
        Seeds 171
    Stir-fried Vegetables with
        Cashew Nuts 172
    Summer Vegetable Salad with
        Hazelnuts 143
    Summer Vegetable Soup 123
    super vegetables 27–8

Sweet and Sour Vegetables
    with Tofu 191
Tagliatelle with Vegetable
    Ribbons 168
Thai Vegetable Curry 175
Vegetable Couscous with Olives
    and Almonds 179
Warm Vegetable Salad 223
Young Vegetables with
    Tarragon 233
see also individual vegetables

vine leaves: Stuffed Vine
    Leaves 110
visualization 18, 51, 62
vitamins 18, 23, 25, 32, 37, 40,
    44, 60, 68, 69, 70
    folate (folic acid) 35, 37
    vitamin A 15, 21, 22, 25, 26, 31,
        37, 41, 69, 90, 97
    vitamin B group 15, 25, 29, 30,
        31, 35, 41, 44, 71, 74
    vitamin B$_1$ 37
    vitamin B$_2$ 37
    vitamin B$_3$ (niacin) 37
    vitamin B$_6$ (piridoxine) 37
    vitamin B$_{12}$ (cyanocobalamin)
        32, 35, 37, 71
    vitamin C (ascorbic acid) 15, 18,
        21, 22, 25, 26, 34, 37, 41,
        44, 69, 81, 90, 97
    vitamin D (calciferol) 31, 34, 37
    vitamin E (tocopherols) 15, 21,
        22, 25, 26, 28, 29, 31, 33,
        37, 41, 69, 91
    vitamin K 25

walnuts 31
    Baked Apples with Figs and
        Walnuts 251

Bulgur Wheat Salad with
    Walnuts 150
water, drinking 6, 14, 33, 55,
    59, 62, 73
watercress 28
watermelons: Lime and
    Watermelon Tonic 83
weekend detox 60–63
weight issues 6, 7, 13, 15, 16,
    24, 74
wheat 12, 17, 24, 29, 35
wheatgrass 41
wholegrains 29, 35, 43, 68

yam: Tagine of Yam, Carrots and
    Prunes 180
yoga 46
yogurt 17, 23, 32, 44, 70
    Minted Pomegranate Yogurt
        with Grapefruit Salad 242
    Mixed Bean and Aubergine
        Tagine with Mint Yogurt 182
    Sesame Falafel with Tahini
        Yogurt Dip 111
    Summer Berry Frozen
        Yogurt 246

zinc 21, 22, 36

Acknowledgements

Photographers: Karl Adamson; Edward Allwright; Peter Anderson; David Armstrong; Tim Auty; Steve Baxter; Martin Brigdale; Nicky Dowey; James Duncan; Gus Filgate; Ian Garlick; Michelle Garrett; John Heseltine; Amanda Heywood; Tim Hill; Janine Hosegood; Dave King; Don Last; William Lingwood; Patrick McLeavey; Michael Michaels; Steve Moss; Thomas Odulate; Peter Reilly; Craig Robertson; Bridget Sargeson; Simon Smith; Sam Stowell.

Recipe writers: Pepita Aris; Catherine Atkinson; Stephanie Barker; Ghillie Basan; Judy Bastyra; Susannah Blake; Angela Boggiano; Georgina Campbell; Carla Capalbo; Lesley Chamberlain; Maxine Clarke; Carole Clements; Trish Davies; Roz Denny; Patrizia Diemling; Stephanie Donaldson; Matthew Drennan; Sarah Edmonds; Steve England; Joanna Farrow; Rafi Fernandez; Jenni Fleetwood; Christine France; Silvana Franco; Sarah Gates; Shirley Gill; Brian Glover; Nicola Graimes; Rosamund Grant; Carole Handslip; Rebekah Hassan; Shehzaid Husain; Christine Ingram; Becky Johnson; Soheila Kimberley; Lucy Knox; Elizabeth Lambert Ortiz; Ruby Le Bois; Patricia Lousada; Gilly Love; Lesley Mackey; Norma MacMillan; Sue Maggs; Kathy Man; Sally Mansfield; Elizabeth Martin; Maggie Mayhew; Sarah Maxwell; Norma Miller; Jane Milton; Sallie Morris; Janice Murfitt; Annie Nichols; Angela Nilsen; Suzannah Olivier; Maggie Pannell; Louise Pickford; Marion Price; Keith Richmond; Rena Salaman; Anne Sheasby; Marlena Spieler; Liz Trigg; Christopher Trotter; Linda Tubby; Hilaire Walden; Laura Washburn; Biddy White Lennon; Kate Whiteman; Judy Williams; Carol Wilson; Elizabeth Wolf-Cohen; Jeni Wright.

Food stylists and home economists: Alison Austin; Eliza Baird; Alex Barker; Shannon Beare; Julie Beresford; Madeleine Brehaut; Sascha Brodie; Jacqueline Clarke; Frances Cleary; Stephanie England; Tessa Evelegh; Marilyn Forbes; Annabel Ford; Nicola Fowler; Michelle Garrett; Hilary Guy; Jo Harris; Jane Hartshorn; Katherine Hawkins; Amanda Heywood; Cara Hobday; Claire Hunt; Kate Jay; Jill Jones; Maria Kelly; Clare Lewis; Sara Lewis; Lucy McKelvie; Marion McLornan; Wendy Lee; Blake Minton; Emma Patmore; Marion Price; Kirsty Rawlings; Bridget Sargeson; Jennie Shapter; Joy Skipper; Jane Stephenson; Carol Tenant; Helen Trent; Linda Tubby; Sunil Vijayakar; Stuart Walton; Sophie Wheeler; Stephen Wheeler; Judy Williams.